The life and times of Thabo Mbeki

The life and times of
Thabo Mbeki

Adrian Hadland
and
Jovial Rantao

ZEBRA

ZEBRA

Published by Zebra Press, an imprint of Southern Book Publishers
(a division of the New Holland Struik Publishing Group (Pty) Ltd)
PO Box 5563, Rivonia, 2128
Tel: +27 11 807 2292
Fax: +27 11 803 1783
E-mail: marikat@struik.co.za

First edition, first impression April 1999
Second impression May 1999
Third impression July 1999
Fourth impression September 1999

Managing editor Kate Rogan
Copy editor Catherine Murray
Cover designer Micha McKerr
DTP Patricia Crain

Reproduction by PG&A, Cape Town
Printed and bound by CTP Book Printers, Caxton Street, Parow, 7500

ISBN 1 86872 260 0

Contents

We would like to dedicate this book to Jackie and Pearl

Foreword

He is an African

It is a summery morning in South Africa and the president-in-waiting is having a friendly meeting with an international investor in an elegant room at Tuynhuys. Thabo Mbeki is alarmingly busy. A European monarch and a prime minister are among those visiting the country at the time, there is an election to prepare for, a security scare in the Western Cape province and, incidentally, a government to run.

One could have expected, and forgiven, an atmosphere of controlled haste. Instead, Mbeki converses like a man who might suggest going out for a bite of lunch later to finish the discussion.

Half-way through the allotted time, however, he stands up abruptly and heads for the door. All eyes in the room follow him. He stops short at a table, picks up two silver pots, and proceeds to move around carefully serving tea and coffee to the dozen or so people seated at the horseshoe table, regardless of their rank.

It is a pointed gesture made all the more telling by its apparent leisureliness. This is a man who has already made his personal transition to the presidency, and who is finding it an agreeable place. The edginess of Mbeki that some have experienced over the years is tellingly absent this morning.

I wondered after the meeting whether the aura of this new sense of presidential ease would quickly filter through to the public in South Africa. I have to say my own answer was: I doubt it. It is interesting to mull over the reasons as to why that might be.

It is in fact difficult to think of another seminal figure in South African politics whose public image was for so long as exaggeratedly indistinct as that of Mbeki.

This will change quickly once he formally occupies the presidential seat, but for now it is true that Nelson Mandela's successor remains something of an unintentional enigma for large sections of the population, for different reasons. No one doubts his great intellect and skill. They question, rather, whether they know what he is really like — which is a different matter.

As his presidency dawns Mbeki's image is rather like a rubber mask which can be pulled and prodded, features elongated or flattened as the mask is stretched this way or that; almost infinitely elastic in the hands of those observing. These days when I hear someone talk with assumed authority about 'the real Thabo', I quietly take it to mean only that they have fashioned a rubber mask to satisfy their own specifications.

The truth is that the ranks of Mbeki's trusted insiders are thin and exclusive, and even those within them cannot be too certain of the completeness of their own understanding or the permanence of their proximity.

The man who has earned the right to lead South Africa into the new millennium has regularly disappointed those who expected him to hunt only with the hawks, confounded those who thought he would share their dovecotes. There are those to whom he is the revolutionary prophet of the African Renaissance, all-wise liberator of the indigenous masses, nemesis of the oppressor and his progeny. And there are those to whom he is a vengeful manipulator whose driving purpose is power and whose wielding of it is an unsettling prospect.

Apart from these caricatures, Mbeki has had an unusual variety of other images attached to him in the course of his eventful adulthood, cumulatively adding to the public uncertainty. You will recognise some of them.

There was the whisky-sipping, Keats-quoting raconteur. The political 'sex symbol' of talk radio-land. The clubbable confidant of that generation of the country's captains of industry. The latter-day hero of the young lions sprung from the loins of ungovernability. The poor judge of character who preferred to appoint loyalists over adopting the Kennedyesque 'best and brightest' approach. The master of close-in political knifework. The lieutenant accused of 'bungling' the tricky tasks handed to him by Mandela, and the opposite: the long-suffering, brilliant, behind-the-scenes 'fixer' who protected his leader's sainted image from being tainted – often resenting the thanklessness of the task ...

The least that can be said about these outer edges of the character spectrum is that they cannot all be right. There is a lot of space in between for something closer to the human truth to be found.

In evoking a slightly mysterious air around the democratic South Africa's second leader, I want to take care not to imply that we are dealing here with one of those political oxymorons thrown up sporadically by history – the reclusive man of the people. Mbeki is exclusive, perhaps elusive, but not reclusive.

He has been described as distant but he is instantly recognisable and no more or less accessible than most other world leaders. He does all the public things that normal politicians are normally required to do, and does them very well indeed; after all, it is often forgotten that he has been a professional politician since he was a teenager.

No, with Mbeki the enigma resides in something else, somewhere else. It is a sense of his enduring untouchability even as he shakes your hand. Not for nothing do people wonder whether he has ever allowed himself the luxury of true friends, rather than just comrades or allies.

His is an unusual aura in another way, for in its distance it is neither haughty nor austere. Mbeki has few peers in his ability to exude polished, practised – often poetic – *bonhomie* under circumstances trying or tranquil. He has simultaneously established a deserved reputation as a writer of great force, learning and originality.

But those of us who try not to mistake a buffed surface for the grain of the wood beneath are aware that we do not really know Thabo Mbeki, irrespective of whether we try to pretend otherwise, or how many times we might have found ourselves in his company. We know that we have not put a finger on what precisely is inside the dapper, powerful frame of the man destined to accept custody of a fragile rainbow. To tell the truth, we doubt that anyone has. It will be intriguing in the coming years to watch the full personality unfold before our eyes, never forgetting that, in a non-party-political sense, Mbeki's success or failure will be South Africa's too.

A basic biography of Mbeki, whether one agrees or disagrees with its conclusions, is much needed because it establishes a detailed starting point from which a comprehensive public record can begin to be developed. Among many other things this book reveals the degree to which current perceptions of the man are drawn from remarkably uneven evidence.

In the book you will find much solid, straightforward factual information about Mbeki, interesting enough merely on the strength of the importance of who he has been and is still to be, and helpful to an understanding of why he does certain things in certain ways. New sources are tapped, too — like a relative of a childhood sweetheart, schoolfriends, political colleagues of all stripes — and it is in those sections which paint a picture of his earlier life that I found myself most engrossed.

To my mind, the authors emphasise foundation stones of Mbeki's character which rank above others as essential to any serious attempt at understanding the man. The first shows that when Mbeki speaks of the African National Congress as having been his life, it is meant quite literally. He was utterly deprived of a normal family life as a young man (Govan Mbeki's sacrifice of a father-son relationship on the altar of the struggle makes for quite uncomfortable — even shocking — reading), and the organisation played that role for Thabo. Literally nothing he does can be properly understood unless it is placed within the context of how he sees it furthering the aims of the ANC.

Bluntly put, Thabo Mbeki had a lonely and largely loveless childhood followed by an insecure life in exile. This explains, among many other things, his vitriolic disapproval of latter-day opportunists who see the ANC primarily as a vehicle to promote their personal careers, and his genuine resentment of the so-called culture of entitlement among some younger black South Africans — as well as his more predictable hostility towards the 'previously advantaged' who want to take what the new South Africa has to offer, but not to give to it.

It explains, also, a striking absence of sentimentality in Mbeki's dealings with many people (one of the most obvious contrasts between him and Mandela) and points to the little-appreciated fact that under the well-cut suit and the air of well-being is a man deeply damaged by the apartheid era, who has paid a profound psychological price and has to fight even now to control his own bitterness. No one should doubt the depth of anger this man feels about the degradation of his people wrought by colonialism, apartheid and their beneficiaries. If some people have experienced him as cold in spite of his winning smile and poet's mien, and as slightly paranoid or prone to fearful anger, there are reasons.

I believe it is true, as is implicit in this book, that Mbeki does not 'hate whites'. But he certainly hates residual notions of white superiority and practical manifestations of continuing white domination. Often the concepts get muddled and the distinction lost, with confusing and even dangerous results.

In this context, one wise observer remarks of Mbeki that even though he was an exceptional diplomat in exile and during the negotiations process (his role in the latter is habitually underestimated because of the public prominence of the charismatic Cyril Ramaphosa), he has not until now been good at making people feel better about themselves. That is a very subtle observation, distinguishing Mbeki in yet another way from the political icon whose position he will fill.

Another watcher of the country's politics puts it this way: South Africans are moving from the era of Mandela the magician to that of Mbeki the super-manager. The style will be, and should be, different.

Another foundation stone is the overarching influence on Mbeki of the late Oliver Tambo. I would go so far as to say that an understanding of Mbeki is not possible without some knowledge of the life and times of 'OR' and his interaction with the younger man.

Many, including Mandela, believe that the character of the modern-day ANC owes more to Tambo than to any other individual. The same can be said of Mbeki's character, from some of his most distinctive mannerisms, to his single-minded workaholism, to his preference for behind-the-scenes, indirect politicking. The lessons he learned at Tambo's knee, lessons not just of politics but of life itself, are an indelible part of his makeup, as this biography makes clear.

It must be quite difficult to be regarded as a mystery man by others when you do not feel that way about yourself. Mbeki professes to be surprised by the persistence of the 'will the real Thabo please stand up?' refrain at home and abroad, and there is no reason to doubt the genuineness of his puzzlement.

As far as he is concerned there are no great mysteries to be resolved, there is no Rosetta Stone of his character waiting to be given up by the desert sands: he is who he says he is. This book is unlikely to give him swift relief on that score: public clarity will come only as hindsight delivers its verdict on the Mbeki presidency.

To their credit the authors, both of them respected and seasoned political journalists, eschew amateur political fortune-telling and make no promises about the book that they cannot fulfil. They resist the temptation to claim to be cracking a code, undertaking rather to provide an introductory biography of an important figure whose most decisive days are upon him. Where they are drawing their own subjective conclusions I think they make it plain enough. The value of the text lies in its gathering together of the salient facts so far of a significant life. Readers can make up their own minds about the meaning of those facts.

It is worth noting that this is neither an authorised biography nor a hostile exposé, and has the benefit therefore of access without spin-control, criticism without malice. It does not stretch attempted objectivity to the point of blandness, but neither need you search for a hidden agenda.

It also provides, in addition to the biographical bricks and mortar, the full texts of Mbeki's most important speeches – essential reading if one wants to grasp the two vital, intertwined philosophical strands of the African Renaissance and the Two Nations.

In the most constructive sense, then, this biography is an Mbeki primer. It will act as a springboard for more detailed thematic work, but for now it will be a standard text. Readers will understand Mbeki – and, indeed, his generation of black South African anti-apartheid activists – better after reading this book, even if it is unable to shine a clear light on his soul.

Shaun Johnson
March 1999

Acknowledgements

The authors would like to thank all those, named and unnamed, who kindly agreed to give interviews on their experiences and dealings with Thabo Mbeki over the years. The University of the Western Cape's Mayibuye Centre was an invaluable resource for archive material while the Independent Newspaper Company, in particular the Parliamentary Bureau, provided a great deal of support without which this book would not have been possible. Our thanks also go to Southern Books for their enthusiasm with the concept and professionalism in helping us carry it out.

Gentle I am, and calm
and with abstracted pace
absorbed in planning
courteous to servility

but wailings fill the chambers of my heart
and in my head
behind my quiet eyes
I hear the cries and sirens

From 'I am the Exile', by Dennis Brutus

Introduction

Thabo Mbeki sits in an armchair, looking dead ahead, the television cameras rolling. His hands are crossed tautly in his lap. Children are gathered round him, one leaning on each of his knees, a couple more on best behaviour surrounding the seated figure. South Africa's deputy president seems stiff and uncomfortable.

'President Mandela has asked me to address you on his behalf,' he says. 'I am honoured to be able to do so.' Ever formal, ever eloquent, the man who will be South Africa's next president appears a stark contrast to the man whose large shoes he must soon fill. Surround Mandela with children and he has light in his eyes and a spring in his step. Place them around Mbeki and he looks awkward and self-conscious. 'I don't imagine there's any such requirement,' he said in 1997 to the charge that he would not be able to fill Mandela's shoes. 'Anyway, he's got very big feet... I don't believe I could grow taller or start wearing strange shirts.'[1]

As one of the children throws an arm casually over his knee, Mbeki reads off the statement he was not expecting to deliver. Until the day before Friday, 9 October 1998, the declaration was touted as being a presidential address. The press gallery in parliament hummed with speculation over what the address would contain: would Mandela announce that someone in his family had HIV/AIDS? Would a major new programme be launched? Why all the hype and the excitement?

As he has had to do on countless occasions over the last two or three years of the Mandela administration, it was Mbeki who was called in to take up the reins as Mandela bowed once more to the pressures of his 80 hard years and increasingly fragile health. While many senior politicians both in South Africa and abroad charge staffers to write their speeches, Mbeki generally does them himself. Frequently, he sits up into the early hours of dawn honing and rewriting his missives, particularly if the speech is an important one.

On this day, he has not had long to prepare. He only received the draft from the ministry of health the day before. The declaration is short and to the point. It is filled, however, with the familiar Mbeki rhythm, the elegant economy which has become the hallmark of his addresses over the years.

'For too long we have closed our eyes as a nation, hoping the truth was not so real,' he says of the threat of AIDS. 'The danger is real ... Because it is carried and communicated by other human beings, it is with us in our work places, in our classrooms and our lecture halls. It is there in our church gatherings and other religious functions. Aids walks with us. It travels with us wherever we go. It is there when we play sport. It is there when we sing and dance.'

His words at times have a lyric conciseness, a rolling syntactical logic that gathers momentum like the utterings of a southern preacher. But where Mandela may have tousled the head of the closest child or pulled him on to his knee, Mbeki wouldn't look more uncomfortable if he were sitting there naked addressing the nation.

This is not to say that a politician's relationship with children needs to be a defining characteristic. Since the invention of the camera, incalculable numbers of politicians have seized public occasions to take hold of the nearest baby in a show of mushy humanity and kindliness. But the contrast with Mandela, who has made children a key symbol of his post-Robben Island life, is a small indication of the difference in style the two men exhibit. Of course, the differences don't stop there, and during the course of this book, readers will hopefully garner a clearer idea of what those differences are and how they are likely to impact on us as a nation as well on those who are required to fulfil the instructions and formulate the policies that will come to define the Mbeki presidential term.

Little more than five years ago, Mbeki was the head of the department of international affairs of the African National Congress (ANC) and was widely tipped to become democratic South Africa's first Foreign Minister.

In 1999, Mbeki, having already secured the presidency of the country's majority party, is almost certain to inherit the nation's top executive post from the legend that is Mandela.

But little is known about Mbeki the man. His successes, and failures, have often been achieved or borne behind the closed doors of the liberation movement and then of the party. His gradual rise to prominence, behind the shirt-tails of his famous father, Govan, and under the tutelage of Oliver Tambo, took place far from South African turf and beyond the gaze of local communities. Mbeki, however, brings to the presidency a wealth of intra-party and international experience together with a radical and original political vision forged in colonial and post-colonial African history and tempered by the dynamics and personalities of the struggle against apartheid.

There has been, and continues to be, controversy and uncertainty about the skills and tactics of Mbeki over the years: speculation about his ruthless political acumen, of his alienation from South Africa's grassroots communities, of his interventions in empowerment deals, of his need to consult to the point of indecisiveness. We intend to touch on these perceptions, illustrating their existence or otherwise with concrete examples from the back rooms and corridors of Mbeki's cloistered life. They also uncover the way in which Mbeki looks at and deals with life on a day-to-day basis, his family and past, his routines and preferences, his major speeches and key interactions, painting as we go a picture of the man who will lead South Africa into the next century.

But Mbeki does not start his incumbency from scratch, far from it. It has been five years since the South African miracle captivated the world. The end of 300 years of colonialism and apartheid, the end of racial conflict, the dawn of democracy were all compelling notions not only to a world still wracked with violence and division but to a nation tired of repression, inter-racial hostility and international isolation.

But few would have guessed, even once civil war had been narrowly averted, the depth of social crises, the economic stagnation and the immense domestic and global challenges to policy-makers in the aftermath of the miracle. It is not often that sports men or women contrive to provide profound insights into the human condition. More usually, clichés such as 'the best side won,' 'a game is made up of two halves' or 'I couldn't have done it without my team-mates' are the order of the day. But in 1998, the manager of the Montreal Expos baseball team in America said the following of an extraordinary period of sporting achievement: 'Sometimes, something has to almost die... for the miracle to take place.'

What was true for baseball, was true also for South Africa. As a nation, South Africa was close to death by 1994. The body politic was in tatters, the economy was ailing and uncompetitive, the pain of the past festered unaddressed, violence was commonplace, the legacy of apartheid – the suspicion, the poverty, the greed, the hatred, the inequity, the anger, the corruption – remained unresolved. By 1994, some 2,3 million South Africans were estimated to be suffering from malnutrition, 30 per cent of the population was illiterate, only 13 per cent of the people in the rural areas had running water in their houses and, in Gauteng, the province around Johannesburg where the most wealth is accumulated, nearly a quarter of the black population lived in shacks made of plastic and tin[2].

But the miracle of democracy torn from the clutches of civil war spurred on the nation, making us believe that if we could survive apartheid, we could achieve anything. We were proud of our indomitable spirit, of our powers of forgiveness, of our ability to sit side by side and reach consensus, of our new president, Nelson Mandela. Buoyed by the spirit of renaissance and hope, South Africa's first democratic government set out to correct the wrongs of the past, to provide reconstruction and development and to forge a new path to a non-racial, harmonious future.

Caught up by the euphoria of the moment, rash promises were made, such as the late housing minister Joe Slovo's claim that a million houses would be built within the first year, and pressing problems, such as the bloated and corrupt public service, were ignored or postponed. Rather like the 'liberation before education' slogan of the 1980s, the end was deemed more important than the means.

But many great achievements have been made since 1994. One of the world's most liberal constitutions was enshrined, a representative parliament was inaugurated, the Truth and Reconciliation Commission began to tease out the pain and suffering of the past, institutions supporting democracy – such as the Human Rights Commission, the Independent Electoral Commission, and the Public Protector – were established and, in virtually every field of human endeavour, initiatives were taken to improve the lot of the ordinary person.

But as time went on and the years began to pass, the enormity of the problems became more and more ominous. Perhaps most important of these concerns is unemployment, now estimated to be well above 30 per cent and climbing – though employment levels in the informal sector are difficult to gauge. With economic growth optimistically predicted to be little more than 0,5 per cent in 1999, the rationalisation of industry in the face of a more competitive, international environment, the need to trim a massive public service, the dwindling contribution of gold to the fiscus and the vulnerability of the emerging, local economy to the global marketplace, have forced the issue of unemployment to the top of the national political agenda.

The Congress of South African Trade Unions (Cosatu), which, along with the South African Communist Party, make up the ruling government alliance with the ANC, has pushed the Mandela administration to temper its economic policy of strict fiscal discipline and debt reduction in the hope of creating more jobs. The Mbeki administration will face similar and perhaps more severe pressures.

But along with joblessness come the attendant social problems of crime, spousal and child abuse, corruption, decay and poverty. With the bulk of the state budget going on either salaries or debt repayments, there is simply little left to meet the aspirations of the millions of South Africans who suffered for so long under apartheid and who continue to suffer. Add to this formula the devastating impact of the turmoil on the world's stock markets in 1997. Like many emerging economies, South Africa took a severe battering. The rand depreciated 28 per cent against the US dollar between January and September of 1997 while 22 per cent was wiped off the value of the Johannesburg Stock Exchange (JSE). Foreign investment, which had soared from R4,3 billion in 1994 to R20,2 billion in 1997, turned into a net capital outflow in 1998. Amongst corporations which lost billions of rands in market capitalisation was a group of black-owned companies which now account for 10 per cent of the JSE.

The companies, including New Africa Investments Limited (NAIL) – of which, until his resignation in February 1999, the deputy chairman was former African National Congress chief negotiator Cyril Ramaphosa – are at the forefront of initiatives to give black South Africans greater ownership of the formerly white-dominated economy. The negative impact of a profoundly bearish global marketplace prompted interest rates in South Africa to climb by 6 per cent between April and October 1998 – with mortgage bonds rising to 25 per cent per annum – surging inflation of close to 9 per cent and the lowest business confidence levels for more than ten years.

The minister of finance, Trevor Manuel, told parliament at the time: 'There are many emerging economies that have been dragged into the vortex of this storm.'

But while the impact of the crash affected the local economy deeply, hindered the reconstruction after apartheid and damaged sorely needed job creation, the fundamentals of the South African economy remain solid. South Africa has a sound and well-capitalised banking sector in which bad debts account for 3 per cent of banks' portfolios, compared to approximately 30 per cent in Japan. The government has reduced its fiscal deficit from 10 per cent in 1993/94 to a targeted 3,5 per cent in 1999/2000. Inflation has been brought down to single digits and has remained there. Sound fiscal policies and reforms in revenue collection and expenditure management have meant cut-backs are not anticipated in health, education, welfare payments or housing projects.

But further ghouls lurk in the shadows. Southern Africa has the highest rate of HIV/AIDS infection in the world, random acts of terror and criminality have scared off investors and tourists, and violence and civil war burst out sporadically but intensely on the subcontinent. Three hundred years of apartheid have greatly lowered the value of human life, diminished respect for individual and community rights and have left income disparities between rich and poor at among the most severe on the planet. These are tough obstacles by any standards, let alone for a government in office for the first time or for its successors in the years to come.

But doom and gloom has never been a South African attitude and reasons to be cheerful abound. In the five years since Mandela took the helm, real differences have been made. Millions of people have received access to electricity and water for the first time, free health care has been made available to the most needy, hundreds of thousands of new homes have been built and in virtually every field, from education to minerals, from welfare to construction, new policies are being framed and implemented.

Among the hundreds of Bills passed by parliament during Mandela's first, and last, presidential term are a number which fundamentally change skewed apartheid imbalances and put in place a process of radical social and economic transformation. In the labour field, the Employment Equity Bill provides our country with what its supporters describe as the most comprehensive anti-discriminatory legislation in the world and a practical framework to redress past discrimination in the workplace. (The Bill's detractors claim it will damage investment, burden companies and dampen economic growth.)

In the face of growing discomfort over current crime levels, legislation has been passed, or is being finalised, dealing in particular with violent and organised crime. New laws have been introduced dealing with bail, parole, and minimum sentences targeting especially violent crime. The Prevention of Organised Crime Bill makes provision for drastic action against gangs. The Domestic Violence Bill and Maintenance Bill look at the special needs of women and children and make it clear that violence and abuse aimed at women and children are not tolerated.

In health, education, land affairs, labour, justice, broadcasting and sport, key legislation has been introduced providing the first few steps toward the overhaul of apartheid, a system described accurately by the United Nations as a crime against humanity.

Little by little, the country is being transformed from an apartheid regime to a thriving constitutional democracy. As a result, Mbeki has been arguing that developments here, as well as on the continent at large, are the first signs of a renewal in the fortunes of Africa, of an African Renaissance. The notion forms part of a growing body of political thought by which Mbeki will come to judge his own successes and failures in the years to come. It is a collection of ideas that have been spawned during the course of his life, some he has inherited or adapted, and honed by his indisputable intellectual acuity. We will attempt, during the course of this book, to explain and elaborate these theories, for they will define the direction of the Mbeki presidency and the future path of the nation.

We cannot hope, in this work, however, to provide a complete portrait of the life of Thabo Mbeki. Even the life of an ordinary person whom most would regard as simple or unremarkable has been coloured and affected by the very things which make us human: our relationships with others, our beliefs and attitudes, our conditions of life and work, our habits and preferences. Even in our own minds, our memories change with time. Sometimes we ignore the bad times and cling to the good, sometimes it is the other way round. Our brothers or sisters will remember events in earlier life quite differently to the way we remember them. Our friends or parents will also have recollections which may not match our own. Indeed, history itself is little more than collecting together the memories of those who were there and who have chosen, or been able, to describe their experiences.

In thinking back on events, especially momentous ones, one is apt to reinterpret things to suit what we might have been thinking at the time or to fit in more closely with what we ought to have been thinking. Memory itself is subjective and fluid, either about oneself or about others. In Thabo Mbeki, the difficulties of gathering a personal history become as complex as understanding the history of South Africa itself. His life spans more than 50 years of an extraordinary period, perhaps the most extraordinary period, in the life of our nation. What more important things could happen than the formal introduction of apartheid and the successful conclusion of a three-decade struggle for liberation and democracy? Nobody was unaffected by this struggle, no life untouched, no past unimportant, no future undetermined.

The period between 1942, when Mbeki was born in the tiny location of Mbewuleni in the Transkei, and 1999, when he assumes the mantle of the presidency, has been nothing short of cataclysmic for the country as a whole. His life, as we will see, is very much a microcosmic symbol of this change. He is its victim and its author, its child and its parent. The skills and experiences, strengths and frailties he brings to bear on our future are the product of his past and of the lives of those who went before him. They grew out of his, and our, history. They are the flotsam and jetsam of a life lived, day by day, in a world gripped by turmoil and change.

Many in South Africa suffered the injustices of apartheid, or enjoyed its privileges, grimly determined to do the best they could. They thought they could not change things, that they couldn't make a difference. They took what life threw at them, acted at times with courage and nurtured the hope that one day things would be better.

Mbeki was not afforded this luxury. Yes, he had hope and courage. Yes, he was as prone to the unexpected twists of life as you or I. But Mbeki knew virtually from day one that politics and the struggle would not just be incidental to his life, they were his life and his life was theirs. This was not a unique state of affairs. Increasingly from the turn of the century, individuals and their families adopted the struggle against racist oppression as their defining objective and accepted its heavy demands and substantial sacrifices with stoic acknowledgement. Normal family relations, under such circumstances, were not possible.

Friends and comrades became family and families became distant and dislocated. They often became a group of individuals operating within a different communal context. Marriages became strained and broke. Communications lapsed, then ceased. Weddings and family events were missed. The upbringing and education of one's children were left to others.

It was no easy task to throw away both the extended and close family ties which have characterised African society for centuries in search of an ideal, democracy, which had existed for as long. But many chose this way. Hundreds paid for the choice with their lives and with the lives of their families.

As Nelson Mandela said in his speech at his daughter Zindzi's wedding: 'It seems to be the destiny of freedom fighters to have unstable personal lives. When your life is in the struggle, as mine was, there is little room left for family. That has always been my greatest regret and the most painful aspect of the choice I made.'[3]

The family into which Thabo Mbeki was born was torn apart and scattered to the winds during the course of the struggle against apartheid. Thabo's father, Govan, was imprisoned for almost three decades, his sister was detained for something she had no knowledge of, his youngest brother is missing, presumed killed, his only child, a son, has also disappeared and is presumed dead. Mbeki himself, after spending much of his childhood in boarding schools and away from home, spent almost 30 years living in exile. His younger brother, Moeletsi, went away to school in Lesotho and then too lived in exile. All that was left of the Mbeki family during these many hard years was Ma Mofokeng, Thabo's mother, who eked out a living in the impoverished countryside of the Transkei for decade after decade. She still does.

This biography is not an authorised or sensitised work. It does not have the official stamp of approval of the deputy presidency, nor have its contents been vetted or changed to suit propagandistic or political purposes. In fact, there are subjects dealt with in this book that Thabo never talks about, not even to his family, and others he will be angry about or will deny.

It is worth pointing out, however, some of the difficulties we have experienced in putting together a work of this kind. First and foremost, the organisation with which Mbeki has been involved since adolescence, the ANC, was not only illegal in South Africa until 1990 but was engaged in a military struggle against the state. As such its officials were constantly in fear of violent reprisals, assassinations and abductions at the hands of the state. This forced the ANC to operate clandestinely. And while this was essential for the survival of the ANC, and for its members, it makes gathering a history of the organisation's policy-making and structure during the exile years especially difficult.

Says Howard Barrell, a journalist who researched a doctoral thesis on the ANC in exile for the University of Oxford: 'Little of value has been made public about how the ANC's inner councils tried to shape ANC political and military operations inside South Africa. ... what has been said publicly has often been rendered bland by the requirements of security or been coloured by the needs of propaganda.'[4]

We have, therefore, had to rely in this work on interviews with people who were there, as well as on the little academic and journalistic work that has been done thus far to decipher Thabo's role in events and developments within the ANC's executive structure. Accounts have often contradicted one another or put a different emphasis on one aspect over another. It is worth adding, too, that at the time the bulk of the research for this work was undertaken, South Africa's second democratic elections were little more than a few months away. People were wary of talking freely or on the record or, if they did cooperate with the authors, they may have done so with the election in mind. We have attempted to verify and cross check information with different sources from all relevant parties and present these as best we know how and as close to the truth as it has been possible to come.

The information was also collated in a relatively short period of time and the works produced in the years ahead as well as events themselves will validate or disprove our assumptions and understandings. We have no doubt, however, that this will be only the first of a number of contributions to the record of South African contemporary history as it unfolds. We look forward to a more complete and scholarly rendition of events and of the people who participated in them. In the meantime, this book is offered as an introduction to a man whom we will no doubt become more than accustomed in the years ahead and whose real role in South Africa has yet to be played.

1

Family life and beginnings

It is the helicopter that brings the crowd. Chattering over the scattered hamlets and kraals of rural Transkei, people look up and come running. In the clean-swept dirt yard of the Goodwill store in Nceleni, a small group know at once who the passenger of the craft is. 'It's Thabo,' they call. 'Thabo has come home.'

Chores in the village are abandoned, livestock left to fend for themselves. At a gravestone unveiling ceremony nearby, solemn guests take one look at the camouflaged machine hovering above and depart as one holding their hats firmly on their heads. It is late 1998, and waiting by the broken, bleached goalposts of Nceleni's only soccer field, a line of dusty police cars and a few dozen intrigued onlookers await the deputy president's arrival.

Soon, the helicopter comes to a rest and the small, meticulously dressed form of Thabo Mbeki is hustled from under the swirling blades and into a vehicle with flashing lights that the villagers guess 'must have been brought over from Butterworth'. The convoy begins its short trip to the white-washed Goodwill store a few hundred metres down a deeply ridged mud road. By the time the line of cars and four-wheel-drive trucks have stopped outside the store, replete with its Sunlight Soap and Joko Tea signs, its chicken-wire protected counter and racks of tinned foods, close to 300 people have gathered. They sing and cheer, begging Thabo to address them.

Inside the modest house, connected by a ragged-topped wooden door to the shop, Thabo's mother, Ma Mofokeng, waits to see her son for the first time in more than two years.

She is a small woman with large, owl-like eyes shining through thick spectacles. She is deeply attentive, sceptical in her questioning and, like the rest of her family, fiercely independent. 'Everybody is so wild and excited,' she says, anticipating the short half-hour visit. 'The community is so proud of Thabo and they want him to come and shake the hand of each and every one of them.'

Thabo's sister, Linda, knows he is coming home that day. Ma Mofokeng's hand-wound telephone is linked to a party line and, more often than not, is out of order. During the severe thunderstorms that occasionally drift over Nceleni from the sea, the lightning quickly wrecks what human hands have temporarily repaired. Thabo, as usual, has called Linda at her shebeen in Umsobomvu, on the outskirts of Butterworth about 30 kilometres from Nceleni, to pass on the message of his homecoming. He will be stopping over in Butterworth, he tells her, but will then be flying on to Nceleni to open a technical college and to see Ma Mofokeng. Linda, who has also not seen her younger brother in more than two years, thinks she will try and say hello to him before he goes on to Nceleni. The taxis, in any case, are infrequent and expensive and the road is very bad.

If the crowd awaiting Thabo at Nceleni is big, it is huge at Butterworth. 'I couldn't get near him with all that security,' Linda said afterwards. Her insistence that she is Thabo's sister is greeted only with cold, disdainful eyes and the security cordon remains unimpressed and unbroken. After waiting for some time, jostling with the crowd, she catches barely a glimpse of her brother. How many more years will it be before she sees him again? At 57 years of age, Linda is the oldest child in the Mbeki family. She is a large woman, shy with strangers and weary of repeated enquiries about her famous brother. Several of her front teeth are missing from the top row, a common feature in South Africa's Eastern Cape province.

In Nceleni, mother and son settle down onto the comfortable sofa in the small lounge. Executive aides wander about the house and, through the window, they can see security officials keeping the crowd at bay. The shop is doing fine, Ma Mofokeng tells her son, but she complains once more about the lack of piped water in the Idutywa district. Thabo's rise to president of the ANC has so far resulted in few material changes in this part of the Transkei and this is beginning to annoy the village elders – as well as Ma Mofokeng. They plan to visit him soon in a delegation to insist on at least some improvement in conditions. She tells Thabo she is doing her bit for the voter registration effort in the meanwhile and has pinned up a handwritten notice in the Goodwill store saying: 'Everybody over the age of 18 must join the ANC and vote.' As they speak, Thabo notices an unseemly white cable stapled high on the living room wall. 'Ah, so you've got electricity at last', he remarks.

Soon the 30 minutes have passed, Thabo's aides start getting fidgety and it is time to move on. Ma Mofokeng goes off to her bedroom and returns with a big bag of sweets. 'Here,' she urges him, 'why don't you go and hand these out to the people?' Thabo shakes his head. 'I don't have time for that, ma,' he replies. He gestures to a couple of his staffers to take the bag out into the yard and pass the sweets around. To cheering and ululating, Thabo leaves the small cottage and climbs back into the security vehicle parked just outside. His handlers scan the crowd suspiciously, jump into their own vehicles and the convoy moves off. Ma Mofokeng returns to her work in the store. Linda is already home in Umsobomvu, frustrated and disappointed by her brother's elusiveness. And Thabo is carried into the overcast Transkeian sky by the camouflaged helicopter that brought him, ever so fleetingly, to the place of his birth.

The pain of familial separation is not new to any of the members of the Mbeki family. It has haunted their lives for decades and continues to haunt them still. 'Things are no different now to the way they were,' says Ma Mofokeng, thinking back over the eight decades she has lived in the district of Idutywa. 'I was staying all alone in the apartheid years, and I'm staying all alone now,' she says, her expressionless face belying her years of hardship. 'The only difference is that, then, I had to, and now, I have a choice. But I am lonely now, as I was then.'

Ma Mofokeng has only recently moved across from the hills to the west of Idutywa, from a tiny village called Mbewuleni, to her current home in Nceleni on the eastern side of town. But it was in Mbewuleni where she and her new husband, Govan Mbeki, first moved in 1940 to start a new life and begin a family. And it was here that Thabo was born and where his story begins.

Ma Mofokeng — or Epainette Moerane as she was known before she was married (Ma Mofokeng is a clan name) — and Govan came from similar households. Academics refer to their class as 'typically progressive' or 'modernising peasant families characteristic of the Transkei region at the turn of the century.'[1] But, in fact, only a few possessions, a little land, some education and a house made of brick separated them from their deeply impoverished and illiterate neighbours.

Ma Mofokeng was raised in the Mount Fletcher district near the rugged, mountainous border between Transkei and Lesotho. Her father was a lay preacher in the Methodist Church who kept some livestock on a small farm. After obtaining a Cape Senior Certificate, the highest school diploma available at the time, she went into teaching and secured a post at the Taylor Street Secondary School in Durban, where her subjects were English and Geography. It was here that she met Betty du Toit, an Afrikaner woman and a Communist Party of South Africa member, who was involved in organising the sugar workers in Natal[2].

Betty du Toit and her communist friends and colleagues were to have a profound influence on Ma Mofokeng and she soon took the plunge and joined up. That was in the mid-1930s, quite some time before her husband-to-be applied for his party membership card. These days, she feels the party has changed too much to attract her continuing loyalty. 'The Communist Party to which I belonged then has changed now. Then, it was purely a workers' party. It had its own newspaper, *Inkululeko*. Now, it is full of contradictions.'

She shakes her head, fingering the rim of the straw hat on her lap. She had planned to go and spread animal dung on her garden until the clouds overhead darkened and we arrived on her doorstep. As we talk, her old telephone signals the approaching storm by tinging every time the line is struck by lightning. The tings become more frequent until rain drives against the tin roof and a booming flash hits the telephone poll by her front gate, sending a shower of sparks pluming toward the moistening road.

Ma Mofokeng remains a staunch peasant activist, deeply rooted in the land and amongst the people she has always known and cared about. It is this, more than anything, which has prevented her from moving from this backward, isolated community to more comfortable surroundings. Her determination to stay in Idutywa and do what she can for her kin and community has caused 'differences of opinion' between her and her

4

husband, Govan, who lives most of the time in a smart, modern bungalow next door to Thabo's official residence about 800 kilometres away in Cape Town.

It was at the Taylor Street Secondary School where Ma Mofokeng met Govan, a fellow teacher with equally left-leaning political inclinations, a talent on the rugby field and a ballroom dancer of some repute. She remembers Govan back in the days when they first met as 'an unostentatious, rather lonely young man: "particular about how he dresses, particular about how he speaks"[3].' The attributes were among many he was to share with his eldest son, Thabo.

Govan, too, came from the modest Transkeian peasant élite. His father, Skelewu, was a devout Methodist and teetotaller who would say grace even before drinking a glass of water[4]. His mother was the daughter of a Methodist evangelist and the large family of eight children were brought up according to strict Methodist principles. Along with religion, education was held in high esteem by Govan's parents and by Govan himself. It was a trait he would hand down, in time, to his own family. Almost all of Govan's seven older siblings became teachers and he too headed in this direction.

At boarding school in Healdtown he was introduced to Latin, to which he took a shine and at which he excelled. He later studied the classical language for two years at Fort Hare University and went on to teach it during his own sporadic career as an educationist.

The late 1920s and 1930s were to be formative years for both Ma Mofokeng and Govan. 'My ideas on politics took shape towards the end of the 1920s and the early 1930s,' says Govan of that time[5].

During the late 1920s, Govan used to travel around the Transkei with his cousin, Robert, who was an organiser for the Industrial and Commercial Workers' Union (ICU). The ICU was the first real mass organisation of black South Africans and was engaged in several battles with employers and with the state during the 1920s. One of the most important of these confrontations surrounded the passage of the Industrial Conciliation Act in 1924. The Act forced collective bargaining with whites-only unions and restricted black workers from taking on skilled or even semi-skilled jobs.

In the 1930s, the decade before Thabo's birth, the Industrial Conciliation Act, together with a number of other pieces of discriminatory legislation known as the Hertzog Bills, were introduced by Prime Minister JBM Hertzog. The Bills were to have an enormous impact on the lives of Thabo's parents and later on Thabo's own life too. The Bills saw the introduction of the pass laws, which meant that blacks wanting to travel or enter 'white areas' would need official permission and documentation. The Representation of Natives Act made their vote worthless, and the Land and Trust Act limited their ability to own land to a tiny 13 per cent of South Africa's territory.

The Bills stirred up great animosity within the black community and heralded a rapid change in how both Govan and Ma Mofokeng viewed the world and their place in it. Crippling constraints had been put in place which were deliberately aimed at limiting their prospects and those of their children. The experience of travelling to ICU meetings with Robert, of helping with interpretations and listening to the debates and arguments, had quite an effect on Govan. But it was really when, as a young man, he began his studies at Fort Hare University in 1932 that his political views began to gel.

Fort Hare at that time was humming with the news of Italy's invasion of Ethiopia, of opposition to the Hertzog bills and of the important African personalities and radical beliefs being expressed at the All-Africa Convention held in 1935.

Also at this time, Govan was befriended by a young South African Communist, Eddie Roux, and his wife Win. The two communists were on honeymoon in 1933, and were travelling the Transkeian countryside with their camping gear and a donkey. One day, while still on their honeymoon trip, they set up their tent on the banks of the Tyhume River, a stone's throw from Fort Hare, and held a few outdoor meetings with the students. In the evenings, Govan would walk across the fields to join them in their tent for late-night chats and discussions. He was enthralled by their talk of equality and class war, of the power of the masses and of the dream of revolution against tyranny and oppression[6].

Govan also spent each holiday during those years with one of his half-sisters, Fanny, in Johannesburg. There he came face to face with the growing realities of apartheid and the politics of resistance gathering steam in the black urban areas. He worked in the holidays as a newspaper vendor for the Central News Agency (CNA), but was fired by his Irish manager for attempting to form his co-workers into a trade union[7]. It was to be the first of many dismissals from different jobs on the grounds of his political beliefs and activities. With a little of the money he earned from selling newspapers, and fresh with the inspiration of Robert Mbeki and the Rouxs, he would buy Lenin books for a penny each from the People's Bookshop in Braamfontein[8].

One of Govan's closest friends at that time was Thabo Mofutsanyana, known as Edwin. White South Africans, and particularly the officials who registered births, would often give their black compatriots 'easier' western names. Edwin was a leading African member of the Communist Party and he and Govan would joust for hours over matters of ideology and political theory. 'We used to talk and talk and talk and talk,' says Govan of Edwin. ' ... he was a very radical person. And he used radical language too ... big words like "nicompoop", things like that.'[9] When Govan's first son was born, he named him Thabo after his best friend.

Govan's growing sympathy to communist thought and his friendships with white and black communists were only partly to blame for his gradual scepticism toward the orthodox, Methodist Christianity he had been taught as a child. He noticed with disappointment and frustration the missionaries' silence when the Hertzog Bills were passed by the government. Where others he knew and respected were angry, the missionaries seemed to accept with resignation the new limitations on black people's rights. 'Gradually the question was taking shape in my mind: But, in fact, is there a God?' he recalls. What little was left of these beliefs, so arduously shaped by his devout parents, soon evaporated. 'By 1933, I had finished with religion,'[10] Govan remembers. But it wasn't all work and no play for Govan and Ma Mofokeng. Govan's exploits on the rugby field saw him becoming the secretary of the Fort Hare Rugby Club and the two were so enthralled with ballroom dancing, they started a club in Durban. Later, alone in his prison cell on Robben Island, Govan would rehearse those steps and twirls and imagine Ma Mofokeng smiling in his arms[11].

After a year at the Taylor Street Secondary School, Govan moved to Adams College near Amanzimtoti. The small town was not far from Durban and it was easy enough for him to see Ma Mofokeng regularly and to continue to build their close relationship. Together they moved in the social circles of Durban's intellectual left-wing élite and danced the tango and the quickstep at the club. Those days were perhaps the happiest of all the many years they were to spend together. Later, when asked whether he and Ma Mofokeng had had much fun during their lives, Govan replied: 'We didn't have fun at all'. He went on to paraphrase a poem by Kipling with the Sisyphian complaint, 'Does the road go uphill all the time?'[12]

But back in 1938, Govan and Ma Mofokeng were in love – though the good times now seem dwarfed by later events. One day that year, Govan received a telegram. It was a job offer from the Clarkesbury Institute, a teacher-training college in his beloved Transkei. He leapt at the chance to return home and soon packed his bags. The decision to return enforced the first period of extended absence between Govan and Ma Mofokeng. Much worse and longer periods of separation were soon to follow. While Govan moved back to the Transkei, Ma Mofokeng travelled to the Orange Free State, where she took up a new teaching position of her own. They saw each other during school holidays and, in 1940, they married.

Besides his teaching, his dancing and his interest in politics, Govan's writing talents had fast developed into a skill he would be able to use to earn some extra money. 'I started writing in Xhosa at an early age, but I was not writing politics. I tried to write plays and poetry. It was only later I shifted to political writings,' he recalls. The year before he was married, Govan published *Transkei in the Making*, a work of political analysis which was deeply critical of the system of local government in operation in the Transkei. While it was generally a restrained piece of analysis, there was 'a decidedly radical edge' to the work which attracted the attention of the left-wing press[13]. He was asked to edit a newspaper, the *Territorial Magazine* – later renamed *Inkundla ya Bantu* – and was appointed a director of *The Guardian*, a weekly journal which had a close association with the Communist Party.

Govan was fired from Clarkesbury for refusing to participate in school prayers, but the two newlyweds decided to settle in the Transkei in any case, in a tiny village called Mbewuleni near Idutywa. Surrounded by the thousand-metre mountains circling the floodplains of the Great Kei River, Mbewuleni is a remote, deeply rural hamlet of no more than a few dozen kraals. Perched on a hillside, swept by cold winds and torrential rain, goats, sheep and cattle continue to roam the shaved fields as they always have.

The Mbeki kraal was relatively prosperous by Mbewuleni standards, due mainly to the small general store Govan and Ma Mofokeng established on their arrival. Govan had read about cooperatives while studying privately for his Bachelor of Commerce degree in Durban and fervently believed they were an excellent means of establishing community cooperation and self-reliance. Gradually, though, as the other partners dropped out, the cooperative part of the venture fell by the wayside and the store became the Mbeki family's alone[14].

As Govan's journalism work was not especially lucrative or regular, they supplemented their income with money earned from the store and from Ma Mofokeng's baking of cakes and scones for a local coffee shop. Govan also earned some extra cash by doing typing and clerical work, such as for the local Cattle Dipping Committee, and by serving for a short while as a councillor on the Bunga, or the United Transkeian Territories General Council[15]. The kraal consisted of two mud, thatched huts: one for Govan and Ma Mofokeng and one for cooking. A third hut was added later for the children.

Their first child, Linda, was born in 1941. 'Then I remember chatting, my wife and I,' recalls Govan. 'Enough now of girls. Why? Because boys remain in the family all their lives and girls have a habit of leaving the family and adopting new names. Also, if anything goes wrong with girls, they become the burden of other families.'

Thabo was born the following year, on 18 June 1942.

'He was, according to my wish, a boy,' recalls Govan. 'But between my wife and I, there was an arrangement. She was Sotho-speaking, I'm Xhosa-speaking and we said all children must have both Xhosa and Sotho names. So I had a great friend, Thabo Mofutsanyana, or Edwin, and I named Thabo after him. Like me, Thabo's Xhosa name, Mvuyelwa (He for whom the people sing), never stuck.' The family was soon extended to four children with the birth of Thabo's two younger brothers, Moeletsi, who was born in 1945, and Jama, who completed the family in 1948.

Thabo's early years fell very much into the pattern of rural Transkeian life in the 1940s. He was a playful but introverted child, average by most accounts and in most respects. The local school, Ewing Primary, was just across the valley from the Mbeki kraal. It only went up to Standard Four and all four classes gathered under the same roof, the local Presbyterian Church hall, which was little more than a tin shed with two mud huts outside for the principal and for preparing the food. Lessons were under the strict tutelage of the principal, Mr Jeffrey Mphahlwa.

9

'Thabo never spoke much,' says Sonwabo Gustavus Mphahlwa, who was in Thabo's class throughout his years at Ewing and who was also a nephew of the principal. 'He was also clever. We played a little cricket and "jump-jump". We also took part in athletics but our favourite was relay. I was good at that and so was Thabo.'

On Fridays, the local schools in the district would take turns in hosting music concerts. All the children would gather together and sing and dance. Thabo and Moeletsi especially enjoyed these outings and would dance happily together for as long as the music continued. All the children at the Ewing Primary School, including Thabo and his sister and brothers, were fed through a government feeding programme. The arrival of the South African Railways truck, crammed with food parcels and supplies for the Mbeki store, was always a cause of great excitement. Classes were abandoned and the children would rush off to help unload wooden boxes full of soap, sacks of maize, tins of sardines and packets of candles. The children's food parcels contained bread, peanut butter, raisins, jam and, on occasion, plums.

While their classmates carried off the food parcels to the school, Thabo and Moeletsi would load up the sledge behind the temperamental old family mule, Dyakopu, with the stocks for the store. Dyakopu, meaning baboon in Xhosa, was a legend of recalcitrant moodiness and was feared around the village. 'If you went in front, it would try and bite you. If you went behind, it would kick,' says Micky Nama, another school friend, now a lawyer in Idutywa. 'Thabo was the only one that Dyakopu would go quietly with. Some days, we would try and take the mule down to the windmill to get water. We would put the water in a big drum on the sledge. When Dyakopu reached the top of the hill, it would turn around and run away, sending the drum rolling down into the nearest donga. It never did that to Thabo.'

After the stocks had been packed away into the Mbeki's tin and wood store, Ma Mofokeng would cook up a big pot of soup for the schoolchildren. On days when a cold front whipped in from the sea and an icy wind thrashed the kraals with heavy rains, the soup was especially welcomed.

Isolated even from the tiny community of Mbewuleni, the Mbeki family settled into a routine. After school, Thabo would walk home across the valley to the family kraal with his sister and brothers. He would wash his threadbare clothes with water brought from the well by Dyakopu and hang them out to dry in the late afternoon sun. While the clothes flapped in the breeze, he would clean out the suitcase in which he kept his clothes. The suitcase was one of many wooden boxes used to transport long bars of blue soap for sale at the family store. Each of the children had such a box, which they kept in their shared hut, and Ma Mofokeng insisted they were kept meticulously clean. After the boxes had been scrubbed and various other chores completed, Thabo would iron his clothes and pack them away into the suitcase. Then it was time to go out into the fields with his brothers and sister to help retrieve the community's wandering livestock.

'We had to fetch everybody's cattle,' recalls Linda. 'In those days, there was no such thing as stock theft. If there was one missing, all the boys would go and look for it. If it could still not be found by nightfall, they would have to get up very early to go and look again.' The morning searches occasionally led to a late arrival at school and this invariably led to harsh punishment being meted out by terrifying Mr Mphahlwa, the stern principal.

'When we were late he used to punish us by administering corporal punishment. He would hit us on our hands with a branch. It was painful,' says Sonwabo Mphahlwa, whose kinship with the principal did not spare him the rod. 'I used to be punished a lot and frequently because I had to go and do some farm work before going to school. I would be late sometimes.' Thabo, however, was almost always on time. Unlike his younger brother, Moeletsi, Thabo did not particularly relish the livestock hunt in the fields but they all feared the painful branch wielded by Mr Mphahlwa. Thabo far preferred, even from an early age, to pull out one of the many books his parents had collected over the years and settle down somewhere quiet to read in peace.

'Thabo's always been a great reader,' says his father, Govan. 'He read a lot of books at home, including my first one which was published in 1939 on the Transkei. There were all sorts of books there, Marxist-Leninist, the Communist Manifesto. They were there and he read them all and other literary ones, novels and so on. My wife used to complain about him. "I don't like Thabo, he's just like you", she would say. "He never does anything with his hands. Moeletsi helps around the house, Thabo doesn't. He just reads books".'

Although they were both communists, Govan and Ma Mofokeng were

11

not extreme about their anti-religious sentiments in front of the children. Thabo's sister Linda, who attended a convent school after her years at Ewing, was permitted to say grace before the evening family meal. Ma Mofokeng chuckles as she remembers how Thabo, when this solemn ritual was being performed, would nip out a hand and quickly tuck a tasty bit of meat from Linda's plate into his mouth.

Linda remembers, however, that in spite of Thabo's desire to read, all the children had their fair share of chores to do around the house and in the shop. 'Ma always kept us busy. She likes to see children busy all the time.' Ma Mofokeng agrees. She fails, undoubtedly out of loyalty, to recall her rebukes of both her husband and Thabo: 'We expect our children to be handy at home. Thabo did what the others did. If there were dishes to be washed, he was there.'

But Thabo's heart wasn't always in the chores, as few children's are. During his duties manning the counter at the shop, he would keep a book on his lap and, at times, the local villagers would find it difficult to attract his attention. It was behind the counter of the shop that he began to establish relationships with white people. Wholesalers and competing white traders would come into the store to sell or buy goods and it was often Thabo who had to deal with them.

After his clothes had been cleaned, the boxes packed, the cattle found and the chores done, it was evening and time for bed. Thabo was considered clever at school by his peers, but was a quiet young lad who didn't speak much. He hadn't been at school long, though, when he started missing classes.

Every morning he would complain of a stomach ache and stay in bed. As the day wore on, he would apparently feel better and would get up or start reading. Once this had happened for several days running, Ma Mofokeng's suspicions were aroused. 'I suspected something was going on,' she says now. Acting on her intuition that all was not what it seemed, Ma Mofokeng contacted the school principal. She discovered that while Thabo was generally performing well at school, he had a particular weakness at mathematics. He had been playing truant from school to get out of maths classes.

Says Ma Mofokeng, who had been a teacher until only a few years before: 'The next morning, as usual, he had a stomach ache in the morning. I asked somebody to bring me a piece of chalk from the school and I started him in mathematics from scratch. I drew on the ground and used objects: "If I have this many cattle outside the kraal, and bring these in, how many are in the kraal?".'

'My wife was very good in that area. In fact, she taught me,' laughs Govan. 'She taught him at home and gave him lessons and Thabo got over his problems; the road was clear.'

Unlike his brothers and sister, Thabo felt most at home and at his most talkative to the members of the community known as the 'red people' or the *amaqaba*: the overwhelming majority of illiterate peasants, the poorest, most traditional rural people who would cover their faces in ochre or red mud and wear blankets. The community at Idutywa at that time were distinctly divided in two: the small group of clerks, shopkeepers and educated petty bourgeoisie who wore European dress and were known as the *amakholwa*; and the red people. 'Thabo was always at his best with the red people,' says Ma Mofokeng. 'He would talk to them for hours and hours. If you got another person coming to the house or the store, he would close up. If a red person came, he would even forget he was reading.'

The shop, as was often the case in remote, rural areas, became more than just an outlet for candles, paraffin and canned goods. It was an advice centre, a medical surgery, a pharmacist and a post office. With many of the men in the community working as migrant labour in distant cities or on the far-off gold mines, and with a high degree of illiteracy, it was the Mbeki children who were called upon both to read incoming letters and to write letters of reply.

Says Govan: 'Every store is some sort of postal agency and we had our own postal bag. There was a high rate of illiteracy in one section of the population ... and you have got to read their letters. Often they would open the letter in the shop and they would get hold of my own children: "Here, come read here". Or write the letter in reply. ... those children got to hear about things at an age when they should not have heard about it. There's a husband working away from his family and he writes his wife at home and the husband has heard reports ... "oh, your wife is doing this and the other thing." Then the husband takes the woman to task in the letter. And the children read it. But, well, it's a service that had to be done.'[16]

Thabo and Linda were called on most frequently to provide the letter service at the store. In hindsight, this didn't worry either of them much.

Says Linda: 'We were so young, we didn't realise when a husband said this to a wife. We just didn't realise what it meant.'

Thabo, too, was unperturbed: 'I would have to read the letters and draft the replies. In the letters, they would tell their lives. It exposed us to the thinking of older people, what their problems were and what they did to resolve them.'

And so the family went about its business, its routines and its chores. Ma Mofokeng was a busy woman seeing to the store, cooking and baking, advising and assisting members of the community. Govan was always preoccupied with his work, wary of being disturbed at his writing or reading and was frequently absent on trips. He occasionally travelled back to Fort Hare where he had been elected a representative of former students on the university's governing council – or to meetings around the Transkei or in the nearby cities of East London or Port Elizabeth.

'I never really had time for the children,' he said later. 'Not that I didn't like them. Not that I didn't love them. But I was doing writing and reading so I didn't have the time to be playing with them. So I pushed them on to the mother. "Come go and play there or get to your mother or leave me alone." So that I don't know how they feel today. Probably they feel that I didn't pay sufficient attention to them as children. I wouldn't blame them if they felt like that. Now even when I get my grandchildren ... I can't be with them for long, I'm doing something else and want to be left alone.'[17]

The unreliable income from odd jobs, journalism and the shop made those early years very difficult at times for the family. There simply wasn't enough money even for the bare essentials. Govan and Ma Mofokeng, Thabo and his sister and brothers were all required to make sacrifices and to endure the hardship of poverty. 'We didn't have much ... we were so poor that for underpants, my wife had to use my pants because we couldn't afford to buy her any,' recalls Govan.[18]

If Govan and Ma Mofokeng could barely clothe themselves, things were worse for the children. They were expected to survive with the most rudimentary of possessions. 'We brought up those children like that,' says Govan, of the grinding scarcity suffered by all six of the young Mbeki family.

In 1953, matters took a turn for the worse. First, a fire damaged the store and the kraal – in the process destroying many of the families'

14

books, records and photographs – and then it was flattened in a terrible storm. Many of the goods held in the fragile wood and iron shop were perishable items and were ruined. The family's economic situation, already perilous, became desperate.

Govan was forced to put aside his written musings and his part-time clerical work and return to teaching. There were no teaching jobs in Mbewuleni, though, and he soon left, never really to return. When Govan had been at home, it was difficult for Thabo to spend much time with him. Now that he had gone, they would spend even fewer moments of familial intimacy together. In a sense, he knew his father better from his books and his writing than he did from their interactions. The family was left to Ma Mofokeng to raise and it was tough, even for her, to spend as much time with the children as she, or they, would have liked.

2

Political awakenings

D uring Thabo's childhood years, in the 1940s, black politics in South
Africa was on the move. The events of those years were to have an
indelible impact on him. The ANC was being reorganised under the
leadership of Dr AB Xuma and the Youth League, in which Nelson
Mandela was a leading player, was forcing the parent organisation into a
more radical outlook. As Thabo was growing up, trade unions expanded
rapidly among black workers, the townships and squatter camps became
increasingly politicised and active national campaigns against the pass
laws and other pieces of apartheid legislation sprouted up. New left-wing
political groupings, such as the Non-European Unity Movement, began
to emerge and became increasingly outspoken. South Africa's political
landscape had begun to shift. The struggle was gathering momentum.

In most cases, the rural areas were the last to be touched by these
events and one could hardly expect a small boy bringing livestock home
at sunset to be caught up in the whirlwind of history. But the Transkei
was not like other rural areas. It had a proud heritage, stretching back
centuries, of producing men and women of calibre who had a profound
impact on national as well as local affairs. Nelson Mandela, who was born
down the road from Idutywa, on the other side of Umtata, is a case in
point. There have been many others.

Thabo's father did his best to awaken the Transkei to the events going
on around it. He served as secretary for the Transkeian African Voters
Association and represented Idutywa as a councillor on the United
Transkeian Territories General Council. When Thabo was only four years

old, his father helped to establish a new organisation called the Transkeian Organised Bodies (TOB) group which was radically outspoken given its rural context. Through the TOB, Govan called for full citizenship rights for all people in South Africa. He urged support for the Miners' Strike underway in Johannesburg in 1946, and supported a cash collection for its victims. He backed the boycotting of the Natives' Representative Council[1].

Slowly, Thabo became aware of his father's activities as he listened to the late-night discussions in the kraal and began to try and understand the many texts lined up on the family bookshelf. When his parents' political colleagues came to visit, they treated Thabo as a person who obviously had to be interested in politics. He was expected, like any adult, to defend his views in debate and to understand that what he considered to be his store of knowledge was not necessarily correct[2]. 'Our parents never initiated any political discussions at home,' says Thabo. 'It was always up to us to raise matters with them, then they would talk about it.'

After the fire and the storm destroyed the family store, Govan found a teaching post in distant Ladysmith. Thabo, too, had to leave. The Ewing Primary School only took scholars up to Standard Four. As his father headed off to Ladysmith and his sister Linda was dispatched to a convent at Ngcobo, Thabo was accepted at a school in Queenstown. He was only ten years old when he was taken to the train station at Butterworth with his few clothes in the old soap box.

The breakup of the family was never to be mended. At first, it was due to school and the need for income, then because of exile, death and, in Govan's case, prison on Robben Island. The family, which even in its early stages was a collection of self-dependent and strong-willed individuals, became dislocated and ever more distanced. Says Thabo: 'By the time we grew up, we were used to being without our parents. We didn't feel the separation, it was a condition of life.' Of the Mbeki family relationship, Thabo's boyhood friend, Micky Nama, observed: 'It was quite unusual. But people understood.'

Govan thought of bringing Ma Mofokeng to stay with him in Ladysmith, but realised his job would always be in jeopardy for as long as he was so involved in political work and refused to condone religious activities. Better, he thought, that she stayed in Mbewuleni and minded the shop and whichever children were left. Govan's concerns were justified when he was once more dismissed from his teaching post in Ladysmith for his political beliefs.

Thabo's uncle, Michael Moerane, was a music teacher and his home in Queenstown was often filled with the sounds of practising, teaching and small concerts. Each of Moerane's six children were encouraged to take up a different instrument and, in the evenings, Thabo's uncle would accompany them all on his piano. Govan remembers going to visit one day and being pleasantly surprised at what he found. 'One evening I got to Queenstown, to my brother-in-law's house and I find him sitting at the piano and each one of his six children has his or her own musical instrument and he is accompanying them. Thabo is playing the flute and would play the piano too. That was very good. Almost every evening, that's what my brother-in-law did with his family.'

Next door to the Moeranes lived the Matshikiza family who were also renowned for their musical talents. It was Todd Matshikiza who wrote the famous musical, *King Kong*, which first brought to the world's notice the richness of South African music. Thabo used to spend time with the Matshikizas too, and it was little wonder that when faced with six essay questions at his matric exams, young Thabo opted to answer the one on 'learning to play the piano'.

It was while staying in Queenstown that Thabo engaged in his first politically conscious act. It was 1952, during the Defiance Campaign, and an ANC convoy drove past the house calling on residents – through loudspeakers – to attend a meeting the following day. Thabo and his cousin Kabeli decided they had to join the party and become part of the campaign. They sneaked out of the house the next day, sold a few coke bottles to pay for the membership fees, but were crestfallen when their money was turned down. They were told to come back later, when they were a little older[3].

When school broke for holidays, Thabo would occasionally travel home to Mbewuleni to see his mother and younger brothers, but more often he would take the train down to Port Elizabeth to be with his father. Govan, by then, was chest-deep in political work.

After leaving Ladysmith, he had taken up the position of local editor and office manager of the newspaper *New Age*, the new title of *The Guardian*, in Port Elizabeth. But if Govan was busy in the 1940s, he was frantic in the 1950s. Following the electoral victory of the National Party in 1948, the screws on black political rights were tightened with new determination and brutal effectiveness. In response, the radical youth wing of the ANC, led by Nelson Mandela, forced the party to adopt a Programme of Action in 1949 which included plans for the Passive Resistance – or Defiance – Campaign as well as numerous other protests against the gathering consolidation and enforcement of apartheid. Each new law further restricted black lives and entrenched white domination. As Albert Luthuli told a gathering in 1952: 'Today we have reached a stage where we have almost no rights at all: no adequate land for our occupation, our only asset, cattle, dwindling, no security of homes, no decent and remunerative employment, more restriction to freedom of movement through passes; in short, in these past 30 years, we have witnessed an intensification of our subjection to assure and protect white supremacy.'[4]

Thabo quickly sensed the maelstrom when the ANC arrived in the very town in which he was now living, Queenstown, for the party's annual conference in 1953. Even for a child, what Luthuli described as 'a sense of divine discontent' would have been palpable amongst the hundreds of delegates who gathered to discuss their worsening situation. On top of the Hertzog Bills of the 1930s which limited Thabo's rights to acquire land, to vote and freedom of movement, a new battery of even more tyrannical legislation had been put in place by the National Party. The Group Areas Act meant Thabo could only live in township or homeland areas, the Suppression of Communism Act ruled that his parents' political beliefs had been outlawed. The Separate Amenities Act meant Thabo couldn't go swimming at the local pool nor use the Queenstown library. The Bantu Education Act set a curriculum fit only for a manual labourer. And the Criminal Laws Amendment Act and the Public Safety Act gave the government the instruments to enforce its other laws with terrifying and violent coercive powers.

Each new law deeply affected the black community and served further to entrench apartheid and curtail black rights. They also served, with the concurrent growth in the membership and radicalising outlook of the ANC, to force what would soon be a showdown between African nationalism and Afrikaner nationalism, a tempest in which Thabo himself would soon become engulfed.

Govan in the 1950s was a full-time advocacy journalist, attending meetings and fund-raising events. He wrote analytical and theoretical articles for *New Age*, as well as for other left-wing journals such as *Liberation* and *Fighting Talk*. Between 1953 and 1956, meetings of more than ten blacks were banned in the Port Elizabeth township of New Brighton and this was extended in 1956 to the entire magisterial district. Having joined the ANC in 1935, Govan now became one of its key organisers. The banning order meant that the party, for the first time anywhere in the country, had to learn how to operate outside the reach of the law. 'It was during this time, 1956 to 1960, that we perfected methods of working underground,' he recalls[5].

Govan gave political education classes to the youth, many of whom would travel down from Lovedale College to receive instruction. But when Thabo went to stay with his father, he did not attend these classes. Instead, he formed his own little organisation and began to discuss political matters with his friends just as his father was doing. While other children of his age were going to the movies or playing in the park, Thabo's friends established committees. The restrictions on the number of black people who could gather in the same place meant, once more, there was no room for Thabo at his father's side. Only this time it was enforced by the police and the punishment for any infraction was arrest and imprisonment.

After two years in Queenstown, at 12 years of age, Thabo was on the move again. This time he returned to Butterworth in the Transkei, just 30 kilometres from Idutywa, to complete his junior certificate. 'Ma wanted him nearer home,' says Linda of the decision to change schools. 'It was my parents' decision but it was a bad one,' Thabo says now. 'I had none of the things at Butterworth, such as a piano, that I had had in Queenstown.'

Though he was barely 12 years old, Thabo was already being called on to advise adults. On his arrival in Butterworth, he was called over by the local chief, CW Monakale, who had a problem with the government's cattle-culling policies. 'He raised it, so we sat down and discussed it,' says Thabo. Meanwhile Thabo's younger brothers, Moeletsi and Jama, had been sent off to Lesotho to further their studies after the government had passed the Bantu Education Act. The Act severely limited the curricula of black schools and was an attempt to force black South Africans into ignorant subservience. As Thabo had already been at high school for a couple of years, this would not affect him. But it would consign his brothers to a markedly inferior education and even bleaker prospects.

Thabo's talents at school, which had begun to be noticed in

Queenstown, became starkly apparent in Butterworth. He was consistently scoring first class results in every exam and was academically head and shoulders above his peers. Physically, though, he was a small boy, as today he is a small man. 'The principal was a friend of mine and he said the boy was brilliant,' says Govan. As expected, Thabo achieved his junior certificate with a first class pass and the family agreed to send him to the famous Lovedale College in Alice, Govan's Alma Mater. He was by now only 14 but was put straight into the matric programme.

With his father operating underground in Port Elizabeth, Thabo now travelled home to Mbewuleni more frequently. His bookishness had become his main passion in life and he would irritate his mother by spending most of his days reading in bed. Some mornings he would collect a great pile of books around him and refuse even to change out of his pyjamas. He would just stay in bed and read, the whole day. When he was seen wandering about Mbewuleni, he always looked distracted and remote. Says Micky Nama: 'Even when he was walking, he always looked in a very plaintive mood.'

At Lovedale, Thabo's nascent political interests began to form and he became increasingly active in student politics, joining the school branch of the Society of Young Africans in 1955, which was affiliated to the Non-European Unity Movement, and then the school branch of the ANC Youth League in 1956. In response to the government's Bantu Education policies, the Youth League at Lovedale agreed to launch a mass action campaign and a strike was called. Thabo's deep involvement in the organisation of the strike at a college (he served on the executive committee) that had spawned so many great leaders of the democratic movement led to his being noticed by important figures within the ANC. It also led to his expulsion from school. Says Govan: 'They [pupils] were expelled and the parents were expected to go back and plead and accept some conditions. I didn't. When I received a letter from my wife saying Thabo was back at home, I ordered a full set of his subjects from a correspondence college, and said to him: "You study at home and get your matric". If he wasn't applying himself, my wife would tell me.' In spite of the threats, Ma Mofokeng was not as vigilant as she could have been and Thabo only got a second class pass.

Thabo arrived back in Mbewuleni in 1959 and set about trying to complete his matric, which he was due to write at St John's College in

Umtata. Besides the books and the politics, though, 16-year-old Thabo was developing an eye for girls. Having girlfriends in the kind of rural setting he grew up in was strictly taboo. It was marriage or nothing. Neither his friends, nor even his family, knew when he started seeing Olive Nokwanda Mphahlwa. She was the daughter of the same strict principal who had occasionally rapped his knuckles with a branch at the Ewing School just a few years earlier. Now, she was attending school in the nearby village of Blythswood, a few kilometres from Nqamakwe and about ten kilometres from Butterworth. They met for secret rendezvous, beyond the prying eyes of the villagers and developed a relationship on the quiet. Soon, however, the innocence of first love made way for more intimate contact. Nokwanda became pregnant.

'We never saw Thabo and my sister walking around as lovers but we did see her big stomach,' says Sonwabo Mphahlwa. The pregnancy, while not unheard of amongst the young, urban or rural, caused a stir in the village. Meetings were held behind closed doors between the families of the two miscreants and voices were raised in anger and insistence. With Govan away, it was left to Ma Mofokeng to face the principal's wrath. It was agreed that Thabo, still only 16, should pay the usual penalty for making an underage girl pregnant: five head of cattle. 'The girl's family was cross but what could they do?' says Ma Mofokeng. 'I was not happy myself either.'

Kwanda Monwabise, Thabo's only child, was born in 1959 and lived with his mother and her family for ten years. Nokwanda trained as a nurse and is currently a pensioner in Port Elizabeth. She often calls Ma Mofokeng to see how things are and to keep in touch – when she can get through on the unreliable party line. 'Kwanda was a lovely child,' says her brother Sonwabo Mphahlwa. He was quite different to his father in that he was very naughty and chatty, an extrovert compared to his introverted dad. When he reached the age of ten, Kwanda was brought back to the Mbeki kraal and was raised by Ma Mofokeng until he had passed his matric.

Thabo, meanwhile, was struggling to adapt to the birth of his child and to complete his matric when South Africa erupted. The death of 69 unarmed protestors at the hands of police in Sharpeville on 21 March 1960 sparked an unprecedented wave of protests, riots and harsh counter-measures by the security forces. The government declared a state of emergency and one of the first to be detained was Thabo's father, who was dragged off to jail in Port Elizabeth. Thabo knew how brutal the security branch could be, what methods they used to torture and interrogate political inmates. He feared for the life of the small, stubborn man whom he loved so much but who forever seemed to slip from his grasp and life.

It was little wonder, with all this going on, that Thabo did poorly at his matric exams and attained only a second class pass. But he was still hungry to learn and wanted to continue his studies. There were precious few options for such advanced learning in the Transkei, so it was inevitable that he would have to move further afield once more. The Eastern Cape was, by now, familiar territory. He had been to Port Elizabeth and to Butterworth. He had spent time in Queenstown, Alice and Idutywa. The action was happening about 800 kilometres away, in Johannesburg. There, in late December 1960, 40 black leaders together with a number of liberal and progressive whites met for a consultative conference in Orlando, Soweto, to devise a way of stopping the National Party from proceeding with its plan to turn South Africa into a republic. The move to a republic looked certain to allow the government to pursue headlong its dream of black subjugation, unfettered by colonial reluctance or global restraint. The consultative conference rejected the notion of a republic and, instead, called for an 'all-in-conference' to demand a new constitution in which blacks, and indeed all South Africans, would be granted individual, fundamental rights. It was a familiar call to Thabo: one which his father had been urging for ten years and which he had come to accept as his own passionate belief. Johannesburg, or at least, Soweto, had become one of the last bastions of opposition. It was here that Thabo knew he must go.

The well-known Sowetan advocate, Duma Nokwe, who was also secretary-general of the ANC, agreed to let him stay in his home and Britzius College in Johannesburg was prepared to sign him up for a course in GCE A-Levels. The decision made, Thabo set off.

Almost as soon as he had arrived at the Nokwe home, he received a message from Nelson Mandela. Says Thabo: 'I met Nelson Mandela for the first time in 1961. I had travelled from the Eastern Cape to Johannesburg and on my arrival received a message that he wanted to see me. I was taken aback that Mandela wanted to see me. He invited me to his house in Orlando West for lunch. We sat and chatted for a long time about a whole lot of issues, about the problems in the ANC Youth League and the youth movements in general. At that point I was active in the ANC Youth League. When I recollect that meeting, I realise how our discussion illustrated Mandela's ability to be in touch with developments on the ground. To date I do not know how Mandela knew that I was in town.'[6]

Surrounded by the hustle and bustle of South Africa's largest city, mixing with the leaders of the increasingly militant struggle for black liberation, destiny had taken Thabo by the hand, willing as he was, and he was pushed inexorably toward a life of hardship and struggle. He had already spent so much of his young life fending for himself. But until then, a short train ride would have carried him home to his mother's cooking, the sound of sheep drifting in from the fields, or to Govan's cluttered Port Elizabeth bedsit.

Even after busy Alice, the strikes and protests, the lectures and late nights arguing with his friends, Johannesburg – and the huge dormitory township next door to Soweto – was an intimidating and overwhelming place. Gangsters roamed the township streets and jazz and kwela music echoed from smoky shebeens. The police were a constant, menacing presence, checking for passes, hammering on the door late at night, watching and waiting in the shadows.

How could he not have been haunted by the thought of distant Nokwanda, raising their small child? Where would he find money to send them something at Christmas? When would he see them again?

He was wise enough to know that not all whites were brutish racists. Like Betty du Toit, who had so impressed his mother, and Anne Welsh (later Yates), his teacher at Britzius College who also helped run the South African Committee for Higher Education. Anne Welsh took an instant interest in Thabo. She recognised immediately that here was a student with extraordinary potential. Well-read, hard-working, amiable and engaging, he seemed wasted in the clutches of the apartheid education system. He needed a real challenge: tutors who would push his intellect to its limits, libraries full of demanding texts and the space and freedom to pursue his thirst for knowledge unhindered by midnight raids or by police machine-guns.

In March 1961, on the eve of the declaration of a republic, the all-in-conference, with 1 400 representatives from across the country, called for negotiations to begin on a new, democratic dispensation for South Africa. Nelson Mandela, one of the delegates, was asked to draw prime minister

Hendrik Verwoerd's attention to the resolutions. He wrote a letter to Verwoerd arguing that the rising tide of unrest spreading around the country 'could be averted only by the calling of a sovereign national convention representative of all South Africans to draw up a new, non-racial and democratic Constitution.'[7]

As they awaited a response, a national general strike was launched which ground the economy temporarily to a halt. A massive Defiance Campaign began in which thousands were arrested. Finally, the government responded. It declared a republic on 31 May 1961, and declared the ANC as well as the nascent Pan-Africanist Congress (PAC) 'unlawful organisations'. Govan was arrested once more for furthering the aims of the now banned ANC.

Grimly pursuing his academic responsibilities, Thabo – as Anne Welsh had anticipated – scored first class passes for virtually everything he did. His writing was already very advanced, sometimes almost lyrical in its structure, his arguments well ordered and convincing. Where others with his depth of reading would have over-elaborated or used long, pretentious words, Thabo's style had a natural, beguiling simplicity. He wrote as he spoke and all who read and listened carefully were quickly won over. He was a forward thinker who had a way of conjuring a vision that was as desirable as it was attainable. It was little wonder, then, that when the ANC, now underground, decided to reach out to the youth, it was Thabo to whom they turned.

As had been the case at Lovedale with the student protests, he had to be convinced to stand for the position of organising secretary of the new African Students' Organisation (ASO). His modesty and introverted nature made him reluctant to pursue the limelight or subject himself to the public approval of his peers. But put to the vote, the support was overwhelming, and justifiably so. He threw himself into this work and, as unwilling as he was to abandon his books, travelled from school to school, from college to college, talking, arguing and convincing as he went.

A report of his first speech as the new organising secretary of the ASO appeared in the newspaper *New Age* on 4 January 1962. African students were breaking with their past of submissiveness and parochialism, the young Thabo told his audience. African students now identified themselves with the struggle of their people. Where they used to strike over such matters as food, treatment by the boarding master and similar complaints, 'today students will go on strike as a sign of their revolt against the system as such, expressing opposition to a principal whose remarks and policies are objected to, or to a teacher who is believed to be spying on the students. Even local grievances among students take on this larger, political character.'[8]

The ASO grew and grew and Walter Sisulu, Duma Nokwe and the other party leaders looked on Thabo with pride and hope. Some people argue that even then certain of the party's top officials, including his father Govan, Walter Sisulu and Nelson Mandela, had already decided that, one day, Thabo would be president. If such a pact was undertaken, Thabo didn't know about it. He had more immediate things on his mind. His studies became a night-time activity and, after long days in the field, he would settle down to his books, to his other world where the hardships and frustrations of daily life would melt away in the words of great thinkers and writers.

News soon reached Thabo that his father had been arrested again and thrown into jail in Port Elizabeth. Already detained for five months in 1960, Govan was charged with furthering the aims of a banned organisation in 1961. How far home now seemed, in the middle of all this turmoil. In the midst of these events, Thabo was at the heart of things as never before. Still trying to continue his studies, still hustling his peers into political action, still missing his family and worrying about his father, he soaked up the heady atmosphere.

Besides the activity inside the country, much of the rest of the world also appeared to be on the brink of revolution in 1960 and 1961. The air was thick with anti-colonial and revolutionary struggles, from the uprising in Cuba to the Portuguese colonies, where the seeds of civil war were germinating.

Thabo, in spite of the maelstrom around him, successfully completed his A-levels with the usual outstanding results. He began a Bachelor of Arts in economics by correspondence with the University of London. Anne Welsh, his former teacher, knew she had to move quickly. Before long, he too would be thrown into some dark cell or be cut down by police bullets. She wrote a letter to Thabo's parents. It said: 'Your boy has a gift. I have written to the University of Sussex in Britain recommending him for a scholarship to study for a Masters in economics. If you can see to him getting there, I will see to his fees.'

26

3

Exile

R eleased from his second prison term in 1961 for furthering the aims
of a banned organisation, Thabo's father knew the struggle was
heading for an ugly place, a place of violence and of confrontation. Like
his father before him, he knew education was the key to a child's future as
well as to the future of his people. Since the ANC's banning in 1960, he
had become involved in the establishment of a secret military wing of the
party. The wing was to be called The Spear of the Nation, Umkhonto we
Sizwe (MK), and Govan was one of its founding members and part of its
High Command. He created a small sabotage unit in Port Elizabeth which
was gathering the resources to launch a mini-guerrilla war. He agreed that
Thabo should be sent abroad but knew that, like him, Thabo had no travel
documents. This would mean that leaving the country would be a
hazardous exercise and also one from which there would be no return.
Not until liberation.

A few ANC activists had already fled, with the security branch hot on
their heels, but the route was not well established and danger lurked
everywhere. Some had not made it and were already cooped up in
apartheid jails. Flying out from Johannesburg airport, or indeed from any
airport, was not an option, not without papers. Thabo would have to
cross into one of the neighbouring countries by foot and try to reach a
small group of ANC sympathisers who had gathered in Tanzania (then
Tanganyika). Lesotho was landlocked and would lead him to a dead end.
Mozambique and Angola were Portuguese colonies, heavily protected
and sympathetic to the Verwoerd regime. That left either Swaziland or

Botswana (then Bechuanaland), both of which were British protectorates. As he was travelling to Britain to study, British territory seemed like the best and, in fact, only alternative. It was decided that Thabo should make for Botswana and from there try to reach Tanzania.

But before Thabo and a group of friends could bolt for the north, he once again received a message from Mandela. Mandela had by now gone underground and was on the run from the police but insisted on meeting with this, the first group of ANC students to go into exile. Says Thabo: 'We met him at a secret venue in Mayfair where he conveyed his best wishes to the group and issued his last instruction before our departure. As part of the final instruction, he made two points to us. The first was that we were ambassadors of South Africa abroad and that we needed to behave properly. Secondly, he said that as one of the first groups of ANC students leaving to study abroad there was an immense responsibility on us to succeed. He said when the struggle against apartheid was over we would be expected to play a leading role in the processes of reconstruction of a post-apartheid South Africa. What struck me about this meeting was that Mandela was underground, under a lot of pressure evading the police, but still found the time to meet with this group, wish them well and boost their morale. To reach Mandela, we took all sorts of routes before we finally got to him. When we met him he was in a disguise. What struck me during our meetings in 1961 and 1962 was that despite all the pressure he was under, Madiba had a genuine concern for ordinary people. He risked his life to come and bid farewell to ordinary members of the ANC.'[1]

In September 1962, Thabo joined a group of 30 fellow students bound for exile. Among them were Mantu Shabalala-Msimang, Mandela's deputy minister of justice, and Simon Makana, South Africa's current ambassador to Russia. To conceal their intentions, their story was that they were a football team, together with supporters, headed for a match in Botswana.

Filled with trepidation, lacking documents and money, they set off in a small convoy of minibuses and made it as far as Zeerust in the Northern Province before they were pulled over and arrested. A team of special branch police officers were called up from Johannesburg and they quickly identified Thabo as one of the leaders of the group. He and a friend were kept in custody, charged with failing to produce a reference book, and the others were sent back to Johannesburg.

Thabo appeared in the Zeerust Magistrates' Court the next morning. He knew, however, from his time with the famous Sowetan advocate Duma Nokwe, that the law allowed him to appeal for time to present his reference book. The argument was accepted by the magistrate, Thabo was acquitted and he returned to Johannesburg to pick up the football team once more. This time they took the small dirt roads, avoided the police, and made it safely to Botswana. From there, they were escorted by foot across the border into southern Zimbabwe (then Southern Rhodesia) by guerrillas from the liberation movement ZANU. The group was again apprehended, this time in Bulawayo, for not having valid travel documents and were kept in jail for some six weeks. The authorities decided to deport them all but, following Thabo's arguments – this time informed by a helpful court clerk, Cyril Ndebele, who is currently Zimbabwe's parliamentary speaker – agreed to send them back to the country from which they came, Botswana, and not to South Africa, as they had feared.

Once back in Botswana, the group made their way unhindered by plane to Dar Es Salaam in Tanzania. The delay had cost Thabo weeks and it was some time yet before the passage to Britain could be arranged. He knew the university term in Britain had already started and that each day he was stuck in Africa he was falling behind. Autumn in the northern hemisphere turned to winter as September, then October passed and November began.

Back home, Thabo's family had been torn apart and scattered to the winds. His baby boy, Kwanda, now almost three, was growing up in the distant hills of the Transkei. Nokwanda, the boy's mother, was training to be a nurse, which seemed a good occupation. His two younger brothers, Moeletsi and Jama, were at school in Lesotho, having been sent away to escape the inadequacies of Bantu education. His father, Govan, was soon detained a third time under the Explosives Act, acquitted and then placed under house arrest. His sister, Linda, had moved to Cape Town to do a course in commerce. Ma Mofokeng was alone at the store in Mbewuleni, minding an empty kraal with winter approaching.

Finally, Thabo arrived in London. He contacted the University of Sussex, where he was to meant have begun his studies in September, only to be told he was too late and that he should register for the following year. He was devastated.

Once again the support network at home kicked into place. Anne

Welsh contacted the university and pleaded with them to let him start. Explaining the circumstances, she argued that his extraordinary intellect would enable him to catch up comfortably. The university authorities, like the officials in Botswana, at last agreed. Thabo rushed to Sussex, a few hours train ride from London, to begin his studies.

Already renowned for its leftist leanings and scholarship, Sussex was another critical period of experience-gaining and learning for young Thabo. For the first time in his 21 years, he could study in peace and to his heart's content. He could argue and debate without fearing arrest. He could read books that hadn't been banned and hear speakers who were free to speak their minds. He could drink his preferred whisky in bars with friends of all colours and persuasions and walk the streets without the heavy presence of his passbook in his pocket.

After the Rivonia arrests in 1963, the mass detentions of activists, the widescale unrest and the ruthless attentions of the security forces, the democratic movement was left in tatters. Some estimate that inside South Africa by 1964, the ANC, South African Communist Party and MK literally consisted of three or four active, scared members and another 50 or 60 part-time sympathisers. The only functioning components of any of the organisations were in exile.

Leaders of MK who had gone into exile in South Africa's neighbouring countries attempted in 1967 and 1968 to launch two military campaigns aimed at infiltrating guerrillas back in to the country and rebuilding political structures. Both were disastrous failures. The Wankie and Sipolilo campaigns, as they became known, succeeded in planting a few landmines just inside South African territory, but the MK casualties were high and many lives were lost. The South African security forces were just too strong, too heavily armed and mobile, knew the territory too well and had a network of informers in place that prevented successful infiltration. And while the ANC tried for the next ten years to launch military actions inside the country and to build cells of political activists, these initiatives inevitably floundered.

While Zambia, Tanzania and Zimbabwe hosted small groups of ANC and SACP cadres, London became the headquarters of the democratic movement in exile. Thabo, again uncannily at the centre of things, was perfectly placed to make his mark. As he had done at home in the early 1960s, Thabo began to build the youth and student sections of the ANC in exile. His work was noticed by Oliver Tambo, who developed a special

30

affection for the young man and who was to have a profound influence on him.

Adelaide Tambo recalls the first time that Thabo came to Oliver's notice. 'A group of six or seven young ANC students came round to our house in Highgate one day. Oliver gave them all assignments and asked them to report back the following day. When they came back the next day, some had done half the job, and the others had done nothing. Only Thabo had done all he was required to do. Oliver was angry with the others. They had all been asked at the same time, given assignments at the same time, and now some had not produced. Thabo had done perfectly everything he was required to do. Oliver said to me, "There are a lot of leadership qualities in that young man".'

During his time at Sussex, Thabo was allowed to branch out into the areas of reading and research that he loved. Besides his economics studies, he wrote a thesis on the poetry of Percy Bysshe Shelley and John Keats. Their words would remain with him in the years ahead and would be used on some surprising occasions.

In Thabo's first year at Sussex, in July of 1963, news came from home that Govan had been arrested along with several other of the ANC's highest-ranking officials at Lilliesleaf Farm in Rivonia near Johannesburg. Govan and his colleagues were put on trial for high treason, a charge which carried the death sentence. The Rivonia trial was to become one of South Africa's most famous court cases. At Sussex, a massive campaign was launched to save the lives of the accused.

Under the very real threat of being hanged – along with his colleagues – for his activism, Nelson Mandela made one of his best-known addresses to a packed courtroom: 'During my lifetime I have dedicated myself to this struggle of the African people. I have fought against white domination, and I have fought against black domination. I have cherished the ideal of a democratic and free society in which all persons live together in harmony and with equal opportunities. It is an ideal which I hope to live for and to achieve. But if needs be, it is an ideal for which I am prepared to die.' It was the last time Nelson Mandela, or Govan Mbeki, was to be seen in public for almost three decades. They were both sentenced to life imprisonment in 1964.

Caught up by the heady activism of those days, and now a member of the university's Socialist Society, Thabo attempted on two occasions to leave his university studies and join the ANC's armed wing, Umkhonto we Sizwe, to take a more active role in the struggle. Both times, ANC president Oliver Tambo refused. Disappointed, he nonetheless pursued his academic work with passion, determined that soon he would devote his life's work to the freeing of his father and his people. One of his most important influences during that time was a Hungarian-born professor of economics, Tibor Barna. One day, a despondent Thabo told Barna that in the face of the viciousness of the apartheid regime, there was little one could do so far from home. Barna replied: 'Therefore, what are you asking us to do? Are you saying we should do nothing, simply because the enemy is vicious?' The words still ringing in his ears, Thabo led a group of students on a march 60 kilometres from the university to the South African embassy in London to demand the release of the Rivonia prisoners[2].

At Sussex, Thabo also began to experience a bit more of the outside world. He often led ANC student delegations to conferences in different parts of Britain, from London and Birmingham to Manchester, as well as overseas to the United States and Europe. Essop Pahad, one of Thabo's closest friends at Sussex and later deputy minister in the office of the deputy president, recalls how, even at university, Thabo sought to take on the giants of the South African economy in debate. 'When we were at Sussex, there was some Christian society which invited an MD of Anglo American to address them on the South African economy. The meeting was held in Gower Street and Thabo said to me, "let's go". We went and listened ... and [Thabo] requested to pose a question. His question was, "Is it not true that apartheid is not good for profits?" At the end of the interaction, the MD, who had been placed in a difficult position ... agreed with him and was ultimately convinced that Anglo American had to become a bigger opponent of apartheid.'

Upon completing his economics Masters degree in 1966, Thabo received the first and only message from his father during his years on Robben Island. It was contained in a letter sent to his mother and was relayed through the channels to him in London. It said 'continue with your studies and get your doctorate'. Thabo had never asked for advice from his father before, not personal, political or otherwise. But Govan felt that a doctorate would open new doors for his son, would win him respect and admiration wherever he went. He felt it so important he broke the unwritten, unspoken contract of a lifetime to convey his wishes. Study on, he said. Achieve your doctorate. Make your family and your people proud.

Govan received no response and did not bother to try again. As he said later: 'In my family, no one depends on one another, no one looks to the other for this or the other thing … we work as a team as I work with my comrades in the ANC. We have the same goal. Thabo has never asked for advice. We strengthen ourselves.'

Thabo ignored his father's recommendation and was employed by the ANC's London office full-time to work with Tambo and Communist Party leader Yusuf Dadoo. As Thabo soon learnt, life in exile within the formal structures of the democratic movement was a very different proposition to studying full-time with the occasional organising thrown in. The late 1960s and early 1970s were an extremely bleak period for the movement. Inside South Africa, the ANC had been crushed and humiliated, outside, they squabbled over strategy and ideological preference. The movement was determined to proceed with its vision of armed liberation. It hoped initially to build a peasant-based revolt along Cuban and Vietnamese lines, originally spurred on by the thinking of Thabo's father. But the Rivonia arrests and the state of emergency put paid to that idea. Between 1963 and 1976 no armed actions by the liberation movement took place at all inside South Africa.

Externally, the bickering continued. Factions were formed and factions within factions. Members, on several occasions, were expelled, sometimes in groups of five or eight at a time. The workerists fought with the black liberationists, the hardline communists challenged the less radical socialists. The need for secrecy amid concerns over infiltration by agents of the South African state covered the debates and communications with an opaque shroud which, more than ever, divided and confused the exile community. The movement was a hotbed of insecurity.

Into this quagmire, Thabo gingerly stepped. As a young, competent, western-educated intellectual he was immediately aware of the danger. Power in those days was about position, allies and knowledge. Thabo had knowledge and people feared him because of it. It meant he was a threat to their positions and to the perks and patronage that went with it. Thabo had the ear of Tambo but needed to protect himself in the same way everybody else did: with trusted, loyal allies. Whether or not they were good, or able or clever was unimportant. If they could be relied on, if they would warn him of the ghoul in the shadows or of the conspiracy afoot, if they could protect his back, they were more to be valued than a sackful of doctorates.

During his years at Sussex, Thabo had grown especially close to a number of other South African exiles to whom he now looked for allies. The Pahad brothers, Essop and Aziz, were two of these, as was Pallo Jordan. Before long, Thabo's brother Moeletsi joined him in London. While they had their individual faults, they were all Thabo had. Essop and Aziz were bright but nowhere near matched Thabo's intellect, Moeletsi struggled to find the same commitment to politics as his brother and even became known as a 'Maoist' on the far left of the spectrum of ANC ideological positions, and while Pallo came close to being Thabo's intellectual peer, he was considered a lazy procrastinator. But he trusted them and they were loyal, and that was the only really important requirement.

'Thabo, Aziz, Essop and Pallo were a close group and were always together', says Adelaide Tambo. 'At Christmas at my place [Highgate], we used to have a big lunch with sometimes 20, sometimes 30 people. Each and every room in the house was a bedroom with sleeping bags everywhere. On Boxing Day, the four of them would go out and visit their friends and they would come back in the evening to eat a big pot of curried turkey. Thabo used to stay at our house during the holidays and used to take up holiday work. One job was clipping time cards at a building society. He said it was very boring. I saw Thabo in a suit for the first time at his graduation in Brighton where the University of Sussex is. I'd never seem him that smart. Essop and Aziz and Thabo all graduated at the same time and they all used to dress scruffily. But on that day, they all wore suits.'

Looking around him, however, Thabo knew his friends could not be relied on to understand or even implement his vision. He understood the importance of the military struggle but knew this would never work without solid political foundations. If he wanted something done, he would have to do it himself. On top of the bookish solitude and empathy with the peasants he had cherished as a child, he now accumulated a reluctance to delegate and an appreciation of loyalty. These were all to become hallmarks of Thabo as he walked the path of his future. Add to this a long-sightedness rooted in his intellectual acuity and an easy manner with people honed during his years of organising the youth, and his armoury was almost complete. The only other piece of the jigsaw was sheer luck: the kind of good fortune that had dropped him into

Queenstown in 1953 and into Soweto during the early 1960s. The luck which had carried him safely into exile.

It was during this time in London that Thabo befriended Zanele Dlamini. They had met years ago in Johannesburg, according to Zanele, while Thabo was an organiser with the African Students' Organisation – but Thabo doesn't remember that first contact. Zanele was a social worker who was also studying for a post-graduate degree at the University of London. Her family lived in Alexandra township near Johannesburg and she was one of six sisters and a brother. Her father was a priest and, like nearly all of her sisters, Zanele decided initially that she wanted to be a nurse. She soon realised, however, that nursing was not what she imagined and enrolled for a bachelor degree in social work at the University of the Witwatersrand in Johannesburg.

At the university, she was active in student politics, but not at a leadership level, says Aziz Pahad, now the deputy foreign minister. She was particularly interested in campus issues as well as in human rights matters and was a keen sportswoman who excelled at tennis.

Soon, Thabo and Zanele had fallen in love. But it was to be a love they would have to nurture from afar, for both Thabo and Zanele would be heading off to different parts of the world. Though Thabo had excellent struggle credentials, criticism was never far off. While he had joined the Communist Party and had been able to quote Marx since childhood, Thabo had been educated in the west. Those who had gone to political academies in the Soviet Union or in East Germany found him insufficiently radical. They questioned his commitment and hinted at the worst kind of weakness: his apparently liberal tendencies. Those who had received military training questioned his courage.

The ANC's consultative conference in Morogoro, Tanzania, in 1969, once more reaffirmed the movement's dedication to the armed struggle. A Revolutionary Council was established to oversee all political and military activities in South Africa. Thabo knew that to have any authentic legitimacy in the organisation, he needed to go for military training, preferably in the Soviet Union. His application was approved this time and soon he was heading for Moscow.

Back at home, so well informed were the security branch, they knew Thabo had disappeared from the scene in London. They realised he was a rising star within the ANC and assumed he would be returning to South

Africa. Surveillance measures were stepped up around the home of Ma Mofokeng in far distant Mbewuleni in the Transkei in the hope he would appear. Members of the community were approached and asked to report immediately to the magistrate's office in Idutywa if they saw Thabo. These same people, who knew Ma Mofokeng so well and were regular patrons at her shop, whispered to her what was happening.

Late one night, the security branch came knocking at Ma Mofokeng's window. They knew where she slept and that the window was right above her bed. Angrily, she demanded to know why they were disturbing her. 'Where is Thabo?' they asked. They entered the hut and carried the wardrobe out into the street, where they sifted through everything in it under the moonlight with the aid of bright torches. By her bed there was a pile of letters that members of the community had entrusted to her to post. They opened each one, giving letters written in Xhosa or Sotho to black constables and letters in English to white ones. In the meantime, another group of policemen stripped her bed, sheet by sheet, blanket by blanket, looking for documents or messages. They carried the bed out into the open too and turned it upside down. Boxes of correspondence, family photographs and documents from the store were confiscated. It was to be a pattern that was repeated with wearying frequency.

'My life was not my own. The Security Branch called any time of day. They ... knocked on my window at midnight. "Open up, it's Captain Cronje",' says Ma Mofokeng, remembering those trying days. She had not heard from Thabo since he left the country some eight years earlier, though occasionally she heard news of him through her friend Adelaide Tambo, the wife of Thabo's boss. With her children scattered and her husband jailed she had only her grandchild, Thabo's son Kwanda, for company. At the age of ten, Kwanda had been brought back to the Mbeki kraal. 'It is our practice. Kwanda was Thabo's son. He should be an Mbeki. He had to come to his father's kraal,' said Ma Mofokeng. Kwanda was formally adopted, with Govan's approval, and remained with Ma Mofokeng until, at 18, he had finished his matric. Friends say that before he disappeared, he went off to become an apprentice welder at the state ironworks, Iscor, at Sasolburg near Johannesburg. The silence from most of Ma Mofokeng's family diaspora, though, was difficult to bear at times. 'My life was not an ordinary life so in most cases I had to make allowances.'

In 1969, Thabo arrived in Moscow and began the improvement of his struggle credentials with a year at the Institute of Social Sciences. The following year, in 1970, he was joined by Albertina and Walter Sisulu's son, Max, and together they made their way to a remote military camp near a town called Sekhodia.

It was to be the toughest year of Thabo's life. If ever he had felt isolated or miserable before, nothing compared to the drilling and marching he was forced to endure that winter. The task to which Thabo and Max had been assigned was an officer's training course for commanders of any unit size from small detachments to full companies.

Says Max: 'Thabo was more comfortable with a book than with a gun in his hands. Not that he couldn't shoot. He didn't find it easy being told what to do and what not to do. He was too well-educated and too independent-minded for that.'

One cold night, the South African contingent, led by Thabo, was sent off on a training exercise. They walked for hours through the Russian wilderness, in full kit, searching through the endless silver birches and rugged undergrowth for one marker and then the next. Thabo, as the platoon leader, carried the only map. Some way into the exercise, the platoon floundered and began to feel lost. 'Thabo, where is the map?' they asked him. Thabo looked down to where the map should have been fastened to his jacket, and to his dismay it wasn't there. He searched frantically for it, while his platoon grew increasingly irritated. 'I can't find it. It's gone,' he told them woefully.

After a few minutes it became evident that Thabo had dropped his map somewhere in the darkness. Grumbling mightily, the weary platoon retraced their steps, step by step, kilometre by kilometre. They spread out and scanned the ground, until eventually the map was found and the platoon completed their arduous exercise.

'Nobody was pleased. We were exhausted,' says Max, smiling as he recalls the incident from a comfortable armchair in his parliamentary office. He has since been redeployed from his position as ANC Chief Whip to the state arms manufacturer, Denel. 'I could never imagine Thabo as General Thabo,' Max says lightly of his friend's military acumen. 'I could see him then as a political leader, but not as a military one.'

The only person Thabo communicated with during these hard times in the Soviet Union was Zanele. Thabo arranged to have his letters delivered to the head of the South African Communist Party, Dr Yusuf Dadoo, at his offices in London. Dr Dadoo then handed them over personally to Zanele, who in turn would keep the Tambos and Thabo's circle of friends informed of developments.

Thabo, however, had served his time in political and military training and silenced, for the time being, his critics. He was now a fully qualified military officer with political leadership and weaponry training conducted in the authentic surroundings of the Soviet Union. On returning to London he was promoted and dispatched almost immediately to Lusaka in Zambia where he took up the post of assistant secretary to the newly created Revolutionary Council, which was chaired by Oliver Tambo. Fate, or luck, had once more intervened. For in the creation of the Revolutionary Council, the headquarters of ANC and SACP activities, particularly inside South Africa, had shifted to Lusaka. As the power flowed south, so Thabo was caught up in its rhythm. Zanele, in the meantime, had completed her Masters at the University of London and headed off to the United States to begin a doctorate.

After almost a decade of little action at all in southern Africa, things began to change for the ANC in the early 1970s. Small groups of activists who had been detained during the upheaval of the 1960s were released – including Harry Gwala, Jacob Zuma and Joe Gqabi – and began to rebuild ANC underground structures both inside the country and in the neighbouring 'forward areas' (areas that were as close as the ANC could get without being in South Africa proper) of Swaziland, Lesotho and Botswana. The left-wing *coup d'état* in Portugal in 1974 led to the independence of Angola and Mozambique headed by new black governments with whom the ANC had enjoyed close, fraternal ties. This helped break the *cordon sanitaire* which surrounded South Africa with friendly states and allowed the transportation of MK personnel and weaponry closer to home turf.

Within South Africa, where the ANC had failed substantially to imprint its mark in organisational terms, the Black Consciousness (BC) movement was beginning to radicalise a new generation. Thabo was intimately involved with each of these developments. He made frequent trips from Lusaka to Swaziland as well as to Botswana, shoring up structures and briefing new exiles. On occasion he acted as a courier, transporting weaponry and ammunition from Mozambique for storage in caches near the

South African border in Swaziland. As the Swaziland authorities remained cooperative with the South African government and with infiltrators and spies about, this was dangerous work. But it was to the political side of things he devoted most of his attention. Slipping past police, he made contact with supporters and built a network of activists in Swaziland.

Thabo was also desperate for information from South Africa and took it on himself to personally interview as many of the new exiles as possible. Often they were sent back with instructions to do what they could in their own communities, to use what talents and resources they had to build the underground resistance. Thabo became increasingly aware of the potential of the Black Consciousness movement not only to contribute to the groundswell of opposition but also, more worryingly, to undermine the leadership of the ANC as the vanguard of the liberation struggle. Steve Biko, the charismatic leader of the South African Students Organisation, enjoyed a groundswell of support amongst the youth. Many, too, of the exiled ANC cadres who had fled South Africa in the early 1960s were approaching middle age. Black Consciousness threatened to strip the ANC of the new blood it needed to resurrect its fortunes and its prospects for the future.

Thabo started to identify the leadership of this new movement and began working on them with a view to bringing them under the broad ANC flag. The vice president of the South African Students' Organisation, Nkosazana Zuma – then Dlamini – was invited to travel down from the University of Durban, where she was studying to be a doctor, to visit Thabo in Swaziland. (Nkosazana and Zanele are related by clan – both are Dlaminis.) There he recruited her to the ANC and sent her back with instructions to recruit others, to form ANC cells, and to 'influence debates and discussions within the Black Consciousness movement towards ANC positions.'[3] Zuma, who was later to become minister of health in South Africa's first democratic government, is another who has remained loyal to Thabo over the years and whose loyalty has been rewarded. This was true also of Jacob Zuma, Nkosazana's future, and now, ex-husband who worked closely with Thabo in Swaziland and later in Lusaka.

The improved organisation in the forward areas, in which Thabo was a key player, served a couple of crucial purposes. First, it allowed MK to begin more visible military activities within South Africa from safer and better equipped bases. As a result of this, the ANC's symbolic leadership was re-established internally and young militants, even if they were BC-aligned, headed for the ANC in exile – rather than the Pan-Africanist Congress – to acquire military training. Second, once the floodwaters broke in the aftermath of the 1976 Soweto uprising, only the ANC was in a position to channel the thousands of willing new recruits into active liberation structures. The PAC simply wasn't equipped to deal with 14 000 new members.

Shortly before June 1976, however, Thabo, Jacob Zuma and Albert Dhlomo were placed under 'protective custody' by the Swazi authorities. This was as a result of a growing crescendo of threats from the South African government that it was on the verge of capturing the three ANC officials. After a month in custody, Thabo and his two colleagues were escorted to the Mozambique border and ordered to leave. They missed experiencing the 1976 uprising from Swaziland by only a few months[4].

From the start of the party's rebuilding, Thabo was infinitely better informed and more in touch with internal developments than most people inside South Africa itself, let alone those sitting in Lusaka or London. As information was power, Thabo was fast accumulating both. It was not much of a surprise, then, when in 1975, Thabo was appointed acting chief representative of the ANC in Swaziland. He was emerging from one of the organisation's outstanding young intellectuals to becoming a *de facto* leader in command of one of the most critical forward areas established by the movement. In the same year, he was elected to the ANC's most powerful policy-making body, the National Executive Committee.

During this time, Thabo and Zanele managed to stay in touch and to keep the fire of their love burning. Thabo would send a telegram saying he would be in London at such and such a time and Zanele would fly over to meet him. They decided, in spite of the obvious logistical difficulties, that they wanted to get married. This, however, was not a simple matter within the exiled ANC community. All marriages of ANC cadres had to be approved by a committee. Says Adelaide Tambo: 'The custom was in the ANC that people didn't just go and get married. They must get permission from the organisation. They had no money, they were refugees. Even the ring had to be bought. But the weddings were always nice; everybody came together and made the weddings great successes. Sometimes the leadership would say, "no, you didn't come here to get married", or, "no, you have been marked for another assignment and can't get married now".'

Thabo was deeply concerned the committee would not approve his request. He confided his worries in Adelaide. 'Thabo came to me one day and said, "Mama, I want to marry Zanele." "Well, put in your application and see what happens," I said to him. "Mama, if Papa [Oliver Tambo] doesn't allow me to marry Zanele, I'll never, ever marry again. And I'll never ask again. I love only one person and there is only person I want to make my life with, and that is Zanele." He was very determined to marry her.' Fortunately, the request was approved.

Zanele's older sister, Edith, had in the meantime gone to work as a nurse for a while in Zambia and there had met the man who was to be her husband. He was none other than a cousin to the Queen of England, a member of the British aristocracy with a residential seat in Farnham, Hampshire. Edith became Lady Edith Glanville-Grey and she insisted that Thabo and Zanele should celebrate their marriage at the Farnham estate. The couple was married in 1974 at a registry office in the north of London followed by a small party at the Tambo's house. Essop Pahad was the best man. That weekend, though, the official celebration was held at the country manor in Farnham.

It was a wedding of virtually unparalleled dimensions for the betrothal of two impoverished refugees. More than 300 people attended, including a good many of the British aristocracy – lords, earls and dukes – and the leadership of the liberation movement. The ANC, as usual, supplied the rings.

'Zanele was always down-to-earth, never pushy,' says Adelaide Tambo. 'She would not go out of her way to catch the limelight, she is a very private person. They never grew up in my eyes. They were children then and I still regard them as my children now. South Africa is very lucky to have children like that. When I was speaking at the wedding, I said "As we grow older, these children will take over the leadership of our organisation, our communities and our nation and we expect them to carry the struggle forward". I was surprised that it has come to be exactly that.'

At the wedding, telegrams of congratulations were read out from all over the world by Essop. They included messages from both Ma Mofokeng and from Govan Mbeki, which had both been requested by the Tambos. The Tambos had asked Ma Mofokeng to supply Zanele with a Sotho clan name, as was the custom, signifying her welcoming to the family. The name chosen was Ma Motlalekhotso (one who brings peace).

Later, Govan said of the wedding: 'I've not attended a single wedding of anyone in my family. I married alone with my wife. My family was not there. Each one, when they decide to marry, has married and I did not miss the marriages.'

After their marriage, Zanele returned to the United States to complete her doctorate, after which she was hired by the United Nations High Commission for Refugees. In this role, she was able to travel widely and soon moved to Lusaka in Zambia to be with Thabo. She then accompanied him to Nigeria when he was transferred there.

Zanele, like Thabo and the rest of the Mbekis, is determinedly independent. Now the head of the Women's Development Bank in South Africa, she demands to be seen as a person in her own right and as a result pointedly rebuffs any enquiry of her relationship with Thabo. Similarly, Ma Mofokeng, even today, says she feels positively insulted when she is introduced to someone as 'Thabo's mother'. Considering Thabo's reserved nature, it is incredible that once Ma Mofokeng had met Thabo's bride, she described her as 'more reserved, not as open, as Thabo'.

'Zanele is a good-hearted person,' says Adelaide. 'She is very good with Thabo's parents. When the Mbeki shop was burgled [in 1997], she left immediately for Idutywa to give [Ma Mofokeng] support and to find out what had happened. Zanele regards Ma Mofokeng as her mother. I think she can handle being First Lady. She has her own way. Zanele is not the type of person who imitates anybody. She is very shy but very strong.' Thabo and Zanele have not had any children. 'That is a private matter about which I have never asked,' says Adelaide.

But back in Swaziland, Thabo was taking to his new, if temporary role, with his usual zeal. The first generation of exiles had spent many years undergoing military training in Cuba, East Germany and the Soviet Union. By the time they returned, they were out of touch with their communities and easily picked up by the police. Thabo started giving crash courses in basic explosives, weapons and grenade skills and then sent the exiles back to strengthen the still weak underground. One of the youngsters to seek out Thabo for help was Tokyo Sexwale, later the first Premier of the Gauteng province, who had been trying fruitlessly for months to make contact with the ANC underground in Soweto. Through

Thabo, Sexwale joined the ANC and left for military training in the Soviet Union. A few years later, it was Sexwale who spilt the first blood for MK in almost ten years when he tossed a grenade at two Swazi policemen blocking his path home, seriously injuring both of them.

But just as some semblance of happiness was restored to Thabo's life, through his marriage to Zanele, so tragedy struck once more. What was almost worse than the terrible result was the part Thabo himself played in the course of events, events that were to lead to the death of both his nephew and of his only son. Thabo was in close contact with the ANC structures in Lesotho, where his youngest brother Jama was now becoming increasingly active, and agreed to forward what was then the princely sum of R400 to Lindiwe (aka Lindi) Sisulu. Lindi, who was Max's sister and the daughter of Walter and Albertina, was working with MK commander Chris Hani.

Thabo called over his relative, Phindile Mfeti, and asked him to act as the courier for the money. But there was a misunderstanding. Phindile thought Thabo had said he should take the money to Linda, Thabo's sister, not Lindi. To add to the confusion, Linda had written to Thabo asking for some money to help Ma Mofokeng who was going through some bad times. Thabo, who was battling to secure enough funds for his own purposes, had chosen not to respond to this request. He was usually diligent in sending money home for books and for the education of his son, says Adelaide Tambo. 'He was very concerned about his child and helped with what he could from his meagre allowance. He sent money from wherever he was.'

Phindile crossed covertly onto South African soil and was immediately put under surveillance by the security forces. He travelled south to the Transkei and handed over the R400 to Linda. She was greatly surprised by the generosity of the gift, but thought nothing amiss. She gave it to her mother, for whom it was welcome and timely relief.

Then, the security police swooped. They arrested both Linda and Phindile, thinking that such a large amount of money could only be used for recruiting purposes for the ANC. Linda was held in detention for ten months and didn't know why. 'She didn't know anything about it,' says Govan. But far worse was in store for Phindile.

He was brutally and repeatedly tortured. Eventually, he was allowed to leave. Nervous of returning to Swaziland just yet, he enrolled at the

University of Durban to read law. But in the upheaval of 1976, he decided to leave the country once more. During his period of detention, he may have been turned into a police agent, but nobody knows this for sure. What they do know is that Phindile asked Kwanda, Thabo's child, now 17, to accompany him into exile. Kwanda undoubtedly had heard from Phindile that Thabo was in Swaziland. He called his father's friend, Micky Nama, at his law practice in Idutywa and told him he was leaving the next morning to meet with Phindile in Durban. That was the last time anyone from the Mbeki family heard Kwanda's voice, or Phindile's. Nothing was heard from the two young men for some time. They just disappeared, as so many young activists did at that time. While South Africa's Truth and Reconciliation Commission succeeded in the mid-1990s in uncovering the remains of dozens of those who had gone missing – and who had been killed by the security forces and buried in unmarked graves – Phindile and Kwanda were not amongst them.

In an interview in late 1998, Govan said of Kwanda, 'We were able to trace his movements up to Tanzania, but thereafter we don't quite know. Some of the people with whom he worked at MK say, no, he went to Cuba or to the GDR to further his studies. The last report says he left the camp and went to study in Nigeria [where Thabo would then have been stationed]. We are still trying to track him down. I don't know if he is still alive.'

What was suspected then is a virtual certainty now. Somewhere, somehow, Kwanda and Phindile were killed. Though in Swaziland, Thabo was aware that something had gone amiss, that Linda and Phindile had been arrested and that thereafter Phindile and Kwanda had gone missing. More terrible news awaited.

His youngest brother, Jama, also went missing, presumed dead. Govan thinks he was killed in a clash with the South African security forces on the Lesotho border. There were stories that he had been executed at an ANC camp in Angola and more rumours that he was killed in Botswana. But news of Jama stopped and nothing has yet been heard of his fate. The struggle has been bitterly cruel to Thabo and to his family. As his mother, Ma Mofokeng, says, 'Thabo has paid the price, he really has'. The struggle for democracy had splintered them as effectively as a bolt of lightning would a blue gum tree. It had caused untold suffering and loss. It had deprived him of a father, a brother, a mother and a son. But there was no way back and no other cause worth sacrificing so much for.

44

After a short period as acting chief in Swaziland, and as the forward areas were becoming increasingly dangerous – due to security force raids and assassinations – Thabo was forced to leave by the Swazi authorities and was dispatched to Nigeria in December 1976. In Lagos, he was appointed the ANC's chief representative and began to fashion a new arrow for his quiver. While the ANC battled, virtually in vain, to establish either a political or a military presence in South Africa until the mid-1980s, and was divided over policy within the exiled leadership, internationally it began to gather enormous prestige as the authentic voice of the South African majority. Much of this was due to the role of a few well-spoken, intelligent, affable ambassadors. Individuals with Thabo's gifts became inordinately important. As head of the ANC's mission in Nigeria, Thabo put his diplomatic skills to the test and impressed African and western leaders alike. Little by little he was becoming a well-rounded, consummate politician: well connected, well read and highly articulate. His inner pain was covered by an overt reasonableness. The ease with which he conversed with all kinds of people, from peasants to kings, was to push him to the forefront of the ANC's image-building – as well as strategic – initiatives.

One of Thabo's jobs during his stint in Nigeria was to assist young South African exiles settle in and begin their studies at Nigerian universities. In Nigeria, too, Thabo became ever more aware of his, and his country's, Africanness. He had been in close contact with political movements from other countries in the region, including Swapo in Namibia, Zanu in Zimbabwe, Frelimo in Mozambique and the MPLA in Angola. He had been for years an admittedly ageing member of the Pan-Africanist Students' Organisation as well as of the Pan-Africanist Youth Movement. He also got to know a whole new and young generation of African leaders, such as Botswana's future president Festus Mokae, who would go on to lead South Africa's regional neighbours in the years ahead.

During his time in Swaziland, he had succeeded in persuading the BC movement, through Jacob Zuma and others, to organise and host a Black Renaissance Convention[5].

The seeds for his vision of an African rebirth, an African Renaissance, had long been nurtured during his travels, his studies and in his interactions with other African political leaders. He had read the poetry and political philosophy of Aime Cesaire and Leopold Senghor. He had heard Ghana's former president and renowned orator Kwame Nkrumah and the calls for African unity even from his own countrymen. He knew, too, that while he favoured negotiation and politics, the armed struggle had an important symbolic role to play in the ending of apartheid and in the rebuilding of the pride and self-respect of the oppressed.

In 1978, Thabo, now 36, was interviewed by the American television channel, CBS. He said: 'A gun is a very important weapon in itself but it also has got a tremendous symbolic significance. You know, when you've grown up in a society and the only person who's walking up and down the street every day, the one who's carrying a gun, is the fellow who is oppressing you, the first thing that is going to occur to you is that if I want to be equal to him, I must carry a gun.'[6] The words echo those of Frantz Fanon, the psychiatrist from Martinique who was a spokesperson for the revolution that gave Algeria its independence from France in 1962. Fanon said: 'At the level of individuals, violence is a cleansing force. It frees the native from his inferiority complex and from his despair and inaction: it makes him fearless and restores his self-respect.'[7]

After three years in Nigeria, Thabo was recalled in February of 1978 into the political mainstream at ANC headquarters in Lusaka. He was appointed Oliver Tambo's political secretary and then director of information. He held more sway now over the divided theorising and plans of the party and his influence began to be more deeply felt. As Tambo's speech writer, and confidant, he had his fingers on the pulse of the liberation struggle. But it was a struggle that had reached a strange kind of impasse.

The party's military objectives continued to bear little fruit and its efforts at political organisation inside South Africa were making painfully slow progress. The leadership of the ANC and SACP remained determined that the way to detonate revolution was to infiltrate trained guerrillas who would be responsible both for the odd military action as well as for political work. Invariably, the teams of keen cadres embarked on military actions too early, before they had a chance to become settled or establish any structures, and they were quickly killed or arrested by the security forces.

In 1978, a high-ranking team of ANC leaders travelled to Vietnam to learn how to conduct a successful revolution. The Vietnamese stressed that political work was as important, if not more so, than the military. The military should flow from the political and not, as the ANC believed, the other way round. This caused some consternation amongst the ANC leadership and a special meeting of the National Executive Committee was called for 27 December in Luanda, Angola. There, a copy of the report from the Vietnamese trip was due to be tabled[8].

The Luanda meeting elected a small commission, called the Politico-Military Strategy Commission (PMSC), to consider new strategic options. Thabo was elected to the commission under the chairmanship of Oliver Tambo. The other members were Joe Gqabi, Moses Mabhida, Joe Modise and Joe Slovo. Other than Thabo and Tambo, the four fell solidly into the MK, and therefore pro-military, camp.

The recommendations which the commission came up with in March 1979, favoured the political over the military and are considered very much the work of Thabo. The four strategic lines recommended by the commission, and adopted by the National Executive Committee, were that the ANC should, first of all, work at mobilising the masses inside South Africa, second, that a broad national front should be established (the genesis of the United Democratic Front (UDF) so prominent in the 1980s), third, that promising activists should be directed into under-ground structures and fourth, that military operations should be developed out of political activity, not the other way round.

Dullah Omar, South Africa's first minister of justice and one of the founders of the UDF, said later: 'That strategy was the product of the work of Thabo Mbeki.'

But in spite of these intentions, not enough effort was made to translate the decision and to create the structures that would allow the party to shift radically its approach to the struggle. Howard Barrell, in his doctoral thesis for the University of Oxford on the ANC's operational strategy between 1976 and 1986, concludes: 'The lasting impression is of an ANC which is eloquent in its reasoning and its resolutions but hidebound or incompetent in implementation.' It was a charge that was increasingly to be levelled at the party deep into and even beyond its first term of office. Narrowing the gap between the framing of policy and its implementation will be a key objective of the Mbeki presidency.

As Thabo began to spread his wings in exile, he did so under the careful and empathetic gaze of Oliver Tambo. They had worked on and off together for more than a decade and a deep understanding, founded on loyalty and closely matched intellects, developed into a formidable union. Thabo watched closely the methods and manner of the man everyone called 'OR' (for Oliver Reginald), while Tambo leaned ever more heavily on the instincts, knowledge and speech writing skills of his aide-de-camp.

Max Sisulu, in an interview in November 1998, says: 'There's a lot of Oliver Tambo in Thabo. He was a father figure to all of us, but for Thabo in particular. Tambo was very persuasive, rarely gave orders and consulted to a fault. That's why he (later) got a stroke; he was overworked, flying all over the place. He was also an intellectual.' In Lusaka, the president and his political secretary set about forging a new pathway for the liberation movement. It was a route which favoured negotiation and the mobilisation of democrats within South Africa and the world and was to bring the pair into conflict with their more militarily inclined comrades in MK, the ANC as well as within the Communist Party.

Following the National Executive Committee decision in 1979 to adopt the proposals of the Politico-Military Strategy Commission, ongoing disputes broke out between different factions of the party. The intended unification of the political and military wings threatened individuals' positions as well as the existence of their departments and empires. This was true at headquarters as much as it was evident in the forward bases of the frontline states. The result was a continuing inability of either the political or the military initiatives to make any headway.

The first seeds of the bid to establish a broad democratic front of opposition to the apartheid government inside the country were sown in the early 1980s. After a series of clandestine discussions, the ANC-aligned Soweto activist Popo Molefe publicly called on the mushrooming civic and trade union organisations to join forces. One of Thabo's most important roles as political secretary to the ANC president was the writing of Tambo's new year addresses, which were read over Radio Freedom and broadcast around Africa and the world. Thabo, in the style of his boss, went to elaborate lengths to consult with different sections of the party and its leadership, as he went about framing the speeches. It was a technique that had been used to satisfying effect when the two of them pushed the Politico-Military Strategy Commission and the National Executive Committee into its new leaning toward a struggle that was also political, rather than purely military.

In the broadcast aired on 8 January 1983, which was drafted by Thabo, Tambo called once more for the formation of a united front. Around the same time, the Revolutionary Council, which had been charged with overseeing political and military work in South Africa, was restructured and renamed the Politico-Military Council. Chaired by Tambo, party secretary-general Alfred Nzo, another ANC dove, was elected the body's deputy chairman. Also brought into the fold was a new member of the Tambo–Mbeki axis, Joel Netshitenzhe – also known as Peter Mayibuye – who served on the council's political committee. Netshitenzhe was soon to become to Thabo what he in turn had been to Tambo: his most trusted adviser. But in spite of the urgings from afar and the secret talks inside the country, the formation of the United Democratic Front later that year came as a shock to Thabo, as well as to the rest of the ANC leadership.

Says Mac Maharaj, another extremely influential player during this period who had been one of Mandela's closest confidants on Robben Island before his release and departure for exile: 'They didn't believe it would happen.'[9] Even though the party had been pushing for such a front, gathering up church, civic, union and student groups under a broadly anti-apartheid and ANC-sympathetic umbrella, it was from within the country, at the hands of activists such as Allan Boesak, Terror Lekota and Dullah Omar, that the initiative was nurtured to fruition. The UDF became a powerful force inside South Africa and while the ANC contributed to its development, not even the party was aware of the extent of its own influence.

In his other guise as the international, affable face of the ANC, Thabo was also playing a vital role. The ongoing credibility and legitimacy of the ANC both inside and outside the country arguably had as much to do with Thabo's efforts on the diplomatic circuit and with the international media as it did with the mostly feeble and costly efforts of MK. In recognition of this role, Thabo was made the head of the ANC's department of information and publicity when it was created in 1984.

But while some gains, if limited, were gradually being made militarily and politically by the ANC in the early 1980s, the signing of the Nkomati Accord in 1984 was to prove a severe blow to the organisation. Preceded by a similar pact of non-aggression signed between Swaziland and South Africa, the Nkomati Accord between South Africa and Mozambique virtually closed the vital link between Lusaka, the forward bases and

South Africa itself. The ANC's admittedly tenuous, if growing, military capacity was devastated as both Mozambique and Swaziland assured South Africa that their countries would not be used as a platform for aggressive acts by the liberation movement.

As the ANC recoiled beyond the borders of South Africa, another wave of popular protest was erupting inside the country. The protests were sparked in part by President PW Botha's move to pass a new tricameral constitution in which two new Parliamentary chambers were to be appended to the white House of Assembly, the 'coloured' House of Representatives and the Indian House of Delegates.

Blacks, once more, were excluded from the franchise, their representation confined to the Bantustan homelands. The two new houses, in any case, were little more than a failed attempt to co-opt the Indian and coloured communities and allowed their new representatives little power and no legislative veto. The UDF, encouraged by the ANC, launched a highly successful boycott of the elections to the two new houses.

From Lusaka, Thabo urged on the protests. In a Radio Freedom address in early September 1984 he sought to encourage confrontation while moderating expectations: 'In our planning, in our thinking, in our mobilisation, we must proceed from the basis that we inflicted a humiliating defeat on our enemy (the election boycott). As revolutionaries, as fighters for liberation, we must plan how we should continue our offensive, knowing very well that the enemy will, as it must, hit back to stop the emergence and consolidation of the revolutionary situation that Pretoria fears so much ... We must answer the question, without seeking to create illusions among ourselves: Are we − as a democratic movement which the people have accepted as their authentic representative − doing all that is necessary to move this organised, conscious and active army of liberation into a continuing all-round offensive for the seizure of power by the people?'[10]

Answering his own question, he coined a phrase that would shake the very foundations of the apartheid regime. Thabo called for a campaign to make South Africa 'ungovernable'. The notion of ungovernability became a totem for the liberation movement in South Africa during the mid- to late 1980s. It recalled an appeal made in 1958 by Nelson Mandela ('In every locality and in all parts of our country, we must fight to ensure that we remove the enemy's organs of government'), but was given new life and new vigour. The results were extraordinary.

Between September 1984 and April of the following year, the homes of 814 police officers were destroyed or badly damaged. The first half of 1985 saw 12 police officers and local black councillors killed and more than a hundred injured. Over the same period, almost 300 township councillors resigned in response to demands that they should do so[11]. The apartheid state was being dismantled from within.

There was great excitement in Lusaka at these developments. At last, conditions for a popular revolution appeared to be gathering strength. A consultative conference, the first since Morogoro in 1969, was called. The venue was to be Kabwe, Zambia. The date, June 1985. The mission: to formulate a strategy that would carry South Africa through to liberation.

Thabo began drafting a new basic strategy document aimed at taking the ANC into the next and, he hoped, final, phase. Assisted by Netshitenzhe and Joe Nhlanhla, who was later to become democratic South Africa's first deputy minister of intelligence, the document was broad but, for the ANC, a radical departure. For the first time, the possibility of entering into 'talks' with the apartheid regime was mooted.

Rumours of these contacts had already begun to ripple around ANC structures in exile. The month before the Kabwe conference, Tambo himself had confirmed he was 'under pressure' to talk to the South African government. This pressure for talks was mounting from several angles: from the newly formed Congress of South African Trade Unions (Cosatu) and its head, Cyril Ramaphosa, who were achieving extraordinary successes in negotiating new rights, from the international sphere and from the within the movement in exile itself.

Thabo had realised that the ANC in exile knew virtually nothing of the dynamics within Afrikaner nationalism in general and of the ruling National Party in particular. It therefore knew nothing of the divisions, the alliances, the threats or, more importantly, the opportunities. Mandela, years before, had urged liberationists to know their enemy. This simply had not been done. Thabo wanted to correct that. He wanted, as American journalist Patti Waldmeir has argued, to know the answers to questions the exiled movement had not even thought to ask, such as, How did the ruling group think? What did it fear? How could its internal contradictions be exploited?[12]

Backed by Tambo, Thabo began to think of ways of finding out these answers. The first step was to invite important white South Africans to discuss issues with the ANC, either in Lusaka or at the increasing number of international conferences being hosted in different corners of the world. According to Waldmeir, 'the ANC's decision to get under white South Africa's skin ... was probably the most important one ever made by the exiled movement. For Tambo and Mbeki alike, unlike the romantic revolutionaries among their colleagues, were intent on delivering not just the corpse of a defeated nation, but the mind and soul of the Afrikaner people to the new South Africa. No doubt they set out with the aim of wooing merely to weaken – their goal to sow confusion in the enemy camp, not to seek true converts in overwhelmingly hostile territory. But [Thabo], for one, was shrewd enough to understand that behind the façade of the Afrikaner bully dwelt an almost pitiful yearning to be understood, loved and accepted by Africa. Only the subtlest of ANC minds could recognise this truth: that petting, coddling and cajoling the Afrikaner would pay enormous dividends. And, apart from Mandela himself, there was none subtler than Thabo.'[13]

But Tambo and Thabo were heavily outgunned by majority opinion within the ANC. The Kabwe conference, while nodding almost imperceptibly at the possibility of a negotiated settlement, once more rededicated itself to renewed revolutionary confrontation. 'The movement was torn between those – like firebrand guerrilla leader Chris Hani – who were intent on striking fear into white hearts, and those – like Thabo – who preferred to charm whites all the way to defeat.'[14]

Following the Kabwe decision to begin attacking 'soft' targets such as white areas and homes, Thabo bucked popular party opinion in 1985, saying he was 'concerned about the impact on white South Africans of attacks against whites. Our aim is to win them away from apartheid, even if they don't come to us. So, attacks hurt us.'[15]

While Thabo decided to embark on a different route altogether, the thrust of ANC strategic thinking, as set out at Kabwe, led nowhere. Pallo Jordan, one of Thabo's allies from his days in London, was placed in charge of a sub-committee to expand the recommendations on strategy discussed in passing at Kabwe. But he lacked the political authority to force the sub-committee to finish its work. A report was finally completed some four years later, but by then events had overtaken it[16]. Inside South Africa, the ANC conceded it still had 'no organised ANC or MK presence' while in exile the movement noted self-consciously that it was still dogged by 'favouritism, regionalism and even tribalism'[17].

As Howard Barrell pointed out in summary of the Kabwe conference: 'At the most crucial moment in its history, in the midst of the most serious uprisings in South Africa in which its name was being widely proclaimed as a leader of a revolution, the ANC had held a conference and concluded it with no generally-agreed formulation of strategy.'[18] For Thabo, though, the conference once again restated his increasing sway in the organisation. He was re-elected to the National Executive Committee and was appointed the new head of the ANC's department of international affairs. His appointment – already decided at a meeting of the top 38 leaders of the ANC in Norway – replacing Johnny Makhathini who died earlier that year, effectively moved Thabo from fourth to third in the ANC hierarchy. He had been confirmed as the ANC's front man, influential behind the scenes and powerfully collegial in the limelight. Always, though, he remained self-effacing and respectful toward Tambo while increasingly taking charge of the more delicate diplomatic negotiations. A similar kind of relationship and rapport would shortly be developed with Mandela, whose days in prison were slowly coming to an end.

Though Thabo's new department successfully concluded a series of talks with groups of South Africans and pressed on to acclaim with the strengthening of ties between the ANC and the international community, its home-based propaganda initiatives and its capacity to provide information remained severely limited. Some argue the inefficiency was due to Thabo's many other duties and his unwillingness to delegate responsibility; others that he had engaged were people simply not up to the task. This was not the first time these charges were to be levelled at Thabo, nor were they to be the last. In Lusaka, the jovial Tom Sebina was appointed Thabo's lieutenant. Slow-witted and prone to overdoing the booze, Sebina was a far cry from attaining the heady standards required by his boss. He was loyal, however, and thus was allowed to blunder on year after year, further compounding the department's poor reputation.

With South Africa in the midst of an escalating and bloody conflict between the state and anti-apartheid formations in the mid-1980s, small groups of influential South Africans began to travel north to meet with the ANC. Almost always, Thabo was the man who met them. It was he who discussed their anxieties and answered their questions. His breadth of education, high intellect and knowledge of events inside and outside the country made him instantly accessible and sympathetic to the visitors, regardless of their ideological beliefs.

The first group was made up of several important white businessmen and was led by the then Anglo American chairman Gavin Relly. They met Thabo at the isolated Mfuwe game lodge in Zambia in 1985. Tambo was unwilling at first to condone the meeting with this group of capitalists, fearing it would open him to the severe criticism of 'selling out' within the party. He relented only after the personal intervention of Zambian President Kenneth Kaunda, who had himself been meeting with various South African emissaries – including intelligence agents – for some years[19]. The ANC, in any case, already had what Waldmeir describes as 'an improbably close relationship' with the huge South African-based mining conglomerate, Anglo American. The ANC, she claims, used Anglo's headquarters in Lusaka as a postbox for sensitive mail. Later, Thabo was to make use of the home of Anglo-Zambian managing director Vernon Webber as an unofficial clubhouse for entertaining visiting South Africans[20].

Relly and Thabo quickly hit it off, spurred on by their mutual concerns for their country and spiced by their common pipe-smoking habit. The stereotypes began to melt away. Other groups were to follow, including a delegation of influential, liberal white politicians such as the former head of the Progressive Federal Party, Frederick van Zyl Slabbert and his deputy Alex Boraine, groups of students, trade union representatives and, on one occasion, two white Afrikaners, academic Professor HW van der Merwe and journalist Piet Muller of *Beeld*. The frequency and diversity of the trips created a new semi-legal space in which the ANC was allowed to build up the kind of internal credibility and profile it had previously been unable to secure[21]. It was a critical period for the ANC, for South Africa and for Thabo.

'Thabo received us at the airport and sorted us out,' says Colin Eglin, a current Democratic Party parliamentarian who was on the trip to Dakar with Slabbert and Boraine. 'A dominant part of Thabo's make-up was to wear his diplomatic hat. He was very diplomatic, very correct. He was extraordinarily warm to us as individuals for bucking the system and coming to visit them.'

Dullah Omar, who met Thabo for the first time as a leader of the UDF in Lusaka in 1989, said of his first contact: 'He was then, I thought, quite remarkable. A great personality and very personable. At a social level, he was very easy and affable and loved to crack a little joke as well as play practical jokes. When talking of the struggle, though, he was deep-thinking, very serious and clearly fully aware of the dynamics inside South Africa. I was quite surprised in my discussions with him that he was looking so far ahead, envisaging the negotiation process as it unfolded.'

By 1986, the ANC had still failed to make any real impression with its military operations. Their latest scheme was the creation of grenade squads. Rapid infiltration of these mini-sabotage groups and the boobytrapping or capture of their 'pineapples' (grenades) turned the initiative into yet another public relations and military disaster. But in the political realm, real advances were being made. In the creation of the UDF, the stayaway of November 1984 and in the formation of the huge trade union confederation Cosatu, a genuine challenge was being mounted to white minority rule, arguably for the first time since the ANC's banning in 1961. Says Barrell: 'Diplomatically, the ANC skilfully addressed different audiences to its own advantage: it persuaded elements in the white South African establishment that it was a serious and mature contender for power; it cemented alliances with a number of other anti-apartheid organisations, broadening its political base and raising its profile in the process; and it harmonised with the tone of international concern over South Africa.'[22]

In June 1986, Thabo was dispatched by Tambo to represent the ANC at a conference hosted by the Ford Foundation in Long Island, New York. The conference, at which several prominent Afrikaner intellectuals were to be present, was seen as a possible opening gambit in the ANC's wooing of Afrikanerdom. Tambo had attempted to invite two Afrikaner academics – including Willie Esterhuyse, a professor of philosophy at the University of Stellenbosch – to come and visit the ANC in Lusaka in 1984, but PW Botha had intervened and the trip had been cancelled. The Long Island conference, however, began badly. The first ANC speaker, Seretse Choabe, threatened to kill a white South African member of the audience, Pieter de Lange[23].

De Lange was no ordinary white South African, though, he was the chairman of the Broederbond (Brotherhood), a secret but immensely powerful organisation with tendrils of influence reaching throughout

Afrikaner society, from teachers unions to farmers groups, from church leaders to cultural societies. The Broederbond was the keeper of the Afrikaner soul, the mechanism by which power was enforced and extended through every sphere of society from cabinet to the Housewives' League.

As Choabe vowed to shoot De Lange, Thabo 'drew reflectively on his pipe and exchanged a glance with his colleague, Mac Maharaj.'[24] His mission endangered before he had even begun, Thabo sought out the Broederbond chairman after the session and they agreed to meet at De Lange's hotel later that afternoon. The chat over drinks with De Lange turned into a marathon four-hour session that stretched into the early evening. According to Waldmeir, when the Broederbonder's pipelighter broke down, Thabo was able to offer his, a gift from a recent visit to North Korea. As the conversation continued, De Lange asked his wife Christine to join them for dinner. It was the first time, according to De Lange, that Thabo had had dinner with an Afrikaner woman[25].

De Lange, like so many white pilgrims to follow, was entranced by Thabo. Here was a reasonable, articulate, educated man with whom he could discuss touchy issues frankly and directly. At the end of the talk, he promised, on his return to South Africa, to do what he could to enhance reconciliation within South Africa.

Three years previously, De Lange had taken over the chairmanship of the Broederbond after a fierce power struggle with the resident conservatives[26]. He claims that in those few years, the more enlightened leadership of the Broederbond had already come to accept that black South Africans would have to be given the vote sooner rather than later[27]. The great monolith of Afrikaner sensibility, rooted in a passion of self-preservation, had begun to shift. Confronted by the urbane geniality of the ANC's most polished diplomat, the dry cracks wrought by Afrikanerdom's own self-appraisal became leaking fissures.

When he did get back to South Africa, De Lange resigned as principal of the Rand Afrikaans University and set out to do exactly what he had promised. Says Thabo: 'What it meant was that he was going to go on the road as chairman of the Broederbond to convince his people that there had to be movement.'[28]

4

The return

In 1985, Nelson Mandela had written to PW Botha expressing his concern about the rising levels of violence in South Africa and requesting a meeting to discuss the way forward. Though the letter was unexpected, there was already a growing sense within the more enlightened echelons of government that the escalating levels of civil unrest and the stagnant economy together with ever harsher international anti-apartheid measures demanded a new approach to the South African conundrum.

The letter from Mandela, and the subsequent meeting with the then minister of justice, Kobie Coetsee, in a prison hospital room in Cape Town, set in motion a series of events that would lead, in time, to the start of formal negotiations between the government and the ANC which would herald in a new democratic era in South Africa.

Thabo was to play a key role in these developments. For the moment, though, Mandela's painstaking headway with the Botha government continued in parallel with Thabo's mission to understand and perhaps even co-opt the Afrikaner élite in exile.

By late 1986, the situation in South Africa had become desperate. Botha had declared a state of emergency and more than 25 000 people were detained in the six months from June, including virtually the entire leadership of the UDF. Abroad, the superpowers of the Soviet Union and the United States agreed at the Reykjavik Summit to disentangle themselves from regional conflicts which kept them tied down in confrontation. Financial and military support for the ANC from Mikhail Gorbachev's Soviet Union began to dwindle[1].

It was during 1986 that the apartheid state finally decided it had had enough of Thabo. A captain in the South African Defence Force was dispatched to Lusaka with the intention of blowing up Thabo's house, preferably with him inside it. The assassination attempt failed when the assassin was captured, arrested and convicted. He was, however, pardoned by Zambian president Kenneth Kaunda when it was discovered he held New Zealand nationality[2].

Thabo, persevering with his roadshow of charm, headed to London to meet a group of business people with South African interests. Included among the business people was Michael Young, the head of communications and corporate affairs at Consolidated Goldfields (Consgold). Young had been an adviser to British prime ministers Alec Douglas-Home and Edward Heath and had been involved in discussions surrounding Rhodesia's Unilateral Declaration of Independence in the 1970s. Though the London meeting in itself was fruitless, Young took it on himself to push things along. As he went about securing funding for talks he envisaged between the South African state and the ANC, he asked Fleur de Villiers, a former South African political journalist doing consultancy work for Consgold in London, to recommend a good person to approach in South Africa. De Villiers recommended the philosophy don Willie Esterhuyse, a man who had met Thabo before at international conferences and who had powerful connections within government. He also had a reputation for discretion and broadmindedness[3].

As discussions between Esterhuyse and Young gathered steam, the preparations reached the ears of the South African National Intelligence Service (NIS). But rather than stymie things, the head of the NIS, Niël Barnard, had something altogether different in mind. Barnard had already met with Mandela several times as a member of a small committee appointed by justice minister Coetsee to engage Mandela in exploratory discussions. According to its senior officers, the NIS had believed for some years that South Africa's problems would not be solved by a military victory by either side. Such an outcome was, in any case, increasingly unlikely. It was not entirely improbable, however, that the NIS was perhaps looking for the same thing Thabo was searching for – faultlines in the opposition leadership and perhaps the rise of a moderate wing within the ANC that could be co-opted[4].

Barnard asked Esterhuyse to spy for his country. 'He told me the government wanted an informal contact with the ANC and he asked whether I would be willing to report to him on the discussions we were going to have,' Esterhuyse recalls[5]. After a sleepless night and some soul-searching with his wife, Esterhuyse agreed, on condition that Thabo was informed of his anticipated role[6]. Barnard accepted the condition and Esterhuyse became part, from then on, of the unofficial channel between the ANC in exile and the South African state. It was rather like the famous 'channel' that was established a few years later between ANC chief negotiator Cyril Ramaphosa and the government chief negotiator, Roelf Meyer, in the constitutional talks.

Says Thabo: 'He squared with me right at the beginning. I knew all along that he was talking to Barnard and that Barnard was reporting to PW Botha.'[7] The talks, between Esterhuyse and a number of important Afrikaner intellectuals – including FW de Klerk's brother, Wimpie – and Thabo and a few ANC leaders, took place at a Consgold estate near Bath called Mells Park.

The meetings were left very unstructured and delegates were encouraged in the afternoons to stroll around the gardens and woods of the isolated estate, eat dinner together, then sit around the fire in the study drinking Glenfiddich whisky and talking into the early hours. According to journalist Allister Sparks, 'on the Afrikaner side, [these meetings] dissolved the demonised image of the ANC that had been built up by years of propaganda, while on the ANC side they sensitised the black liberators to white anxieties, particularly Afrikaner fears about their survival prospects under black rule.'[8]

More than a dozen meetings were held at the Mells estate from 1987 right up to when the ANC and other liberation movements were unbanned on 2 February 1990[9].

Esterhuyse conveyed Thabo's responses on various issues back to Barnard, who was meeting with Mandela, and who would then pass them on to Botha. Mandela was allowed access to a lawyer, George Bizos, who would keep the ANC in Lusaka as well as the domestic movement appraised of developments. 'It was a round robin of indirect talks,' observed Sparks[10].

But as conditions worsened at home, both sides became ever keener to establish more direct modes of contact. Rumours, too, of the talks began to cause unease both in Lusaka and in South Africa. In mid-1987, Thabo's father, Govan – who had already engaged in a few heated arguments with Mandela on Robben Island – caught wind of Mandela's discussions and called on members of the UDF not to visit Mandela in his jail cell[11]. In Lusaka, some accused Thabo behind his back of being a spy for the state.

'However successfully [Thabo] was triumphing over the suspicions of his Afrikaner interlocutors, he had not yet won the battle for the soul of the ANC ... The fiercest battle, as always, was the battle within. Virtually until the final deal was done in 1993, deep divisions remained between the diplomats and the strugglers in the ANC.'[12]

While it was left to Tambo to smooth these over, Thabo pressed on. In August 1987 he attended a conference in Dakar, Senegal, to which more than 50 Afrikaner intellectuals had been invited. In what was becoming a Thabo trademark – a wryly audacious opening remark – he began his speech with the words, 'I am an Afrikaner'[13]. Repeatedly, those who interacted with Thabo were won over. In the words of Waldmeir, 'they were not convinced by [Thabo], they were converted'[14].

But Thabo was all too well aware of the tensions in Lusaka and knew that mere chats with Mandela in his cell were no substitute for the formal involvement of the ANC. During one Mells Park meeting in late 1988, he made this point forcefully to his Afrikaner colleagues. 'He convinced all of us because it was so bloody logical,' says Esterhuyse[15].

Barnard and the NIS were also aware that in spite of the measures put in place to allow Mandela to consult with Lusaka, problems were becoming evident. Perhaps as a result of the meetings with Mandela and Thabo and given worsening conditions on the home front, they had moved from a position of wanting to split the moderates off from the ANC mainstream to wanting a legitimate and unified negotiating partner. 'The last thing we wanted was for the ANC to come apart,' says Mike Louw, deputy director general of the NIS at the time. In the new democratic dispensation he went on to become head of the South African Secret Service and director general of the NIS, and is now retired. 'We needed to leave Mandela's reputation untarnished and couldn't be seen to be playing one off against the other.'

The stage was set for a move away from informal chats to face-to-face talks between representatives of the South African state and the ANC.

By 1988, both had reached a stalemate. On the state side, forceful repression was losing its efficacy in the face of international and domestic criticism. Sanctions preventing economic, cultural and sporting ties with the outside world were becoming stronger and more effective by the month. A little reform was likely to convince nobody and, in fact, would probably add fuel to the flames of revolt. Within the ANC, a growing number of its leaders knew that armed insurrection leading to the seizure of power by force was a pipe dream. The collapse of the communist governments in eastern Europe meant resources were more difficult to come by and the détente between Russia and the United States made the encouragement of regional conflict unappetising. The atmosphere in southern Africa was changing, and it was moving away from a continuing tolerance of politics by arms. While MK struggled to make any significant impact – other than a few spectacular attacks on targets such as the oil refinery at Sasolburg – the South African Defence Force, too, had shown it was more vulnerable than many had believed when it suffered a significant defeat at the hands of Cuban and Angolan troops at Cuito Cuanavale in 1988.

With military victory looking increasingly unlikely, the ANC began to look more formally at conditions under which negotiations could begin with the apartheid state. In 1989, Tambo successfully lobbied African governments to adopt what became known as the Harare Declaration. Many now say the brain behind the declaration was, of course, Thabo's. Officially drafted and signed by the member states of the Organisation of African Unity (OAU), the declaration contained the first real vision of a transition to democracy in South Africa. Tambo was mindful that if the ANC did not seize the initiative, the international community would be all too happy to step in. This had led to rather more compromises than the liberation forces had wished for in both Zimbabwe and in Namibia.

The Harare Declaration, which was issued on 21 August 1989, called, as a precondition for negotiations, for the unconditional release of political prisoners, the lifting of bans on restricted organisations, the removal of troops from the townships, the ending of the state of emergency, the repeal of repressive legislation and the cessation of political trials and executions. The OAU noted, too, that the ANC believed 'a conjuncture of circumstances' existed which if there was 'a demonstrable readiness on the part of the Pretoria regime to engage in negotiations genuinely and seriously, could create the possibility to end apartheid through negotiations.'[16]

Giving the declaration further weight, Thabo led an ANC delegation to New York later that year, where the General Assembly of the United Nations adopted the document with only a few slight changes. Importantly, all the members of the security council signed the declaration[17].

The ANC's cards had been placed on the table. The state also moved to carry things forward. To facilitate formal contact, an influential group of senior state officials, including Barnard, forced through the State Security Council a vaguely worded proposal that would give the NIS the space to make contact with the ANC. So obscurely phrased was the motion that most of the councillors had little idea of its true intent or substance. It said: 'It is necessary that more information should be obtained and processed concerning the ANC, and the aims, alliances and potential approachability of its different leaders and groupings. To enable this to be done, special additional direct action will be necessary, particularly with the help of the NIS's functionaries.'[18]

PW Botha, who had by now met personally with Mandela and served him tea in his executive offices at Tuynhuys, was aware of the subtleties of the resolution and had also encouraged Coetsee and his sympathisers to expand the talks with Mandela to include the ANC's Lusaka heavyweights, if secretly and carefully. Botha's infamous Rubicon speech notwithstanding – in which he veered away from true reform – it is arguably the case that the first moves toward a negotiated settlement in South Africa were indeed condoned, if not initiated, by him. He didn't, however, have the courage or the vision to proceed.

The NIS, which had by now established a reputation for being a discreet and leak-free organisation and had conducted a number of confidential discussions with several African leaders over the years, was handed the responsibility of making contact with the ANC. The problem was: who should they contact and how? The state began to allow Mandela to entertain representatives of the UDF at Pollsmoor Prison, where he was now occupying a private single cell. It was hoped that by doing this, Mandela as well as the ANC would accept the state's bona fides and would be able to establish more direct lines of communication with Lusaka. Following the State Security Council's endorsement in August, Louw together with a few other NIS and state officials once more went to see Mandela. This time, Louw asked for permission to contact Thabo.

'We didn't know exactly who or how to approach the ANC outside and asked Mandela whether Thabo would be a good person to speak to,' he says. 'He was not very happy about it. He wanted to leave Thabo out of it. The talks could jeopardise the important role Thabo was to play in the future. So he was protective. In his mind, he still thought we were causing mischief.' Mandela's reaction to the idea of approaching Thabo firmed up the conviction within the NIS – as well as within some quarters of the South African government – that Thabo had already been earmarked for a powerful position in a democratic South Africa, perhaps even its most powerful position. 'I never had any doubts Thabo would be the man,' says Louw. 'I was in intelligence for quite some time and when you're not closely involved, it's easier to see the wood for the trees. I knew Thabo was the chosen one.'

Others have also suggested that, in spite of Govan Mbeki's insistence that it was for the younger generation to decide on the party's future leadership, the 'Royal Circle' of the ANC – Walter Sisulu, Oliver Tambo and Nelson Mandela – indeed decided perhaps as early as the 1970s that Thabo would one day become president. One commentator argues the pact to make Thabo president was made between Mandela and Govan Mbeki while Thabo was still tending the goats in Mbewuleni[19].

'You could feel it, it was there,' says Louw. 'Clearly there was no one else. [Thabo] was as good as anyone when it came to manoeuvring if only because he got through the ranks. But my impression wasn't that his rise was due to his own actions but was decided at the heart of the party quite a while ago. The way was opened for him more than he opened it up for himself.' These beliefs add weight to the notion that in spite of the internal wrangling in the ANC over Thabo's future, and of his surprising – at the time – and to some bewildering rise to the top of the party heap, that his path had long before been determined.

In the meantime, in spite of Mandela's wish to keep him out of things at this early a stage, the NIS was convinced Thabo was their man. They decided to press ahead and set up a meeting with Thabo somewhere outside the country. They were still unsure, though, how to approach him. But the good rapport that had been built up between Thabo and Esterhuyse, and the latter's frequent debriefings made the academic the obvious choice.

'We eventually decided on Willie Esterhuyse, a mutual friend, who knew Thabo. It was quite a worry for us, who we were going to choose,' says Louw. In June 1989, Esterhuyse flew to London to meet with Thabo in a pub. It was the first stage of what was known as Operation Flair. Thabo was hesitant but eventually agreed on Esterhuyse's assurance that no trap was afoot. Esterhuyse told Thabo to expect a call from a John Campbell regarding a proposed meeting in Switzerland. Campbell was actually the NIS's chief director of operations Maritz Spaarwater and Thabo was given the codename John Simelane. Over a three month period, Spaarwater and Thabo finalised the details of the meeting by phone. While these enquiries were underway, however, a moment of great importance took place in South Africa[20].

In September 1989, PW Botha – who had had a stroke – was ousted as the leader of the National Party and FW de Klerk took over the reins of power. The NIS, nonetheless, continued with its plan. A few days later, Louw and Spaarwater together with three field agents flew to Lucerne via Zurich. They had chosen Switzerland because only it and Britain allowed South Africans to enter without visas and it was considered easier to operate undetected in Switzerland. They wanted to be sure they weren't spotted by the intelligence agencies of Britain, the United States, France or Germany, or even the locals. Word would quickly spread if their purpose was uncovered and few either of the South African cabinet or the ANC leadership knew yet of Operation Flair[21].

The three field agents waited in Geneva for the ANC delegation of Thabo and Jacob Zuma (using the codename Jack Simelane) and followed them all the way to Lucerne, just to make sure John and Jack Simelane were alone. The venue was to be Lucerne's Palace Hotel on 6 September. Thabo and Zuma flew in from Harare but their flight was delayed and the NIS team spent an anxious 24 hours waiting for the pair to arrive at the luxurious five-star hotel. Finally, they met face to face. It was the first time official representatives from the South African government had met with the ANC in exile to discuss the possibility of a negotiated settlement. Spurning ANC fears that he was about to be set up or compromised, Thabo took it upon himself to investigate the merits and possibilities of the approach.

'Both parties were extremely tense. We were well aware of the historic significance of our meeting and that failure would result in tragedy. Who knows when we would have had the chance again? If we had failed, there would have been nothing left of our country but a pile of ashes. We knew it was crucially important,' says Louw.

Thabo strolled up to Louw and Spaarwater and broke the ice with a joke. 'Well here we are, terrorists and, for all you know, communists too,' he said. The four laughed at this and the tension dissipated immediately. 'I never had any problems with Thabo. He was soft-spoken, well-mannered and very sophisticated. He had been all over the world and had an excellent education. We found him very easy to speak to,' recalls Louw.

During that first meeting, Louw couldn't resist the opportunity of throwing in a few lines of poetry from 'The Second Coming' by WB Yeats. 'Turning and turning in the widening gyre,' he recited, 'The falcon cannot hear the falconer, things fall apart; the centre cannot hold.'

Thabo, to Louw's amazement, completed the verse.

Mere anarchy is loosed upon the world,
The blood-dimmed tide is loosed, and everywhere
The ceremony of innocence is drowned;
The best lack all conviction, while the worst
Are full of passionate intensity.

As well as a love of poetry and a conviction that peaceful negotiation was the only route to peace, Louw discovered that Thabo had a special penchant for his own favourite liquor: whisky. When Thabo offered his preferred brand, Johnny Walker Black Label, this was received with gratitude and enthusiasm by his state counterparts and a relationship forged in mistrust and fear was bonded by mutual respect, common interests and 60 per cent proof liquor.

After that first meeting in Lucerne, and once Thabo was safely back in Lusaka, he spoke for the third time in his life with Mandela. Tambo asked Thabo to call Pollsmoor Prison, where Mandela was now being held, and speak to him directly.

Thabo recalls: 'I called Pollsmoor Prison and asked to speak to the prison officer in charge of Mandela. I explained who I was and the call was put through to Mandela. The first thing that Mandela asked me was about the welfare of my wife, Zanele. That once again demonstrates the attention he pays to ordinary people. Despite being imprisoned for a long time, he knew what was happening outside the prison. He knew about my marriage to Zanele in England.'[22]

As Louw and Spaarwater took the message home to Pretoria that the ANC was willing to negotiate, so Thabo reported back to both Mandela thousands of miles away in prison and to his own leadership in Lusaka. The real talks had begun. Several more meetings were to take place in Switzerland, all attended by Thabo, and all leading to the first across-the-table meeting between the leaders of the ANC and the government at Groote Schuur in Cape Town in 1991.

De Klerk, of course, had become deeply involved by then but was taken aback at news of that first meeting in Lucerne. 'After that first trip to Switzerland, I reported back to FW [de Klerk] for the first time. He was shocked when I said we had been negotiating. He said "On who's behalf are you negotiating?" I said I was sorry, I had used the wrong word. FW knew we had gone over but he seemed surprised. I don't know whether that was because of the word "negotiate" or because of the trip itself.' It was only when Louw showed De Klerk the State Security Council resolution that he relaxed.

As those early 'talks about talks' progressed, De Klerk in late 1989 – as a symbol of good faith – released several high-ranking prisoners from Robben Island and provided them with unrestrained access to Mandela's prison cell. Their number included Thabo's 79-year-old father, Govan. On his release, Govan moved into a house in Port Elizabeth – and not home to Idutywa – and, before long, travelled to Lusaka to meet with the ANC leadership in exile to discuss the gathering momentum of the talks. There he came across both Moeletsi, his youngest surviving son, and Thabo.

'Ah, that was an experience,' Govan said later. 'I didn't think I would be able to recognise people like Moeletsi, because they were still very young when I last saw them. I wouldn't have recognised Moeletsi if I had seen him away from there.'

Thabo, too, had changed greatly since he had last seen his father, not only physically but also in standing. He had a full beard by now and smoked a pipe, he was married and had become an important leader of the ANC. Somehow, over all those years of separation, Govan had lost any emotional bond with his eldest son.

It was raining hard that day in Lusaka when Govan and the other newly released leaders, including Walter Sisulu, climbed off the plane from South Africa. There were the 32 members of the ANC's National Executive Committee, waiting patiently in a line on the wet tarmac. Max Sisulu, his young granddaughter in his arms, immediately broke ranks and rushed to his father. Their eyes were moist as he passed the little girl over into Walter's arms.

As Thabo remained in place, Govan chose the more formal route. He slowly went down the line of the official welcoming party until he came to his son. They shook hands and hugged each other briefly. Govan then carried on shaking hands and greeting his exiled colleagues. It had been almost 30 years since Govan and Thabo had last been together.

Speaking some years later, from his small bungalow home in Cape Town, Govan recalled: 'I saw Thabo again at the end of 1989 after more than 20 years. We met in Lusaka. I don't know if I had any special feelings, but I was pleased to see him.'

There are no family pictures or heirlooms in Govan's house, no big photographs of the moment, in May 1994, when his son became South Africa's deputy president or when, in December 1997, Thabo became the party's president. Instead, two Egyptian pharaoh heads adorn the coffee table in the lounge and a small Chinese lacquer screen stands on the mantelpiece. There is a cheesy landscape of Mount Rundle in the Canadian Rockies on the wall and African sculptures wrestle for space on the sideboard with two candlesticks and a marble urn.

From Govan's lounge, white butterflies skitter over the green lawn that sweeps down the hill to Thabo's house, Highstead, about 100 metres distant. It is too far for an 88-year-old man to walk unaided, but occasionally Thabo pops in for a cup of tea. He never asks for advice and it is never given. Thabo's own house is a beautiful mansion reminiscent of the plantation baron's antebellum residences in the American south. Ma Mofokeng doesn't like it much, though. 'It's big, but it's not homely,' she says.

Govan oozes charm and warmth. He is diabetic now and is limping after an accident in parliament where he is a permanent delegate to the National Council of Provinces. He tripped over a metal mop bucket, slashing his shins. They are taking a long time to heal. His home, called Panorama One, is a neat but sterile place more like an executive holiday apartment than a cosy retreat. As he talks of Thabo he seems sad, lonely and regretful. There seems so little familial warmth either in the relationship or even in Thabo's achievements. 'In the political sphere, a man is shaped by circumstances,' explains Govan. 'If his peers are satisfied he deserves a certain position, they will put him there. I can't influence that. So I never even attempted to build him for higher position in the political sphere. For all his generation, I have the wish that they advance up to leadership positions. We're not getting any younger, but older by the day. It never occurred to me to wish that for Thabo, it was for the younger generation to decide. We did this when the Youth League was formed, we encouraged them. That Thabo took the position he did makes me feel nice, and I'm sure my wife, but I don't think it makes me feel nicer than if someone else had taken that position. My concern is with the struggle, its continuity. Continuity must go with the best of that generation.'

Little more than two months after the Mbeki reunion in rainy Lusaka, President FW de Klerk ascended the podium in the National Assembly in Cape Town to give his opening of parliament address. It was 2 February 1990. To murmurs and gasps from the public gallery and the benches, he announced the unbanning of the liberation movements, the release of political prisoners, together with a series of measures intended to address obstacles to the process of negotiation.

At a stroke, South Africa had plunged into a new era. Nine days later, Nelson Mandela was released from prison. It was a moment of massive importance, both in South Africa and across the world. But much of the hard work, the negotiation of a new, non-racial constitution and the overhaul of apartheid, remained to be done. An advance team of ANC strategists arrived in South Africa from Lusaka in early April to begin preparations for the conference that was to become known as the Groote Schuur talks. Matthews Phosa and Penuell Maduna, both lawyers and members of the ANC's Constitutional Committee, travelled to South Africa with Zuma and were put up in a small hotel near Lanseria Airport about 15 kilometres outside Johannesburg. Technically, they were in the country illegally.

Two weeks later, and four years to the day before South Africa's first democratic election on 27 April 1994, Thabo boarded a twin-engined Zambian jet in Lusaka bound for South Africa. The jet, which had been lent for the trip by Zambian president Kenneth Kaunda, carried a handful of the liberation movement's highest office-bearers including Joe Slovo (SACP general secretary), Joe Modise (commander of MK), Alfred Nzo (ANC secretary-general), and Ruth Mompati (ANC NEC member). When the pilot announced that the plane was about to cross the Limpopo River, the mood on the plane reached a crescendo of excitement, anxiety and a sense of déjà vu. Old veterans of the struggle resembled excited schoolchildren as they clamoured at the windows for a glimpse of their homeland. Only a few years earlier, a similar plane travelling to South Africa or other neighbouring countries ran the risk of being shot down or its occupants arrested on arrival. This time, the ANC in exile was coming home.

'We all stood up and stared out of the window,' recalled Thabo, in an interview with the *Sunday Star*. 'There was a lot of excitement building up as we were moving further south. There was a lot of happiness that people were coming back. But there was also some sadness that it was ever necessary that we should be outside the country for so long. When we landed at the DF Malan [now Cape Town International] Airport, there was no earthquake, no white children died, no bombs went off. Why didn't we do that 28 years ago?

'Why didn't the Government then realise the futility of the apartheid system. But then life in exile has in a way been rewarding. Out there are people who will make a very important contribution to change in this country. Admittedly, it has not been very easy for many of our people. We never got kids at our school in Tanzania who even when schools were closed for holidays had nowhere else to go. What has sustained everybody is that nobody spent a life of idleness. People learned something. The other thing that sustained them is that they never lost confidence that one day the apartheid system will go and that one day they will return home and everybody would have played a role in the process. There is really no bitterness against the people who caused all this suffering. The bitterness is really against the system and not against the people.'[23]

On 2 May, at Groote Schuur, the official residence of South Africa's prime ministers – now called Genadendal – representatives from government, the mass democratic movement and the ANC sat down face to face. Thabo was leading the Lusaka delegation, Mandela headed the Robben Island contingent and Archie Gumede fronted for the UDF/

MDM group. Their first task was to introduce themselves. Round the table they went until they got to Thabo. He told them: 'I'm Thabo Mbeki. I carry the bags of my leaders.'

Ever self-deprecating, Thabo had bowed to the seniority and wisdom of his elders. But a few who sat there, at that large table surrounded by the formidable art collection of Cecil John Rhodes, immediately took note of his canny, political sensibility.

Said Thabo after the meeting and the signing of the historic Groote Schuur Accord, the first formal agreement on the way forward: 'We were all of us a bit surprised ... within a matter of minutes, everyone understood that there was no one in the room with horns – and in fact, this discussion ought to have taken place years ago. And when we closed, the general feeling was that not only is forward movement necessary, but that it is also possible.'

It took nearly two years of formal talks and the signing of several important agreements to remove the obstacles in the path of multi-party negotiations. However, it was not until nearly ten months after these agreements were reached that such negotiations actually started at the World Trade Centre in Kempton Park on 29 November 1991. It is not for us, here, to go into the minutiae of the negotiations, set-backs, deadlocks and breakthroughs which finally led to the adoption of South Africa's interim constitution and the holding of the country's first democratic election on 27 April 1994. But we do need to go into some aspects of the events of that time to gain a better understanding of Thabo's role and of the issues which he devoted himself to resolving.

One would think, perusing the few works that have been produced so far about those years of the early 1990s, that Thabo had little substantial impact on negotiations. In Mandela's autobiography, *Long Walk to Freedom*, Thabo is mentioned only three times. On two occasions, he is listed among a number of delegates attending important meetings with the government. The final, and longest, mention concerns the inauguration ceremony on 10 May 1994, when Mandela noted that 'Thabo Mbeki was sworn in as second deputy president.' Hassen Ebrahim, in his important work *The Soul of a Nation*, also mentions Thabo in passing in only a handful of instances.

Perhaps the reason that Thabo's involvement in negotiations has become so obscured, even in the few years since they took place, was the rising prominence of Cyril Ramaphosa, the former head of the National Union of Mineworkers (NUM), South Africa's largest trade union, and then secretary-general of the Congress of South African Trade Unions (Cosatu), South Africa's biggest trade union federation. Ramaphosa, a skilled negotiator who joined the ANC underground in 1986, was to be the single largest threat to Thabo's destined leadership of the party and of the country. He had been an important figure in the MDM in the mid- to late 1980s. He had much to do with the creation of Cosatu and of mobilising the muscle of the country's workforce in applying pressure on the state for reform. He was involved to a large extent in the preparations both for Mandela's release from prison but also ahead of the Groote Schuur talks. During this time, he became very close to Mandela. He is always pictured at Mandela's right shoulder in photographs of the time. Certainly Mandela was enamoured of the young, articulate unionist. 'Cyril ... was a worthy successor to a long line of notable ANC leaders. He was probably the most accomplished negotiator in the ranks of the ANC,' Mandela wrote of Ramaphosa in his autobiography.

But, right after Mandela's release, Ramaphosa vanished. He wasn't at Groote Schuur, nor at the conclusion of landmark agreements later in Pretoria and at DF Malan Airport. Within four months of Mandela's release, his speeches were being written by Thabo, who was also arranging his private meetings schedule. 'Before July 1991, [Cyril] was never there,' says one of government's former negotiators. 'I had the impression he was shifted aside for some or other reason. I have the feeling that Thabo had a hand in that. Where was Cyril? Why did he disappear? He was one of the three leaders of the MDM and he went back to the union. It was striking, knowing his negotiating abilities, that he wasn't there. At that stage, Thabo and Joe Slovo played a prominent role.'

Then, as quickly as he had disappeared, Ramaphosa emerged once more, this time at the ANC's annual conference in July 1991. The ANC conference in Durban that year was the first the organisation had held inside South Africa for more than three decades. It was an important moment in the party's history as more than a thousand delegates met to strategise the final downfall of apartheid and to plot the path to democracy. Thabo made a big impact on the conference and was elected ANC chairman. Says ANC MP Duma Nkosi, one of the MDM activists who had remained inside the country during the struggle years: 'The conference was a key moment in Thabo's acceptance as a leader of the party. His interventions were excellent and we felt in touch with his commitment; it came seeping through. He made a huge impact ... on me as a person. He would throw the whole world around you.'

But while Thabo impressed the assembled party faithful and led the conference's commission on the negotiations – which included heated debate around Joe Slovo's proposal of a 'sunset clause' to keep white civil servants in their jobs – it was Cyril who took the mantle of negotiator in chief. He was elected ANC secretary-general and now it was Thabo's turn to take a back seat.

'Cyril came to the fore in the multiparty negotiating process. Thabo was right out of it and I never even saw him there,' says DP negotiator and current parliamentarian, Ken Andrew. 'I'm sure in the [National Executive Committee] and [National Working Committee] that Thabo had an influence, but it was a Cyril-Mandela operation. Thabo was only involved so far as Mandela chose to involve him. I saw that period as Cyril's show. Thabo probably took a view that it was Cyril's terrain and wanted to stay out of it.'

Certainly, when things became really tough and the country's future rested on a knife's edge during the testing negotiation era between 1991 and the end of 1993, it was the group of four – Mandela, Ramaphosa, FW de Klerk and Roelf Meyer, the minister for constitutional development and the National Party's chief negotiator – who met to sort the problems out. Thabo didn't figure at all.

It was Ramaphosa who became the focal point of the ANC's negotiating effort and it was Ramaphosa who forged the 'channel' with Roelf Meyer, in which tricky obstacles to progress were overcome in trout-fishing expeditions and back-room, one-on-one discussions. As ANC secretary-general and negotiator in chief, Ramaphosa was touted as a virtual shoe-in for the deputy presidency under Mandela's first democratic administration and was widely assumed to be heir apparent to the nation's top executive job. Observers, naturally, from within and outside the ANC, were left aghast at his total exclusion from Mandela's cabinet following the ANC's 1994 election victory and rumours of a schism between the two crown princes were greatly fuelled.

Few who were witness to the negotiations, or to developments within the ANC, deny privately that tensions indeed existed between Thabo and

Ramaphosa. Some see Thabo's securing of the deputy presidency position as clear evidence of his political guile and ruthlessness. As one senior ANC member has described, 'You don't know that Thabo has stabbed you in the back until you feel the blade against your sternum.' Others argue that Thabo was always destined to become the next president and that his knack for removing potential opponents came not as a result of his own machinations but from decisions taken by the Royal Circle.

'When his competitors were disposed of, it came from somewhere central, not from his manipulating things,' says one well-placed source. Certainly, the list of those who could have been considered competitors with Thabo and who were somehow removed from the race is long: Tokyo Sexwale, a senior MK operative and popular former premier of the Gauteng province who is now in the diamond industry; Terror Lekota, an important MDM leader initially sent off to the Free State to serve as its Premier and then redeployed to be Speaker of the National Council of Provinces; Bantu Holomisa, former leader of the Transkei and consistently one of the most popular of the ANC's leaders, who was expelled from the party and later joined forces with Roelf Meyer to form the United Democratic Movement, to name a few.

Publicly, senior ANC members play down the contest and the tensions between Thabo and his greatest threat to the top job, Ramaphosa. Says Dullah Omar: 'Both Thabo and Cyril had extremely important roles [during negotiations]. Thabo was the great thinker and strategist. He was the one we would go to to obtain final direction. Cyril was the implementer, the negotiator. The negotiations committee used to report regularly to the NEC. Cyril and Thabo's roles were complementary. There was no conflict between them at all. They worked together.' In meetings of the ANC's National Executive Committee and National Working Committee during this period, Omar says: 'There was never an occasion when there was a Thabo versus Cyril situation, not once, never.'

Privately, though, ANC members talk of great, understated and mostly concealed, hostility between the two and refer to Thabo's rise as a triumph of political manoeuvring. They describe Thabo as frustrated and even disconsolate when Ramaphosa was riding the peak of the negotiations wave, reaping the glory and hugging the limelight. Some recall times when whisky was Thabo's only recourse to some peace from the pressures of the leadership race. Others say he was never a particularly ambitious person and required considerable persuasion even to stand for higher office. Omar recalls going to Thabo's hotel room late one night to beg him to stand for the newly vacant position of ANC deputy president. 'When the position of deputy president became vacant [Walter Sisulu stepped down], we had to persuade Thabo to make himself available. He didn't want to and late one night, Aziz [Pahad] and I went to his hotel room to speak with him and plead with him. He wasn't interested. Kader [Asmal] had been nominated but Thabo didn't indicate his availability. When he did finally stand, he won overwhelming support. He never pushes himself. In that period, he was very much self-effacing, as he often is in public.'

But while Ramaphosa did take the high-profile role at the multiparty negotiations, Thabo always kept an eye on things from the wings. Omar says that having framed the Harare Declaration in 1989, which was the first document to set out the ANC's strategic vision for a negotiated settlement, Thabo remained the hidden hand guiding it to fruition. 'We had to ensure clear objectives to the negotiation process and make sure this did not lead to domination in one form or another. De Klerk's first constitutional proposal called for a second chamber, a house of minorities, with the power of veto. The National Party entered negotiations to maintain white domination, not to achieve democracy. There was no guarantee when negotiations began that it would end up where it did and the NP had a different solution in mind. Thabo was one of the great generals ensuring that the negotiation process did end up with a framework that removed white domination. One of the great strategists for that was Thabo.'

Ken Andrew also has a few illuminating insights into Thabo's manner of working during the multiparty talks. Andrew chaired both working group three (transitional arrangements) at the Codesa (Convention for a Democratic South Africa) talks, as well as the steering committee of the same working group. Thabo, too, served on both. 'We were having great difficulty on one particular issue, I forget which one, and Thabo and I had to break off to go and appear on television after the news one Sunday evening. What interested me was that when we were hanging about, having our make-up done and waiting to go on, Thabo said to me he couldn't understand what the government delegation's problem was. He was asking both for my view and my insight. I was impressed. It was a demonstration of a solutions-oriented approach, a bid to try and get inside the skin of others to find a solution, not an attempt at out-manoeuvring. We achieved consensus in working group three (unlike working group two where most of the drama was) and within that group, Thabo and [Arthur] Chaskalson had sufficient self-confidence to negotiate without going all the time for a mandate. I didn't have a sense of, hold on, I've got to go back to my principles. He made substantial contributions to the committee and played an important role, though it wasn't as if everybody else was floundering. It was collection of bright people.'

Though Thabo occupied a back seat during the negotiations, he nonetheless came through at the end of the process to win the position of deputy president in Mandela's first cabinet. Ramaphosa was devastated. For some days after the election on 27 April 1994, as the results began to pour in to the offices of the Independent Electoral Commission in Johannesburg, people who knew Ramaphosa could see the tension he was having to endure. Then, suddenly, just before the new cabinet was announced in early May, Ramaphosa relaxed. He knew he had lost out. The decision, which had been Mandela's alone, had gone Thabo's way.

Some insiders argue the ANC felt it important that the members of the UDF and MDM, who had fought so hard and for so long inside the country, should be given a role in the negotiating process. But, gradually, as things developed, they were moved aside to let the old guard take up the reins. 'Perhaps that was the case with Cyril,' one suggested. 'On the day of the first cabinet meeting, I spoke to Cyril on the telephone,' says a friend. 'The names put forward by the ANC included Kathrada, Nzo, Mandela, Asmal, Maharaj, Modise. I said, "Hell, man, it sounds like an old age home". Cyril laughed and laughed. He couldn't stop laughing. It was a clear sign for me that he didn't agree with the composition. You'll remember that Cyril wasn't present at the swearing-in ceremony. Cyril was offered foreign minister, but declined. I believe that. Why didn't he accept it? Because he had made a principled decision that if he wasn't good enough for deputy president, he would stand down altogether. He also wasn't prepared to serve under Thabo.'

The dynamics which secured Thabo the ascendancy over Cyril and which saw the latter shifted out of the political mainstream altogether – at least for the time being – are dealt with more fully in chapter six.

Perhaps one answer to the mystery of Thabo's disappearance from centre-stage in the negotiations lies in his involvement in other critical sites of potential conflict. Ever the long-view visionary, it is more than likely that without the participation of both the white right wing and the Zulu-based Inkatha Freedom Party that there would have been little left of South Africa in the violent aftermath to have enjoyed in a new democratic dispensation. It was to these two key areas that Thabo turned his attention in the early 1990s, shunning the glory of the World Trade Centre to focus on the equally important if less-publicised terrain of competing ethnic nationalisms.

It is difficult now, even for those who were there, to recall how close South Africa came to erupting into all-out ethnic civil war instead of its rebirth as a fledgling democratic republic in 1994. The Inkatha Freedom Party only joined in at the last possible moment, after decades of violent conflict with the ANC, while across South Africa, according to right-wing Afrikaner leader Constand Viljoen, at least 60 000 battle-ready white troops were armed and ready in late April to launch a separatist coup. Thabo had a great deal to do with preventing both of these aggrieved parties from taking to arms.

5

The right wing

T he white right wing was caught unprepared by De Klerk's famous 1990 speech which unbanned the ANC and the South African Communist Party and heralded the release of Nelson Mandela. At that time, the official opposition in parliament was the Conservative Party (CP), headed by the late Dr Andries Treurnicht. At the time of De Klerk's address, the CP strongly believed it could win a general election against the National Party and felt sure they would be able to reimplement old-style apartheid if given the chance. To force the NP into holding an election and to slow down its reform initiatives, the CP launched a programme of passive resistance in February 1991, which became known as Operasie Spierwys (an action of flexing the party's muscles). The programme included proposals for tax boycotts, the interruption of NP meetings, ignoring call-ups for the defence force and various other forms of protest[1].

It was only after the resounding defeat of the right wing during the 1992 Referendum, in which the NP called on its white voters to declare whether or not they supported reform, that the right wing realised the collapse of white domination in South Africa was inevitable. At this point, the right wing moved from confident, but passive, resistance to determined and aggressive mobilisation. A mobilisation secretariat was established by the CP at the end of 1992 with a view to building a 'people's army', putting in place an alternative government and launching a comprehensive campaign of civil disobedience and ultimately violence. A former officer in the defence force, General Koos Bischoff, was appointed to head the secretariat[2].

Within the right wing, however, as has so often been the case in Afrikaner politics, schisms and splits had begun to develop. As the ANC arrived and talks began in 1990, a more moderate wing sprung up in the CP, headed by people such as Koos van der Merwe, Andries Beyers and Koos Botha. They felt that rather than attempt to reimpose apartheid across the country, a good argument could be made for a part of South Africa to be partitioned into an Afrikaner homeland, or Volkstaat. But the mainstream and hardline faction of the CP rejected this notion, at least at first, and refused on principle to negotiate with 'terrorists and communists'[3].

By early 1991, and after several of its members had been expelled and others had resigned, the CP's official stance to stay out of negotiations came under increasing pressure from both its remaining moderates and from the ANC and the NP. Thabo, already sensing the danger of extremist white opposition, called on the CP to bring its proposals to the table, arguing that all suggestions which might help to dispel right-wing fears would be taken into consideration. He met with Koos van der Merwe at a conference in Switzerland in March 1991 and the Afrikaans press splashed a picture the next day of the two of them together 'in a friendly pose'[4].

At home, the right wing were becoming increasingly militant. An estimated 57 extremist groups sprung into existence during the course of 1990 and were soon responsible for more than 50 acts of terror that year. By December 1990, dozens of right-wing activists had been jailed. But still, the extremists groups grew until, by 1993, they had mushroomed in number to more than 200. The levels of violence rose proportionately[5].

Between December 1991 and January 1992, 14 incidents of sabotage were carried out in Gauteng alone by right-wing militants. By March 1992, there had been close to 100 acts of violence carried out by the right wing in the wake of the De Klerk address. During January 1994, 30 acts of sabotage were conducted against ANC offices and personnel in the western Transvaal and Free State while 41 bombs were set off in the western Transvaal during the first week of February[6].

The radical Afrikaner Weerstandsbeweging (AWB), led by Eugene Terreblanche, began to raise a new 'Boer Army', the Wenkommando (victory commandos), in 1990 under the leadership of 'colonel' Servaas de

Wet. Terreblanche himself warned of a Boer holy war and said the AWB would declare such a war on the day the ANC became part of the government[7].

To add to the picture, right-wing extremist groups began to arm themselves with state weapons. The Orde Boerevolk stole firearms, ammunitions and equipment from Air Force headquarters in Pretoria in April 1990. One of the firearms was used to assassinate Communist Party leader Chris Hani in 1993. Members of the World Apartheid Movement were arrested after a bombing spree in late 1990 amid suspicions they planned to use chemical and biological weapons to kill black leaders. The Boere Krisisaksie raided a defence force arms depot in November 1993 and stole more than three tonnes of equipment including 100 000 rounds, 400 hand grenades and 200 mortars. Obviously, the right wing constituted a grave threat to democracy and Thabo quickly became involved in attempting to dismantle the danger[8].

According to General Viljoen, the former head of the South African Defence Force and leader of the Freedom Front party, which is now represented in parliament: 'In the whole negotiation process, Mandela never really negotiated with the Afrikaner. We met Mandela for the first time on 12 August 1993, and thereafter the discussions were always held with Mbeki. Mbeki was always taking the initiative. He was very reluctant to give up that role, even once he became president of the ANC, Mandela was being phased out and [Thabo] became more and more busy. At times we became impatient with the lack of progress, the lack of reaction, but Mbeki always insisted he do this himself. He was very much aware of the crucially important role of finding peace with the Afrikaner.'

It would be simplistic to argue that the only reason Thabo made the Afrikaner question his personal responsibility was the danger that community posed to the new South Africa. We have seen repeatedly his ability to engage and interact with people of very different cultural backgrounds, from his long chats as a child with the 'red people' — the impoverished rural community of Mbewuleni in the Transkei — to his hosting of numerous groups of South Africans in Lusaka, from his first discussions with intelligence officers in a Lucerne hotel room to his personal interest in the Afrikaner and Inkatha Freedom Party (IFP) leadership.

One view would be to understand this in terms of Thabo's powerful foresight, of the natural ability born of his sheer intellectual acuity, to look into the future and see the pitfalls. Another view is that Thabo's notion of an African, and of Africanism, is an all-inclusive vision that holds within its ambit all the varied strands of ethnic and national identities that make up the mosaic that is this country. One of the longest-serving members of parliament, Colin Eglin of the Democratic Party, says: 'Thabo was quite a factor in Afrikaner self-determination and in keeping the Afrikaners on track. It is part of his Africanist philosophy and, for him, an Afrikaner is an African. He was one of the link men in resolving the issue of the Afrikaner, which was not just a power play, but a manifestation of his concept of the African.'

Viljoen sees it slightly differently, though he agrees with Mbeki's seeming affinity to the Afrikaner people: 'The Afrikaner represents the traditionalists and nationalists within the white community. Mbeki runs into trouble with the black community because he is not a traditionalist. He is a detribalised westerner and he depends very heavily on [IFP leader Mangosuthu] Buthelezi with the black community, as he depends on the Afrikaner with the white community. He is clever enough to realise that he cannot wish away ethnicity and tribalism in South Africa. Mbeki doesn't have the same standing as Mandela. Mandela is a Xhosa chief and a very well respected and important political leader. Mbeki fully realises that he has to deal with Afrikaner nationalism and some black nationalisms too. Mbeki carries the can and the responsibility when Mandela goes, when the euphoria and the grand miracle have passed and the hard work begins.'

According to Viljoen, at the time when Thabo personally became involved in negotiations with Afrikaners in August 1993, the Conservative Party had left the multiparty talks, violence was on the rise and the right wing were faced with three options: do nothing, carry on with talks or resort to violence. 'The possibility of a violent option was very close. But the disobedient way in which the AWB operated in Bop [the homeland of Boputhatswana, when AWB militants stormed the capital of Mmabatho sowing death and destruction in their wake and were rebuffed by the Bop defence force] convinced me that whatever military option we decided to take, the AWB would defeat the objectives of the exercise. Previously they had stormed the World Trade Centre.

After Mmabatho, it became clear to me there was ill-discipline within the AWB which made the option very risky.

'It was never our idea to recapture the old South Africa, to have a coup or take command. We wanted to secure a piece of land termed a Volkstaat for the sake of having an Afrikaner area. But it was impossible, due to the division of ideas at that stage, to get clarity on which area. I had troops ready, everything, but didn't know which area to defend. Had I given the word; countrywide we could have gathered about 60 000 plus. I never worked on dividing the defence force. It was not my idea to cause insurrection. But had I decided on the violent option, there would have been a number of soldiers who would have followed me. It was reassuring, but it also placed a heavy burden on me. It would have destabilised the SADF and would have been a mechanism for instability. I didn't even try to convince the commandos.

'The three areas we had narrowed [the Volkstaat] down to was an area from Mpumalanga, generally favoured by the Volksunie, the North West Cape, which was the option of Carel Boshoff; and the conservatives in Gauteng who wanted to go for the old Boer Republics. The problem was to get a unanimous view and it was not possible to find a view before the operation. I was very upset the Saturday before the election because of Mmabatho. I was strongly considering calling for a violent option but I was very doubtful whether I could really trust the ANC in the alternative option of negotiation. I eventually got the ANC and the NP to sign with the Freedom Front a document on Afrikaner self-determination on April 23, an accord. The signing of that, which also secured the Volkstaat Council, made it possible to call off, on April 23, the violent option and that led to the peaceful transition.'

Viljoen describes how, one night, at Thabo's house in Cape Town, right-wing leaders met with the ANC to thrash out the question of self-determination. 'Mbeki referred to the Freedom Charter. There is a clause there saying all national groups shall have equal rights. Mbeki said to me, "for national groups, read ethnic groups". At that moment, he acknowledged ethnicity and we reached an agreement on including group rights in the Constitution.' Thabo, says Eglin, was indeed instrumental in 'breaking the logjam' and agreeing to attach clause 235 in the interim Constitution, on the right to self-determination and group rights which was seized on by the Afrikaners. 'He found the magic word.'

Equally tricky in the melting pot of South African ethnic and national interests was the Inkatha Freedom Party led by Mangosuthu Buthelezi. Ironically, Thabo was involved in the creation of the IFP when he participated in discussions with Buthelezi in the early 1970s on the objectives and goals of the new party[9]. But while the IFP was conceived as an organisation whose task it was to oppose apartheid from within, it soon began to take on its own characteristics and ethnic profile. By the 1980s, the IFP and the ANC had become open and violent antagonists. With its conservative, traditionalist and free market principles, its willingness to serve within apartheid structures and its feudal organisation, a virtual, low-intensity civil war had broken out with the ANC in the IFP stronghold of KwaZulu-Natal.

The ANC's National Executive Council met in October 1990 to discuss the escalating violence, and resolved that a meeting be called with the IFP. According to the SA Institute of Race Relations, deaths as a result of political violence had increased to 3 699 during 1990, up from 1 403 the year before. A related problem was the growing evidence of a 'dirty tricks' campaign waged by the security forces and their alleged involvement in the violence. The way forward was to be a long and arduous one over the years to 1994. The war between the parties continued to roll on, thousands more lives were lost and the IFP entered the negotiations, left again, then rejoined at the last moment. What made things worse for the ANC was the possibility of an alliance between the IFP and the right wing.

After a meeting between the CP and the IFP in October 1990, CP member Jan Hoon claimed afterwards that Buthelezi had mentioned the possibility of the Afrikaners and the Zulus having to fight the ANC 'shoulder by shoulder'[10]. In November 1993, the AWB signed a solidarity pact with the IFP's eastern Transvaal and Gauteng leadership stipulating 'Boer and Zulu would fight together for their freedom'[11]. Though the IFP's national leadership had not ratified the pact, the AWB admitted later it was providing military training to IFP members. Once again, Thabo moved to sort things out.

'In early 1994, he had a lot to do with bringing Buthelezi back,' says a senior government negotiator. 'There were a number of meetings in Durban between Thabo and Buthelezi in which Cyril [Ramaphosa] did not participate. The outcome of those meetings sometimes surprised Cyril because the ANC made concessions that were not part of the negotiation path. We got the message of what had happened in Durban and it was not received well either by us or by Cyril. Buthelezi will never oppose Thabo. Thabo will make him happy.'

6

The Deputy President (1994-1999)

On the morning of 11 May 1994, Thabo walked up the stairs leading to the office of the president in the east wing of the Union Buildings in Pretoria. He could still see in his mind's eye the multitudes that had gathered the day before on the tiered lawns beneath South Africa's administrative seat of power. In their tens of thousands, they had come to celebrate the swearing in of the new leaders of the country's first democratic government. Thabo could still feel the emotion and hear the voices as the people of the 'rainbow nation', as Archbishop Desmond Tutu described them, sang in celebration. The dramatic fly-past by six air force jets, the black, green, red, gold and white colours of the new South African flag trailing in their slipstream, which had moved the people to tears, were still fresh in his mind.

Barely 24 hours earlier, he had stood at Mandela's shoulder on the podium, watched by the nation and the world, waiting to take his vows and become one of South Africa's two executive deputy presidents in tandem with National Party leader FW de Klerk. There, arrayed before them, were leaders from across the globe: US vice president Al Gore and the first lady Hillary Rodham-Clinton, Cuban president Fidel Castro, the secretary-general of the United Nations Boutros Boutros Ghali, German chancellor Helmut Kohl and more than 100 other presidents and statesmen from every corner of the globe. Behind Thabo, the top brass of the South African military machine sat in braided silence, paying their obeisance to the new regime.

Now, 24 hours later, here he was, arriving for his first day of work as his country's deputy president. His new office was next door to Mandela's in the east wing and had been previously occupied by De Klerk's spin-doctor in chief, Dave Steward. The west wing of the Herbert Baker-designed yellow brick palace was then occupied, and still is, by the ministry of foreign affairs.

The Union Buildings stand alone on a ridge overlooking the city of Pretoria. From its balconies and sash windows, the city can be seen gathered into a bowl surrounded by rocky hills. In early summer there are splashes of mauve as the jacaranda trees that are synonymous with the city blossom along wide avenues. On the slopes of the ridge beneath the Union buildings, sumptuous diplomatic residences and expansive, walled homes blend quickly into the office buildings and shopping complexes of the city centre. But now, the bastion of the National Party government, the very edifice of the apartheid regime, has changed hands.

There was little, however, to welcome the new incumbents. Thabo's new office was stripped bare. There were no pictures on the wall, nor telephones on the desk. The previous occupant's computer had been removed, along with the rugs, glasses, files and teaspoons. With little more than a handful of staff at his disposal, Thabo settled into the comfortable swivel chair behind the dusty desk and steeled himself to start from scratch.

Mandela's announcement, a few days earlier, that Thabo would be the country's deputy president had shocked many observers and a good few insiders too. Cyril Ramaphosa, the ANC's chief negotiator and secretary-general, who had led the party into the new era at the negotiation table, was widely assumed to be the most obvious choice. His complete absence from the new cabinet once more fuelled rumours of Thabo's backroom machinations.

But to understand Thabo's rise to power, one has to look back further than a few days or even a few months before the historic inauguration. While in the last chapter we dealt mainly with his work outside the ANC, Thabo had a number of important battles to fight within it. It is to these we must now turn. Upon his return to South African soil on 27 April 1990, Thabo's most serious competitor for a place at the top of the ANC hierarchy was the then general secretary of the South African Communist

Party and military 'super-hawk', Chris Hani. Born ten days apart, Hani and Thabo grew up in the same area of the Transkei and attended the same high school at Lovedale in Alice. In exile, Hani's reputation for military audacity and dogmatic communist orthodoxy gained him almost iconic status within the liberation movement both at home and abroad. Belligerent, uncompromising and radical, Hani occupied the opposite end of the movement's spectrum of personalities from Thabo, the urbane, pragmatic strategist. Of Thabo's generation, perhaps only Hani came close to being his intellectual equal.

Thabo, along with Oliver Tambo, was regarded as the voice of moderation within the ANC leadership. But Thabo's frequent meetings with white capitalists and Afrikaners, his affected pipe-smoking, his affinity with romantic poetry and the classics and his dalliances on the international cocktail circuit, made him an easy target for the ANC's often militant, invariably impatient, constituency. The rumours that Thabo was a spy for the apartheid regime, which circulated with such impunity in the late 1980s, added further grist to his opponents' mill[1]. On top of this, Thabo's willingness to include whites in the liberation struggle both in South Africa and in exile had also riled the more radical Africanist elements of the movement.

After his arrival back in South Africa, Thabo was afforded little time to engage in any real contact with the grassroots ANC support base, tied up as he was with more pressing matters of state and counsel. With his focus on making compromises in negotiations and dealing with local businessmen and foreign dignitaries, he developed a reputation, especially among the militant ANC cadres, of being soft and distant from the masses.

Hani, on the other hand, enjoyed near-divine status in South African townships in the 1980s, but his standing in the ANC had begun to decline in part due to his perceived recklessness and in part due to the rising fortunes of the party doves. It was Hani, as MK's chief of staff, who had pushed the ANC to change its policy regarding attacks on white civilians at the Kabwe conference – so disdainfully criticised by Thabo – and it was Hani who had masterminded the ANC's most successful bombing campaign during the municipal elections in South Africa in 1989.

Kept apart by their differing roles in the exile years, it was only once Thabo and Hani were back in South Africa that the rivalry between them had a chance to express itself. The first head-to-head came in Durban in

1991 at the ANC's first national conference since its return to legality and to home soil since the early 1960s. The office of the ANC's deputy presidency became vacant, in the light of Tambo's failing health and Mandela's promotion from deputy to president. Hani and Thabo were the two main contenders, though Jacob Zuma – who had known and worked with Thabo for years – was an outside challenge to both.

It is worth saying a little about Zuma, as he will undoubtedly play a significant role in Thabo's administration. Though he dropped out of this particular race, for the party deputy presidency, Zuma would soon become the ANC's national chairman and holds an important place in the party's future plans. The ebullient Zuma joined the ANC at an early age and was arrested for MK activities and sentenced to ten years imprisonment on Robben Island in the early 1960s. He left for exile in 1975 after his release and was appointed chief representative of the ANC in Maputo in Mozambique. Later he was promoted to the ANC's chief of security and intelligence. After the unbanning of the organisation, Zuma played a pivotal role in the negotiation process, was one of the first ANC leaders back into the country and headed many delegations in the technical, behind-the-scenes discussions with government bureaucrats.

Born Gezeihlekisa, Zuma was raised in rural Enkandla, near Ulundi, the son of a police sergeant and a domestic servant. He has a number of things in common with Thabo, including their mutual love of Shakespeare and their age. They worked closely together in Swaziland during the 1970s and Thabo recruited Nkosazana Dlamini – who was later to become Zuma's wife and then minister of health in South Africa's first democratically elected government – to the ANC. Zuma is a man who does everything himself, from driving himself around in his Mercedes Benz, often without bodyguards, to shopping for himself and standing in queues. This sort of independence is relatively unusual for a high-ranking official of the new government, and has led to speculation among his detractors that he is secretive and stubborn.

Zuma's childhood years were spent with family in Maphumulo, in the Midlands and in Durban. As a cattle herd, he did not have the opportunity for formal education and taught himself English by reading magazines and the Bible and by asking for help from those who had been educated. Zuma remembers the song his villagers sang that echoed through his childhood, 'The songs were about [Prime Minister DF] Malan oppressing us ... My brother Muntuakabongwa was a trade unionist and ANC conferences used to be held around here, in Greyville and Cato Manor. It was all that I saw and all that I heard. That's what influenced my politics. I felt the pinch of my mother who was a domestic worker and the humiliation of not being allowed to visit her.'

At the age of 21 Zuma went to prison for his political activities and used the opportunity to learn more formally. Already at this stage his political sensitivity and desire for justice had caused him to clash with a local priest for his interpretation of the Bible. What irked him, he said later, was that in his sermons the minister used to admonish the dirt-poor members of his flock over their failure to make regular contributions, without acknowledging that Jesus was a humble man born into poverty. 'It's my nature,' Zuma said in an interview. 'I've always been determined to do the just thing. When the subjective suffering of the black people became clear I looked for a solution and that is what drives me.'

Zuma and Thabo have had a close, if turbulent, relationship over the years. But in 1991, rather than opting to take on both Thabo and Hani for the deputy presidency, Zuma chose instead to contest with Ramaphosa the position of secretary-general. Zuma lost.

This cleared the way for an all-out fight between Hani and Thabo, the super-hawk versus the ultra-dove. It was clear to all that the contest would be an extremely close-run affair. During the ANC Durban conference, Tambo had caused consternation by calling for the partial lifting of sanctions against the apartheid state. As Thabo and Tambo were considered virtually inseparable, Thabo too suffered the humiliation of a resounding strategic defeat when the call was flung out unanimously by the delegates. Also, Ramaphosa's likely succession to the post of party secretary-general closed another avenue of advancement for Thabo and effectively removed him from the front line of negotiations with the South African state. His options were becoming limited.

In addition to this, the still respected and deeply influential wife of Mandela, Winnie Madikizela-Mandela, had made no secret of her personal dislike of Thabo. She was expected to take the substantial vote of the Women's League on to Hani's side. But while his opponents were being rallied against him, a growing lobby within the ANC believed Thabo possessed the qualities to lead the ANC into the new South Africa and strike an historic compromise with white South Africa and the forces of capitalism. What counted heavily in his favour was his charisma, his intellect and his high media profile.

Even more crucial, however, was Thabo's support from the ANC's Youth League as well as from at least half of the ANC's 14 regions. Thabo had, of course, spent many years working to build first the African Students' Association in South Africa and then the Youth League in exile. Peter Mokaba, then the militant and popular leader of the Youth League – later a deputy minister in the Mandela administration – led the charge for Thabo to be appointed.

Later, in 1994, when the Youth League again backed Thabo for the deputy presidency, Mokaba justified the league's position thus: 'The Youth league will stick to that name.' Mokaba said of Thabo: 'We are satisfied with our consultations with most of our regions and structures such as MK, that Thabo is the choice, whether you go to conference or you do it today. We were not doing it against anybody. He is simply the best candidate suitable for the job. He is highly educated both by the East and the West, he was also a leader of the youth in 1962, and has always showed boldness, for instance when they were opening up new fronts in order to infiltrate arms and ammunition inside the country. He is also the most intelligent – the very same class as Mandela, Tambo and Sisulu. He is also very humble. We have done our own research and we as the youth were hurt by the distortions suggesting Thabo is a snob and never mixes with people. The fact is that ... when Thabo is in South Africa he is in Soweto discussing with our youth league there, organising workshops. That aspect of his life is not known. I myself was surprised that the youth league's decision was quite unanimous. It was not as if there were a number of names and we then chose him. Everyone suggested him. We want Thabo's elevation to the deputy presidency to happen now.'[2]

The huge PWV (Pretoria-Witwatersrand-Vereeniging) region of the ANC, led by Tokyo Sexwale, distanced itself from the call of the Youth League and indicated it would be going with Hani, Sexwale's close friend and MK ally. Sexwale said formally that his region and MK formations had not been consulted. With the ANC rapidly dividing down the middle, the party leadership intervened. Little more than a year after returning from exile, it could not condone a divisive leadership quarrel.

Mandela, together with a group of senior ANC party leaders, asked veteran Walter Sisulu to make himself available as a compromise candidate for the deputy presidency. When Sisulu accepted, both Thabo and Hani withdrew their candidacy.

Many ANC Youth League members still believe that had he defied Mandela and stood at that time, Thabo would have been the ANC's deputy president in 1991. It was significant, they argued, that Hani had not been nominated by any of the regions but was expected to be nominated from the floor – a distinctly less impressive recommendation. The Youth League and some of Thabo's supporters put pressure on him to retain his candidature and stand against Sisulu. But he declined. 'I can't stand against the old man,' he told his lobbyists at the time. 'Because we've agreed that we will step down if he agrees to make himself available.'

ANC officials are at pains to explain that by stopping the contest between Thabo and Hani, the ANC leadership was not trying to stifle democracy. They were just keen that at the first conference of the ANC after its unbanning, there should be no open signs of division. It was not the right time, they recalled, to be engaging in an unseemly contest for leadership positions.

Though both Thabo and Hani stood down, a look at the results of the elections for the party's two highest decision-making bodies, the National Executive Committee (NEC) and the smaller National Working Committee (NWC), is illustrative of just how close the tussle between the two men would have been. In the poll amongst all the delegates for the NEC, Hani edged out Thabo by 34 votes registering 1 858 against 1 824. In the election for the NWC, the tables were turned and Thabo succeeded in beating Hani by a single vote, 66 to 65.

We have dealt, in the last chapter, with Thabo's role in the early 1990s beyond the confines of the ANC. Within it, Ramaphosa's rise had certainly robbed him of considerable power. His failure to secure the deputy presidency at the first attempt also seemed to have sidelined him from the highest echelons of the party apparatus. But he remained in both the NEC and the NWC and, before long, his chance would come round again. In those committees, he continued to exert a powerful influence on party policy.

'We had a kind of rule that the National Working Committee was accountable to the National Executive Committee,' says Dullah Omar, minister of justice in Mandela's administration. 'The NWC came in for a lot of criticism for all sorts of things but Thabo, Cyril [Ramaphosa], Mandela, I and others served on the NEC and we observed a convention that when NWC matters were discussed, we kept quiet. So the NEC never knew who was taking positions in the NWC. There was never an occasion when there was a Thabo-Cyril situation, not once, never. There was generally a free-flow of debate and members not on the NWC were free to speak their minds.'

Two years after Thabo's abortive attempt to secure the ANC deputy presidency, Oliver Tambo died and the position of national chairman of the ANC became vacant. Hani had since been killed by an assassin's bullet, but a far more powerful opponent to Thabo's ascent soon emerged. It was none other than Mandela. Behind closed doors and away from the prying eye of the media, it emerged that Mandela, who by then was ANC president, did not want Thabo in Tambo's stead. He, along with a group of ANC veterans, instead put forward the name of Professor Kader Asmal, a former lawyer and academic who had lived in Ireland until the ANC's unbanning in 1990. On hearing of Asmal's candidacy, with Mandela's backing, Thabo once again decided not to contest.

'Late one night, Aziz [Pahad] and I went to his hotel room to speak with him and plead with him,' says Omar. 'He wasn't interested. Kader had been nominated and Thabo didn't want to indicate his availability.' After weeks of deliberations – marked by many meetings, lobbying to and fro – Thabo agreed to defy Mandela's earlier inclinations and go for the position. Says Omar: 'When he finally did stand, he won overwhelming support.'

The victory, which took place at a special meeting of the National Executive Committee, gave Thabo growing kudos and confidence within party structures. He became known as someone who scrutinised every little detail of the issues at hand in committee meetings. He wanted everything to be perfect. He listened closely during meetings and discussions, allowing fellow comrades to make their points. He was quick to intervene, however, if the debate tended to move off track. 'Thabo is not the kind of person who will say that because we have not done our work we should rush something through,' says an NEC member.

But in spite of Thabo's increasing authority and the backing of his new high rank, many still expected, in May 1994, Ramaphosa's name to be at the top of Mandela's new cabinet list. It was thought at the time that

Ramaphosa's non-Nguni origins would stand him in good stead with Mandela's wish that the ANC leadership must not be seen to be Xhosa dominated. It was not. Instead, Thabo got the nod. 'In reality, Mandela had to make a choice [between Thabo and Ramaphosa],' says Omar. 'I don't know on what basis that choice was made.' The decision was, however, Mandela's alone. Whether he remembered some old pact made in a far-off Transkeian kraal or was swayed by the opinions of his closest advisers and friends, whether he was won over by Thabo's vision and his mobilisation of the youth or was subject to the subtle consolidation and expression of power and influence of Thabo himself, has yet to be divulged. In likelihood, though the pact remains unproven, it was a combination of all these.

Once he was settled in his office in the Union Buildings, Thabo spent the next few days creating his new administration. One of his most important tasks was the choice of a small group of key advisers. Top of the list was his old friend, university buddy, best man and exile ally, Essop Pahad. Pahad was appointed as Thabo's parliamentary adviser. The position was an important one, serving as Thabo's link to the legislature and to the party caucus. It was not uncommon, after the appointment, to see Pahad casually strolling over to a minister or MP on the floor of the National Assembly to whisper a few words from 'the chief'. Pahad's reputation as Thabo's hatchetman grew with every reddened ear. The seniority of Pahad's post was later acknowledged when it was officially upgraded to the status of deputy minister. Pahad's title became deputy minister without portfolio in the office of the deputy president – a bit of a mouthful – but none in the ANC parliamentary caucus was oblivious to Pahad's credentials.

Surprisingly, for his legal adviser, Thabo opted for Mojankunyana Gumbi, a former Black Consciousness activist with the Azanian People's Organisation (Azapo) and a member of the Black Lawyers Association. Her appointment, while applauded by gender activists, stirred some bitter emotions within and outside the ANC. Why had someone been appointed who was not even a member of the party but instead was associated with the radical, if small, Azapo?

Next, Thabo chose Vusi Mavimbela as his political adviser. A former official in the ANC Youth League, Mavimbela had worked under Thabo in exile at the Lusaka office of ANC president Oliver Tambo. Mavimbela, also known as Maphepha, had intelligence credentials too and, at the time of his appointment to Thabo's office, was employed by the National Intelligence Agency. He was later made Thabo's security and intelligence adviser.

For his adviser on economic policy, Thabo turned to Moss Ngoasheng, a highly articulate, western-trained economist who had worked in the ANC's economic policy unit.

While many were surprised at the youthfulness and diverse backgrounds of Thabo's team, the fact that all of them were black led to allegations from some quarters that Thabo was a staunch Africanist with anti-white tendencies. Later, however, as his office expanded at a rapid pace, Thabo would add two other advisers, Titus Mafolo and Willie Hofmeyr. Mafolo is a former United Democratic Front activist who chaired parliament's committee on housing. Hofmeyr is a white, Afrikaner human rights lawyer who was a senior member of parliament's highly efficient Justice Committee. The committee produced over 30 pieces of legislation during the Mandela administration, far more than any other committee, aimed at transforming South Africa's criminal justice system.

With his team in place, Thabo was ready. But much of what he would do depended on the ability and inclination of President Mandela to delegate duties. The constitutional arrangements prior to the election meant that Thabo was, in title, senior to the other deputy president FW de Klerk. And cabinet was a coalition of three parties, including the National Party and the Inkatha Freedom Party melded together with the majority ANC into what was called a Government of National Unity (GNU). The GNU was an idea Thabo had hatched himself during the negotiations. He first mooted the notion at a bilateral meeting between the ANC and the NP in 1992, calling it 'unmandated' but inviting the meeting to discuss it[3].

The first few months saw Mandela delegating more and more duties to Thabo and fewer and fewer to De Klerk. The frustration lead eventually to De Klerk taking his ministers and deputy ministers out of government, claiming the National Party's views were being ignored and its opposition co-opted. By the end of the first year, Thabo's succession was virtually assured when, in December 1994, he was finally elected the deputy president of the ANC. Jacob Zuma defeated defence minister Joe Modise in the race for the national chairmanship.

In cabinet, Thabo began to exert a very different style of management to Mandela. If ministers made mistakes or duties were unfulfilled, Mandela took a very conciliatory and supportive stance. He would say to the errant minister: 'We all support you and we know you are trying to do the correct thing. You must do what is right.' If ministers were subject to harsh criticism in the press, Mandela would call on the phone and tell them not to worry. 'Don't let them take you away from the path you are following,' he told Omar when the justice minister found himself in a pickle. Thabo, though, is very different. 'He gets angry when things don't get done,' says Omar. 'He is impatient. Thabo is an interventionist leader. He doesn't just accept what ministers are doing, he makes an input and tells us what he expects. He does that with all the ministers.'

Opposition party cabinet members express few concerns about Thabo's administrative talents or efficiency but have been amazed, on occasion, by the ferocity of Thabo's anger even toward his own colleagues.

According to Colin Eglin of the Democratic Party, while Mandela has an imperial style of governing, Thabo is more collegial. 'He has a managerial style that is much more collegiate than individual like Mandela. He surrounds himself with people and whether they be good or bad, they form part of a college of people. This might well begin to pervade the entire administration and allow for a more hands-on style.'

But while Thabo was still deputy president, he always deferred to Mandela. 'In the relationship, he was very correct, always respectful,' says Omar. 'He always kept the president informed and would always say "we have to report to the president". There was never any tension or conflict, which is not to say they didn't disagree. But a difference of opinion doesn't mean a dispute.'

Little by little, though, Mandela handed the reins of power over to Thabo. The deputy president barely let a comment pass unnoted in cabinet or allowed a cabinet committee meeting to take place without him at its head. Says Jay Naidoo: 'I'm fascinated by his ability to absorb detail. He chairs all cabinet meetings and most cabinet committees. His style of leadership breeds responsibility. He allows cabinet ministers to make suggestions and allows them to execute their plans. He is a very competent chairman but sometimes too lenient because he would allow discussions sometimes to go off the boil. He works a lot in building consensus. He allows ministers to do what they want but within a framework. He is very tough in extracting commitment from his team. I deal with him on the economic side. During the Telkom privatisation transaction, we had some difficult areas, such as deciding where the proceeds must go. He was there to help. I find when you go to him with an issue and say to him "These will be the obstacles and this will be the reaction", he will back you. Thabo likes people who deliver and have got bright ideas. He encourages you to define your own tasks and helps you implement them.'

By the end of the fourth year of Mandela's five-year term, culminating in Thabo's election as president of the ANC in December 1997, Mandela had become little more than a symbolic figurehead with little exercised executive authority. And while this indeed caused considerable tension and conflict between the president and his deputy, it at least prevented any uncertainty over the succession. Such doubts, had they been allowed to develop, could easily have fuelled the wide-scale flight of foreign investment, greatly damaged business confidence and caused a state of limbo and crisis in domestic politics. As it was, from relatively early in the Mandela term, it became common knowledge that Thabo would be his heir.

Thabo was not content, however, just to assume power in an *ad hoc* fashion as a hand-me-down from the great man. He began to create new bodies and remould the structure of government to suit his purposes. In 1996 he established a secretive, 24-member think-tank called the Consultative Council to give him political advice on a variety of issues. Committee members included cabinet ministers, business people and civic leaders such as ministers Sydney Mufamadi, Joe Modise and Aziz Pahad, trade unionist Sam Shilowa, sports administrator Sam Ramsamy, Advocate McCaps Motimele and businesspeople Khulu Sibiya, Eric Molobi, Dr Anne Letsebe, Linda Zama, Bobby Makwetla, Gabriel Mokgoko, Dr Vincent Msibi, Seth Phalatse, Windsor Shuenyana and Professor Wiseman Nkuhlu. The council met monthly at Thabo's house in Pretoria with Essop Pahad, then deputy minister, acting as a convenor.

The same year, on 26 February, Thabo unveiled the Growth, Employment and Redistribution (GEAR) economic policy, an ambitious blueprint aimed at stimulating South Africa's economy to 6 per cent growth by the year 2000 as well as creating 500 000 desperately needed new jobs. Widely acclaimed by the international and domestic business communities for its free market, non-interventionist outlook and its emphasis on fiscal discipline and privatisation, GEAR caused consternation within the ANC's labour movement allies. Thabo, 'the father of GEAR', was nonplussed by this opposition and his office took direct responsibility for implementing the new policy along with the finance ministry headed by Trevor Manuel.

Around the same time, Thabo was behind the scrapping of the Reconstruction and Development Programme (RDP) ministry whose task it was to coordinate an equally ambitious attempt at overcoming the strictures and inequities of apartheid through development. Responsibility for overseeing the implementation of the RDP rested with Jay Naidoo, minister without portfolio in Mandela's office. At Thabo's behest, the RDP office was closed, Naidoo was demoted to posts, telecommunications and broadcasting and line-function ministers were required to incorporate RDP initiatives into their policies.

Besides bringing economic and development policies under his ambit, Thabo reached out into other fields. Responsibility for Youth Affairs, the disabled, the office of the status of women, the Central Economic Advisory office and the Government Communication and Information Service were all corralled into a consolidated deputy presidential administration. To allow Thabo to take a broader view of these new responsibilities and work on co-ordination and strategy, Essop Pahad took the line-function responsibilities with his new title of deputy minister. Thabo's critics saw these developments as evidence of his desire for power and his determination to build an empire. They insisted he was determined to concentrate as much power as possible in his own hands.

Further changes were to come, including the appointment of a redeployment committee within the ANC aimed at switching talented party officials into key parastatals and state institutions such as the armaments company Denel, the management of state prosecutors, the railways and transportation company Transnet, the military, the South African Reserve Bank and the tax body, the South African Revenue Service.

Ever the visionary, Thabo knew that unless direct action was taken, vitally important parts of the state's machinery would never be transformed from their apartheid moulds into something appropriate to the new, democratic South Africa. They would instead continue to be sites of resistance and white-oriented privilege.

In an expression of this, Thabo penned a speech in 1996 outlining the shift in priorities he anticipated putting in place once Mandela's power had finally waned. The speech was delivered on 8 January, the day on which the party was founded in 1912 and the day on which the ANC traditionally announces its most important missives. Based on a document entitled Strategy and Tactics, the speech declared that the ANC would no longer be content to minister primarily to the fears and needs of whites and the privileged but would now focus on the organisation's black constituents. Employment and poverty, rather than job security and minority protection, would be set at the top of the national political agenda. The reconciliation rhetoric of 1994 had to replaced, Thabo argued, with the actual transformation of society. The election of April 1994 had not marked the complete transfer of political power in South Africa. In fact, the struggle to transform the country into a united, democratic, non-racial, non-sexist and prosperous society was far from over. 'The democratic majority has won only some of the important elements of that political power necessary for the advancement of the struggle towards the completion of the current phase of the democratic revolution,' he said.

Thabo committed himself to the political, economic and social emancipation of the black majority. He regarded the black working class, the black rural poor and the black middle class as the main motive forces of the democratic transformation. 'The act of restructuring and transforming organs of State power constitutes one of the most important tasks in the process of broadening and consolidating the national democratic settlement. It's with the completion of this process that the revolution can truly be said to set firm foundations for its permanent defence.'[4]

The changes began to irk Mandela, whose weaning from authority was taking place at a quicker pace than he would have liked and whose signature policy of reconciliation was being put to one side. In the knowledge that Thabo would soon be president, Mandela repeatedly used his public speaking engagements to shore up Thabo's reputation and credentials. Privately, though, he began to resent the speed at which his responsibilities were being taken away from him.

On one occasion in 1998, Mandela was particularly upset with Thabo and repeatedly tried to call him at home one morning. Time and again, Mandela was fobbed off. 'Thabo is in the bath,' he kept being told. Finally, Mandela put on his shoes and his coat and walked up hill from his own residence, Genadendal, about half a kilometre to Thabo's house. There he rapped on the kitchen door until he was let in and allowed a meeting.

Thabo, however, continued for much of the Mandela presidential term – up to his election as ANC president – to play down the likelihood of his assuming the presidency. 'I've not given any thought of becoming president,' he said in 1997. 'I joined the ANC in 1956 and grew up in the ANC. When I joined the ANC and the ANC Youth League, there was no idea of getting into government. We were fighting for the liberation of the country. We had that generation of activists of the movement who had no conception of state positions. You joined the ANC knowing that you were MK and you might die or you might receive a bomb that will kill you. The idea that politics had anything to do with state positions did not arise. Politics had everything to do with liberation. This might be different for someone who joined the ANC much later – someone who joined the ANC in the context of natural ambition. Someone in any political setting would have, but it was not there in my generation.'

But in spite of his modesty, Thabo's new-found power brought with it a series of crises that badly dented his reputation.

One of the many problems that landed on Thabo's lap was a bitter quarrel between the minister of public enterprises, Stella Sigcau, and ANC renegade Bantu Holomisa. Holomisa told the Truth and Reconciliation Commission in 1997 that Sigcau, a former prime minister of the Transkei homeland, had received a R50 000 bribe from hotel magnate Sol Kerzner, to secure casino rights for the Sun International chain of hotels. In the ensuing row, Thabo was forced to intervene. Publicly defending Sigcau – who had been deposed by Holomisa from the Transkei in a military coup in the 1980s – Thabo had Holomisa thrown out of his deputy ministerial position and out of the ANC.

The Reverend Allan Boesak, a powerful ANC leader in the Western Cape and one of the founders of the United Democratic Front in the 1980s, also caused Thabo some headaches. When allegations surfaced that Boesak had used millions of rands earmarked for the poor to line his own pockets, Thabo decided to investigate. Boesak had by then been appointed South Africa's ambassador to the United Nations and such allegations could not go unexamined.

In clearing Boesak, the investigation – headed by Mojankunyana Gumbi – heralded an avalanche of criticism. The press and opposition parties called it a flimsy cover-up. The *Mail & Guardian* argued that the attempted 'rehabilitation' of Boesak 'very quickly took on the look and feel of a crude whitewash intended to pre-empt a police investigation'. The case eventually went to the courts and was still being heard in the Cape High Court in early 1999.

Further crises tested Thabo's diplomatic and disciplinary skills to the full. Mandela's former wife, Winnie, was sacked from her deputy ministerial position in 1996 after consistently refusing to heed the commands of the party executive and abusing her ministerial privileges. Thabo became personally involved in an ugly and embarrassing dispute following the announcement by a small group of South African researchers that they had discovered a cure for AIDS called Virodene. Panned by the medical community, Thabo backed health minister Nkosazana Zuma to the hilt, allowed her to present the research to cabinet and became embroiled in punting a product whose efficacy has still not been proven.

When the Nigerian military government announced it had executed human rights activist Ken Saro-Wiwa and several of his supporters, it was Thabo who was dispatched to Abuja. In spite of his knowledge of Nigeria, having been the ANC's head of mission there in the 1970s, Thabo failed to gain any assurances from the Nigerian regime that no further executions would take place nor would Nigeria at that stage commit to re-establishing democratic governance.

In 1997 Thabo led an ANC delegation to the Truth and Reconciliation Commission (TRC), an instrument created to avoid Nuremberg-style trials and to enhance the process of healing in the wake of apartheid. In the delegation's presentation, the ANC admitted for the first time that things did go wrong in its military camps in exile. Those who were deemed to have worked against the ANC and for the apartheid system were tortured, some were killed and Thabo submitted the names of those who lost their lives at the hands of the liberation movement. Thabo was unhappy, however, when the TRC found in its final report that the ANC was guilty of gross human rights violations just like the South African state. Thabo's attitude to the TRC – particularly his attempt to interdict it from publishing its interim report – indeed caused further tension and disagreement between him and Mandela.

It was to the TRC, though, that Thabo turned in a final effort to find his only son, Kwanda, who probably died at the hands of the notorious death squads that operated between South Africa and Swaziland. Kwanda's mother – and Thabo's schooldays sweetheart – Nokwanda, now a retired nurse, was among those who petitioned the TRC to help find Kwanda. Kwanda went missing between Vereeniging and Durban in 1981 while looking for another relative of Thabo's, Phindile Mfeti, who disappeared mysteriously around the same time. Friends of Kwanda said they had seen him in Europe and a military camp in Tanzania. But no new evidence was found by the TRC and the disappearance of both Kwanda and Phindile remains a mystery.

With all these new responsibilities, crises and worries, Thabo began to gain a reputation for turning up late for appointments or failing to arrive altogether for important public appearances. Parliamentary debates had to be rescheduled at the last minute at times because he was not available. He was accused of dragging his feet in talks with the Inkatha Freedom Party and concerns that he was not able to delegate or administer his office efficiently began to plague him, just as they had all those years ago in Lusaka.

Said one former National Party cabinet minister: 'Thabo has not proved himself a competent administrator. He leaves too many loose ends.' As an example, the former colleague pointed at South Africa's decision to send troops into Lesotho in 1998 to quell unrest and prevent a coup. 'Thabo and Mandela were both out of the country, and a week after something happened – which never should have been allowed to happen – he was still out, in spite of the fact that South Africans were killed. Then he came back a week later, and said the wrong things. My sense is that he doesn't have his hands on the administration.'

In an article in *Leadership* magazine in 1998, Professor Robert Schrire expressed similar sentiments: 'Thabo has not shown himself to have organisational ability, energy or physical drive – which is critically important. He has to become organised and disciplined. He will need to be a tough figure, the pragmatist trying to climb the leadership ladder with all the coalitions he can make.'[5]

Thabo's mistakes have certainly generated much criticism from the press, both locally and internationally. *The Star* of Johannesburg has rebuked him for never being on time and has accused him of being lazy. *The Economist* of the United Kingdom reported that his critics made much of his jet set tastes and faint arrogance. South Africa's *Financial Mail* has argued he is weak, partly because he does not like confrontation and partly because he botched the handling of the Winnie Madikizela-Mandela dismissal and the Allan Boesak affair. A columnist in the Afrikaans *Beeld* newspaper characterised his mission to Nigeria as a failure that 'followed other failures' – the dismissal of Winnie, the alleged cover-up of the Allan Boesak fraud allegations and the stalled 'negotiations' with IFP leader Mangosuthu Buthelezi.

During his five years as deputy president, Thabo has had a combative relationship with the press, insisting on the press's freedom, as enshrined in the Constitution, but seeing the Fourth Estate as one more institution in need of fundamental transformation. In an interview with *Finance Week*, Thabo responded to the charge that he was embroiled in a fight for the presidency with Ramaphosa and alluded to some of the other accusations made against him in the press: 'If you find any two people that claim that [the fight with Ramaphosa], tell them you have an agreement with me for them to come with you and tell me what leads them to that conclusion. Because the same as with other allegations levelled against me, such as lateness, once you ask the source, no one can give an answer.' Thabo wonders privately, and publicly, whether the persistent rumours that have dogged his career are part of some broader conspiracy to undermine him or whether they are just the result of what he calls 'poor journalism'.[6]

Thabo's political opponents lay part of the blame for his perceived inefficiency, unwillingness to delegate and the occasional poor strategic decision – such as Lesotho – at the door of his advisers. They express continuing exasperation at Thabo's apparent preference for surrounding himself with weak people and for his intolerance of capable, if politically threatening, characters. Certainly many of those who could have been considered rivals for power within the ANC have been disposed of. Bantu Holomisa was immensely popular within the ANC before he was thrown out of the party. Tokyo Sexwale looked set for high office when he left politics after a public disagreement with Thabo. Mac Maharaj, the competent transport minister under Mandela, resigned in 1998 amid rumours he was not prepared to serve under Thabo. Ramaphosa moved into the business world on the back of his disappointment at losing out on the deputy presidency. Terror Lekota, now ANC national chairman, was stripped of his premiership of the Free State and redeployed to the more symbolic if less important role of chairperson of the National Council of Provinces.

'Thabo is paranoid about opposition, particularly internal opposition,' says a former cabinet minister. 'Holomisa, Maharaj, Ramaphosa, Sexwale – all of them left for one reason: either Thabo couldn't tolerate them or they couldn't tolerate him. Though one was expelled, all the others were smoothly manoeuvred out. They left by themselves. They were individuals who are strong and who could have been competitors.'

Some observers have warned that the removal of Thabo's competitors could yet have severe ramifications on his own presidential term. Says journalist Lester Venter with more hope than foresight: 'Time will probably show that the manner in which the Mbeki succession was managed was far too ruthless. Mbeki would have got to the presidency without drawing the stiletto from its scabard. But it has been done, and its effect has been to parcel a dark collection of grudges that will follow him into government and add to his burden there. When the time comes, he will regret the entrenched animosities, for the full drama of his burden will be to preside over the dissolution of the ANC.'

One ANC member who wishes to remain anonymous bemoans Thabo's unwillingness to appoint people close to him who would be prepared to play devil's advocate or even to genuinely engage him on important issues. He has instead surrounded himself with 'yes men'. 'Communications adviser Ronnie Mamoepa, Sydney Mufamadi, Essop Pahad and Aziz Pahad are all unlikely to tell Thabo he is speaking crap,' he says. 'Tom Sebina in Lusaka was a congenial pisscat. He was useless. So was Billy Modise. Thami Ntenteni [who is currently in jail serving a seven-year sentence for culpable homicide] and Ricky Naidoo [who resigned at the end of 1998] never opposed Thabo. He has chosen to surround himself with weak people. As a result he failed to read the TRC report situation and the Lesotho intervention. The way that Lesotho was handled was bad. Everyone was out of the country, there was a lack of

TJ Lemon *The Star*

I am an African. Thabo has openly identified himself with an Africa that must resurrect itself.

The main entrance to Mbewuleni, Thabo's birthplace.

The original building of Ewing Primary, Thabo's school in Mbewuleni.

Ma Mofokeng at home.

The Goodwill store in Nceleni.

Linda Mbeki outside her home-cum-shebeen in Umsobomvu in Butterworth.

ADRIAN HADLAND

ADRIAN HADLAND

Sonwabo Mphahlwa, Thabo's schoolfriend and brother of Nokwanda, the mother of Thabo's child, Kwanda.

Thabo in an interview in his new Union Building office on 15 June 1994.

Thabo shares a light moment with safety and security minister, Sydney Mufamadi.

The Star

Zanele Mbeki, wife of
the deputy president.

TJ LEMON *The Star*

Thabo is granted an honorary law degree, the DBL (*honoris causa*), by the University of
Pretoria in September 1995.

Thabo, Frederick van Zyl Slabbert and Breyten Bre

Thabo ascends the steps to power – Inauguration Day, May 10 1994.

The Star

...uring a meeting in Dakar, Senegal on 26 July 1987.

Ettienne Rothbart *The Star*

Thabo signs the oath of office on Inauguration Day at the Union Buildings in Pretoria.

Thabo and communications minister Jay Naidoo share a joke during a meeting with businessmen, 25 November 1997.

Thabo, Free State Premier Ivy Matsepe-Cassaburi, Walter Sisulu and deputy minister of education, Rev Smangaliso Mkhatshwa, at the funeral of Mark Shope, the founder member of the South African Congress of Trade Unions.

Thabo with British pop sensation, the Spice Girls, and Prince Harry, youngest son of Prince Charles and the late Princess Diana.

Thabo addresses a group of Independent Newspaper members led by owner Tony O'Reilly.

Uncomfortable moments: Thabo and South African Communist Party deputy secretary general, Jeremy Cronin, during the SACP's tenth congress.

THYS DULLART *The Star*

Thabo and then labour minister, Tito Mboweni, at the NEDLAC summit, 1 June 1996.

Thabo with the Archbishop of Cape Town, Njongonkulu Ndungane, and New National Party leader, Marthinus van Schalkwyk, at South Africa's first moral summit.

CHRISTINE NESBITT *The Star*

Thabo dressed as a Zulu warrior during the festivities to mark Reconciliation Day at the Ncome (Blood River) Monument.

JOVIAL RANTAO

Thabo and Zanele relax in the tranquil surroundings of his birthplace in Idutywa, Transkei.

JOHN HOGG *The Star*

A child from Ethembeni Shelter for Children with AIDS is fascinated by Thabo's AIDS badge just prior to his broadcast on HIV/AIDS.

JOHN WOODRUFF *The St*

Thabo at the presidential job summit on 25 February 1999.

explanation or briefings and this indicated the weakness of those around him combined with his inability to delegate. This creates a small problem he must address when he is president. He is a sophisticated thinker but he needs a devil's advocate, not a praise singer. Cyril [Ramaphosa] should not be where he is. There are very few people of his ability. All of them have been allowed to escape. It's true, you don't want everybody good in the State. The trend has been to limit state power, but much there's so much to do.'

There are many, of course, who argue that this perceived propensity of Thabo's to accumulate weak people is unfair. Essop Pahad, one of Thabo's closest advisers, begs to differ with this view. 'There's no truth that he has surrounded himself with weak people. It's not that we as his advisers don't differ with him, but when you differ with him you must be clear and be able to sustain your argument during the course of the conversation. He engages with his advisers and he has a very powerful and deep intellectualism as well as political instinct. He does take advice, and he also listens very carefully. One of his greatest strengths is his capacity to listen and that enables him to put himself in another person's shoes, and that enables him to better understand the issues that are being discussed. This is also true for the way he runs cabinet committees. He wants to learn from his cabinet colleagues. That is part of the strength he will bring [to the presidency]. He also has the capacity to go beyond narrow confines. He does not like failure, but who does?'

Mixed in with all the crises and criticism, however, has been a fair amount of success. Internationally, it was Thabo's diplomacy that led to the resolution of a five-year legal battle between South Africa and the United States over alleged sanction-busting activities during the late 1970s and 1980s. Seven officials from the national armaments group Armscor were indicted in Philadelphia in 1991, along with Kentron and Fuchs electronics companies, for conspiring with International Signal and Control – a US company – to smuggle weapons technology from the US to SA in defiance of the US and United Nations arms embargoes. The resolution of the dispute, and the lifting of the continuing US arms boycott of South African products, was made possible largely as a result of the Binational Commission set up by both Thabo and his American counterpart, vice president Al Gore.

Within South Africa, the 'broad church' of the ANC, including the labour movement and the Communist Party, has been held together under Thabo's tutelage while South Africa's economic policies, framed by Thabo, are held in wide esteem in spite of difficult global conditions.

More favourable opinions of Thabo's skills abound too. According to Adelaide Tambo: 'Thabo is an intelligent man with lots of charisma and a very good manner of communication. He goes out of his way not to hurt people, not to offend anybody. At times when people are trying to be rough with him, he is quiet, showing his disapproval by body language.' The editorial board of *Africa: the time has come*, Thabo's book of speeches published in 1998, had this to say: '[Thabo's] ability to listen to other voices, even if they are seriously dissenting, and to put himself into his opponents' shoes so that he can better understand their views, contributed to the negotiated settlement with the IFP and the Freedom Front.'

A key part of any politician's armoury is their ability to deliver speeches, to present to their peers and the nation their vision and their ideas. In this respect, Thabo has few equals, either locally or arguably internationally. And though before he became deputy president, Thabo had written hundreds of speeches for Tambo and Mandela and delivered hundreds more at international conferences and conventions, he – like all ANC MPs – had little experience of doing so before heckling opponents in parliament.

For the second time in his life, Thabo's father, Govan, offered his advice. Govan called one day and told Thabo he didn't like the way he was reading his speeches in parliament. He was looking down at his papers and not looking his audience in the eye. 'He suggested that I hold the paper up a bit so that I'm looking ahead. But it's not easy,' Thabo said in an interview. Govan insisted, of course, that he was not correcting Thabo because he was Thabo's father, 'but as an activist'. Nonetheless, Thabo, for the first time, heeded his father's advice.

There is considerable unanimity across the political divide on the style and effectiveness with which Thabo delivers his speeches. Says justice minister Dullah Omar: 'He is never over dramatic, never presents his points in a sensational way. He doesn't think in terms of gimmicks. His arguments are simple, straightforward: "This is what I say". Every single speech is packed with ideas. He has a vision, knows what he wants. He is low-key in manner, speaks without raising blood pressures. His speeches never evoke emotion, but he does make you think every time.'

Colin Eglin says Thabo 'doesn't grip or transport you – but he can be very compelling. He doesn't have a rabble-rouser approach to politics; you have to listen to what he is saying, and he often speaks quietly. He is not a populist demagogue. I have, however, been riveted by a couple of his speeches.'

What is often not obvious is that Thabo puts a great deal of painful effort into writing his own speeches. Though dotted with classical and even obscure literary and philosophical references, they are inevitably simple in construction and presented at a lilting rhythmic tempo. Writes one former parliamentary correspondent: 'His public speech is calm, delivered in a subdued voice, and is stripped of the imagery and epigrams of podium oratory.'[7]

The unadorned simplicity, however, conceals an arduous perfectionism that has kept Thabo awake many a night. Thabo confesses, for instance, that on the evening before his contribution to a parliamentary debate on the important concept of nation-building, he sat down in his study at Highstead at 7 pm and started tapping away at his speech. He only stopped when he was satisfied with his work some 12 hours later, at 7am the following morning. But while many writers prefer the quiet peace of late nights, Thabo can't stand silence. He far prefers to work to the sounds of smooth jazz, blues, classical, local or even western music blaring from his sound system. This was a habit he developed at Sussex University. 'I would never work in a library, for instance, because it was too quiet,' he says. 'Silence becomes distracting, so normally when I work at home, I put on music to create some background noise. I listen to all sorts of music but not pop. I listen to jazz, or European classical music or things like that. But to sit there and say "it's time to listen to some music" is not possible. It's normally in the context of work.'[8]

On a handful of occasions, the extra effort has resulted in speeches of outstanding quality. Perhaps the most famous of all these was presented at the formal adoption of South Africa's completed Constitution on Wednesday, 8 May 1996. Now referred to as Thabo's 'I am an African' speech, the delivery ranks as one of the most definitive utterances of African liberation since the addresses of Kwame Nkrumah, Julius Nyerere and other African nationalist pioneers three decades ago. In it, Thabo sought to redefine what constitutes a modern day African, what challenges the African is facing and what steps he should be taking to meet those challenges. Punctuated by the refrain 'I am an African', the speech was startling in the radicalism of both its conception and its language. This is how it began:

I am an African. I owe my being to the hills and the valleys, the mountains and the glades, the rivers, the deserts, the trees, the flowers, the seas and the ever-changing seasons that define the face of our native land. My body has frozen in our frosts and in our latter day snows. It has thawed in the warmth of our sunshine and melted in the heat of the midday sun. The crack and the rumble of the summer thunders, lashed by startling lightning, have been a cause both of trembling and of hope. The fragrances of nature have been as pleasant to us as the sight of the wild blooms to the citizens of the veld. The dramatic shapes of the Drakensberg, the soil-coloured waters of the Lekoa, iGqili noThukela, and the sands of the Kgalagadi, have all been panels of the set on the natural stage on which we act out the foolish deeds of the theatre of our day.

The speech went on to embrace South Africans of all origins and join them in a ringing pact of unity both national and continental:

I owe my being to the Khoi and the San whose desolate souls haunt the great expanses of the beautiful Cape — they who fell victim to the most merciless genocide our native land has ever seen, they who were the first to lose their lives in the struggle to defend our freedom and dependence and they who, as a people, perished in the result ... I am formed of the migrants who left Europe to find a new home on our native land. Whatever their own actions, they remain still part of me. In my veins courses the blood of the Malay slaves who came from the East. Their proud dignity informs my bearing, their culture a part of my essence. The stripes they bore on their bodies from the lash of the slave master are a reminder embossed on my consciousness of what should not be done ... I am the grandchild who lays fresh flowers on the Boer graves at St Helena and the Bahamas, who sees in the mind's eye and suffers the suffering of a simple peasant folk, death, concentration camps, destroyed homesteads, a dream in ruins ... Being part of all these people, and in the knowledge that none dare contest that assertion, I shall claim that − I am an African ... The constitution whose adoption we celebrate constitutes an unequivocal statement that we refuse to accept that our Africanness shall be defined by our race, colour, gender or historical origins. It is a firm assertion made by ourselves that South Africa belongs to all who live in it, black and white ... Whatever the setbacks of the moment, nothing can stop us now! Whatever the difficulties, Africa shall be at peace! However improbable it may sound to the sceptics, Africa will prosper!

Thabo placed South Africa firmly at the head of a movement that will seek to drag Africa out of the abyss of poverty, civil war and coups, that will spawn an African Renaissance to reassert the place of the dark continent as a source of knowledge, compassion and hope.

All who work with him or know him agree that Thabo is a workaholic. Little has changed in that respect since he spent full days reading in his hut in rural Transkei during his youth or travelled from college to college mobilising the students. Says Dullah Omar: 'He takes too much on himself; that makes me worried. He is a hard task-master and sets very high standards. When he sees shabby or mediocre work, he thinks that is not acceptable and does it himself ... He does not like white domination and does not like privilege at the expense of others. In South Africa, white people tend to interpret criticism of white domination as criticism of white people. But he is also aware of the concerns they have been raising. He wants to create space for them so they feel secure.'

Mandela has repeatedly warned Thabo to take leave to prevent a collapse from stress and Thabo's rapidly greying hair − even more so than Mandela's − is a sure sign of the kind of pressure he is under. Mandela has also made numerous appeals to Thabo's wife, Zanele, and recently even appealed to his clan, the Mazizi in Idutywa, to urge their son to listen to advice and not work himself to death. This is rich, of course, for an octogenarian who walks five kilometres every morning and who continues to work his way through a schedule former British Prime Minister Margaret Thatcher warned would wear out the fittest young person.

But Thabo pays no heed. He is as stubborn and single-minded as ever.

He gives himself no time at all for introspection or relaxation, taking solace still in the works of great writers, sleeping when he can. Among his most treasured books are the writings of Dostoevsky and Immanuel Kant, both of whom he read at the age of ten (though he confesses to not really understanding the latter at the time), Shakespeare's *Merchant of Venice*, Noel Mostert's *Frontiers*, John Prebble's *The Highland Clearances* and the writings of Langston Hughes. As he did in exile, Thabo continues to travel the world but this holds little glamour for him these days.

But it is with some satisfaction that Thabo now sits atop the pile of political power in South Africa. He has endured half a century of turmoil and pain, joy and deprivation, isolation and victory. Many of his habits and beliefs remain intact: his high regard for loyalty, his solitude, his work ethic, his reading. And though the struggle has changed, it makes new demands now that are as consuming as they ever were. They will require every ounce of his will and energy, every aspect of his intellect and long-sightedness and every moment of his waking life. To this fate he has consigned himself, willingly and without hesitation. At stake is no less than the renaissance of Africa and the prosperity and unity of his homeland.

7

The enigma

Towards the end of 1998, Thabo's brother Moeletsi was dispatched on a mission to Britain. The trip was kept very low-key. Few even in the office of the deputy presidency knew of it. The British government, having agreed to an official request from Thabo, made its preparations and duly welcomed this unusual emissary to London. What was unusual about the visit was that Moeletsi has no official role or position within Thabo's office or indeed in government. He is generally referred to as a media consultant and runs his own practice in Johannesburg. He has, on occasion, involved himself as a conduit for black businessmen, in particular, keen to win government contracts and to participate in the gradual privatisation of state corporations. And yet, the purpose of the mission had a very specific political dimension. It was to observe and understand the functioning of Britain's Cabinet Office, the body which administers and coordinates the executive arm of the British government.

With some important changes due to take place in the near future to the structure of the South African presidency, following the recommendations of Professor Vincent Maphai's Presidential Review Commission report of 1998, such a trip was by no means unimportant. It involved participating in the very reshaping of South Africa's executive. Suddenly, and quietly, Moeletsi had begun to work on matters at the heart of the state machine, arguably beyond his area of knowledge and emphatically — at least as far as members of Thabo's office were concerned — none of his concern or business. The British government was puzzled by the request but, considering that it came from the office of South Africa's future president, allowed Moeletsi full access of a kind not easily granted to ordinary foreign citizens. When details of the trip were learned at home, key officials in Thabo's office expressed their extreme dissatisfaction. Was Thabo involving himself in nepotism? What was so secret that he needed to exclude his own staff? How does he plan to reorganise the office of the president into the nerve centre of the governmental system?

While the full repercussions of the incident are still to be played out, and may yet be explained satisfactorily, it highlights an aspect of Thabo's style that has persistently caused him problems: an uncomfortable sense among colleagues and opponents alike that behind the suave façade lurks a Machiavellian and ruthless manipulator, a dark horse.

The examples abound. Take Jay Naidoo, for instance. The charismatic general secretary of the Congress of South African Trade Unions (Cosatu) was taken onto Mandela's cabinet in 1994. His title, Minister without Portfolio in the Office of the President, was disarmingly vague but carried immense power. Naidoo's task was to ensure every ministry embraced and adopted the Reconstruction and Development Programme (RDP), a hugely ambitious scheme aimed at forcing all government policy, from the awarding of contracts to the framing of legislation, to make provision for restoring the inequities of apartheid. In a very short period of time, the RDP became the mantra of the new South Africa, the lodestone by which companies, individuals and government itself moved forward into the new democratic era. Naidoo's office grew exponentially and his breath was felt on the neck of every civil servant and his eye on every politician's budget. Such power was intolerable for Thabo. A showdown was inevitable.

A cabinet minister at the time recalls how the growing animosity between Thabo and Naidoo became a common feature of cabinet meetings. 'Thabo gave off strong indications that he hated Jay Naidoo,' says the minister. 'He used to refer to Jay in the most aggressive and frustrated terms. It got so aggressive at times, I couldn't believe it. But Jay was trying to coordinate all the activities of the cabinet for the RDP. I thought to myself: "This guy's going to go and the RDP's going to go too." The way in which Thabo handled cabinet, I can't speak negatively about. He was efficient. But Jay, in the office of the president, a minister without portfolio, this was too much for Thabo.'

Unsurprisingly to insiders, but to the shock of many beyond the inner sanctums of government, the RDP office was closed down shortly afterwards. Naidoo was stripped of his post and moved to the junior ministry of posts, telecommunications and broadcasting. The balance of power was restored. The cabinet reshuffle also provided a good opportunity to ditch another thorn in Thabo's side, Dr Pallo Jordan. Though they studied together at Sussex University, Thabo and Jordan have seldom seen eye to eye. Of Mandela's entire cabinet, only Jordan, and perhaps Mandela's water affairs and forestry minister Kader Asmal, came close to Thabo's intellectual level. Jordan is known as one of the few, and more often than not the only, cabinet minister who is brave enough and confident enough to challenge positions taken by either Mandela or Thabo at ANC National Executive Committee meetings.

Naidoo, however, denies this was the course of events that led to the closure of the RDP ministry or that he was the subject of aggressive attacks by Thabo in cabinet. In an interview, he spoke highly of Thabo, whom he first met in Harare in what was the first contact between the trade union federation, Cosatu, and the then ANC in exile.

'I first met Thabo Mbeki in Lusaka and thereafter in London,' says Naidoo. 'It was clear in those early days that he was a strategist, a deep intellectual with whom we could debate some strategic issues. In the late 1980s there was a debate between workerists and populists. It was divisive debate. What was refreshing was to meet people from outside the country such as Thabo and the late Joe Slovo with whom we could debate issues and disagree. It was an important lesson. We forget how it strengthens democracy by allowing differences to manifest themselves through debate rather than to squash them. Our first interaction was important in trying to define Cosatu as an entity in the tripartite alliance as an independent body. The role that Thabo played was very constructive. He was always the one who was committed to finding a solution. That is his strength and perhaps a weakness. He is always seeking a solution even if none may exist.'

Although Thabo was never in the limelight during the multi-party negotiations at Kempton Park, it was to him that the ANC negotiators turned when they hit difficult obstacles, according to Naidoo. 'We relied on him for his considerable intellectual power to put our position. His other strength is his ability to go to the nitty-gritty of details in diverse fields.' Naidoo conceded, however, that Thabo in a state of annoyance was a terrifying prospect. 'When he gets irritated he gets into another world,' Naidoo says.

Thabo, like any powerful person, has made enemies on his way to the top. This has been the case since he first started out in the full-time employ of the ANC in the late 1960s. We have mentioned a few, such as Winnie Madikizela-Mandela and Bantu Holomisa. In one of the most ferocious attacks on Thabo, Holomisa said the following shortly after his expulsion from the party: 'He is a manipulator and he uses the media and manipulates to get to the top. He used [Mandela's] stature to climb the ladder to the top of the ANC leadership. He always crushes opposition as he did with me. Thabo will never make a good president. He is not presidential material.'

There is a considerable degree of disgruntlement felt toward Thabo within the confines of the South African Communist Party, too, and a good proportion of Thabo's antagonists within the liberation movement can be found there. Key examples are SACP deputy general secretary Jeremy Cronin and SACP general secretary Dr Blade Nzimande. Since his return from exile, Thabo has allowed his SACP membership to lapse and his aggressive pursuit of free-market economic policy, in the form of the Growth, Employment and Redistribution (GEAR) policy, has aggrieved both SACP members and some important representatives of the labour movement.

Says one top ANC official: 'If you check the history of the SACP you will find that there was a time when people were saying that African intellectuals within the SACP were being marginalised. This was when people like Joe Slovo and Ronnie Kasrils were at the helm. Thabo was highly respected within the party for his intellectual capacity. Top-ranking officials of the SACP have never been able to forgive him for leaving the party because traditionally all the intellectuals within the ANC/SACP/Cosatu alliance were found in the SACP. Even those who hate him know that they can't fault him anywhere. He is probably more communist in his beliefs and statements that most SACP members. He is always talking about the working class, the poor, rural development, improvement of the quality of life and the need to address the needs of Africans as the majority who suffered mostly under apartheid,' the official said.

It would not be true to say that all communists oppose Thabo. Many high-ranking party members consider themselves his close allies. These include Charles Nqakula, the SACP's national chairman and ministers Sydney Mufamadi, Jeff Radebe and Steve Tshwete. These ties are evidence perhaps of Thabo's strategic *modus operandi* and do little to quell the mutterings surrounding his ability to manipulate and co-opt. But then again, which senior politician anywhere in the world has not consolidated his or her position by a little backroom wheeling and dealing?

Writer Ingrid Uys, in an article published in *Millennium* magazine, observed that an aspect of Thabo that was frequently overlooked was that his political support system extended into almost every major sector of black politics, from left to right. 'His critics are right when they refer to him as a consummate politician. Thabo has kept his hands everywhere, like it or not. He keeps his lines open to the President's disgraced ex-wife, Winnie, because he understands power and Winnie still has it. He had his lines open too, to the firebrand youth league leader Peter Mokaba, at precisely the time the youth league threw its support to him. And yet the media have often portrayed Thabo as a fumbler, seemingly casual in his public appearances, inclined to a lack of punctuality, somewhat aloof from his audience. The more serious criticism is that the men and women he has appointed around him are not on the whole in the top league. Another criticism, although why it should be conveyed as one is not clear, is that under the bland exterior lurks a ruthless politician. The question can be asked – so what? Which successful politician, at the bottom, is not ruthless? Mandela himself is known to have an authoritarian streak,' Uys wrote.

The cases of several other important personalities within the ANC who were sidelined or bumped out of politics altogether by Thabo are worth mentioning. These are the former Premier of the Free State, Terror Lekota, the former Premier of Gauteng, Tokyo Sexwale, and the current Premier of the province of Mpumalanga, Mathews Phosa.

When, in February 1999, Judge Johan Kriegler announced his resignation as chairman of the Independent Electoral Commission (IEC), a body charged with running South Africa's second generation elections, the public was stunned.

Kriegler had had a running battle with the ANC, and through it the government, on the exclusive use of bar-coded identity books in the elections. He believed that all forms of ID books, bar-coded or not, should be allowed. He was also grossly unhappy that he did not directly account to parliament and that he depended on the Department of Home Affairs for his share of the budget.

When he failed in his fight to deal directly with the ministry of finance on issues of funding, Kriegler resigned, citing the threat to the independence of the IEC as the main reason. However, unknown to the public, he and Thabo had been exchanging angry letters.

An ANC cabinet minister who did not want to be identified said the organisation was unhappy that Kriegler, who was appointed to the bench during the apartheid years but was liked by the ANC because of his 'progressive judgements', was using 'retired white conservative males' as consultants for the IEC, ignoring the government pronounced policy to give non-white professionals access to state contracts.

What also irritated Thabo, insiders said, was that Kriegler had a 'hidden agenda' and some anti-ANC tendencies. This assumption was made after information reached Thabo that the judge had flown especially from Gauteng to Ulundi where he met with home affairs minister and president of the Inkatha Freedom Party, Chief Mangosuthu Buthelezi.

Kriegler's mission was to get Buthelezi to go against the government decision that only bar-coded IDs should be used in the election. When Buthelezi, who has worked closely with Thabo in and out of government, refused, Kriegler was angry. He flew back to Gauteng and later told a senior government official that Buthelezi had declined an opportunity to 'screw' the ANC. That, top government officials believe, was the last straw. That comment was seen as a strong indicator that Kriegler might have had another agenda other than protecting the independence of the IEC.

Kriegler has been replaced by Judge Ismail Hussain from the Johannesburg High Court.

Currently the chairperson of the National Council of Provinces, Patrick 'Terror' Lekota, still blames Thabo for his removal from the premiership of the Free State. Reports at the time argued that Lekota's 'redeployment', along with Holomisa's earlier banishment, was evidence of a strategic move within the ANC by its exile faction. The point was to bolster its own position while undermining the power of former United Democratic Front and home-based activists such as Ramaphosa and Lekota. Thabo was identified as being the mastermind of the alleged power play. 'Thabo may be setting up his own people in important positions,' one of the beleaguered UDF faction complained.

The beginning of the end for the charismatic Sexwale happened during the course of 1996, when Thabo requested his co-deputy president, FW de Klerk, to investigate allegations that Sexwale was involved in drug trafficking. De Klerk, who was head of the cabinet committee on intelligence at the time of the request, succeeded in uncovering a document which indeed linked Sexwale to the smuggling of narcotics. The single document, however, was from only one source and was not backed up by any further evidence. It was passed on to Thabo. It claimed that the National Intelligence Agency had been approached by a man demanding money for information on Sexwale's involvement in drug trafficking. The allegations were compounded when Bantu Holomisa added that he too knew of Sexwale's activities, though he also had nothing additional to back up his claims.

In a meeting to clarify the circumstances surrounding the investigation ordered by Thabo, De Klerk told Sexwale that the 'long knives' were out for him. Sexwale was furious that Thabo had seemingly betrayed him and thrown him to the wolves. He wanted his name cleared. Thabo, however, denied he had been behind the investigation and an unseemly row developed behind the scenes. In a bid to impose some damage control and stifle the bad press, the ANC created a special committee to look into developments surrounding the whole fracas. The result was a public reconciliation between Thabo and Sexwale, together with an apology from the ANC in which it expressed regret 'for the deep hurt that has been inflicted on the person and reputation of Sexwale and his family.'

The damage had been done, though, and the bad blood between Sexwale and Thabo continues to run thick. Sexwale, who soared to prominence following the assassination of his friend and MK colleague, Chris Hani, was being widely touted as a leader of national and international stature at the time of the dispute. His willingness to get directly involved in crises, for example visiting rioting prisoners in their cells, won him widespread public support. Sexwale's political ambitions and his desire for the premiership of South Africa's wealthiest province to be recognised within the ANC hierarchy were common knowledge. His tactical error, political observers said at the time, was to attempt to go one-on-one against Thabo. Press reports said Sexwale, who soon left politics altogether, claimed he had been a victim of Thabo's intolerance of rivals within the party. Jordan and Ramaphosa were cited as clear examples of contenders for the ANC throne who had been systematically sidelined.

Sexwale had indeed often expressed to members of his own inner circle his doubts that Thabo was not up to the job of running the country. 'The president's shoes are huge and Thabo has tiny feet,' was a quote that was often heard. Keen not to burn his bridges completely, however, Sexwale sung Thabo's praises on the eve of his departure from politics and his entry into the lucrative South African diamond industry. 'South Africa would be in good hands after the 1999 elections,' he told top businessmen in New York.

The case of Mpumalanga Premier Mathews Phosa's fall from grace within the ANC illustrates another dimension to the Thabo mystique and has some important parallels with the deposing of Sexwale. According to his critics, one of Thabo's difficulties since his rise to the presidency of the ANC has been his inability to separate genuine problems from the power games played by some provincial officials. The nine provinces, seven of which are governed by ANC majorities, have proven to be hot-beds of political in-fighting since they were created under the interim constitution in 1994. It was felt by the writers of the Constitution – including Thabo – that the establishment of provinces and provincial governments would assist in preventing the Balkanisation of South Africa after liberation and head-off any descent into aggressively internecine and intra-ethnic conflict. The result has been a continuing struggle by provincial governments for greater devolution of powers and resources and the exacerbation of regional political in-fighting. On several occasions since 1994, provincial ANC branches have contrived to strip their premier of his party chairmanship polarising their own organisation into the bargain. It is not for nothing that the ANC's National Executive Committee decided in late 1998 that it would be selecting the provincial premiers itself rather than allowing the process to be fought out in the far-flung provincial capitals at the whim of regional party factions.

In early 1998, news reached Thabo that Phosa had been accused by a few members of the Mpumalanga Provincial Executive Committee of self-enrichment and corruption. The manner in which Thabo sought to resolve the allegations angered many ANC members in the province who believed that Thabo's determination to investigate had more to do with his own ambitions and his relationship with Phosa than it did with the veracity of the charges.

The provincial cabinet members who had levelled the accusations at Phosa were called for an audience with Thabo at Luthuli House, the ANC's headquarters in Johannesburg. Thabo then undertook a special trip to the seat of government in Mpumalanga, Nelspruit, to examine the evidence further. The allegations proved false, but many argued they had been decidedly flimsy to start with and that Thabo's involvement had served merely to highlight them and exaggerate their import at a strategic moment. With the ANC's fiftieth annual conference looming in Mafikeng in December 1997, Thabo had already identified Phosa as a potential threat within the party. Phosa was considered a very strong candidate for the ANC's deputy presidency and had proved himself consistently popular with party delegates over a number of years. Thabo was the sole candidate for the presidency and felt Phosa was unsuited to serve as his deputy.

Behind the scenes moves led by Thabo persuaded many, including Mandela, to believe that Phosa, an excellent premier and political leader, was too young to be deputy president. His appointment, Thabo argued, would be in violation of the decades-long ANC tradition of succession, according to which Jacob Zuma was the next in line for the second most powerful job within the ANC. Delegation after delegation met Phosa in a bid to convince him to step down. When it looked, however, like he was not quite prepared to let go of an opportunity to make a quantum leap in his political career, Mandela stepped in.

He announced, without discussing it first with Phosa, that the premier would step down. The announcement placed Phosa in an invidious position. He could not be seen publicly to be defying his president. So, bitter as he was at the treatment, he conceded and stepped down. Zuma was elected deputy president, but only after another candidate, Winnie Madikizela-Mandela, had also been forced to set aside her ambitions of high political office.

So, shortly afterwards, when Thabo accepted the delegation from Mpumalanga, led by Public Works MEC Jackson Mthembu, and a dossier was tabled which the delegation believed implicated Phosa in shady self-enrichment deals, the emotions and disappointments of Mafikeng were stirred once more. Although the details in the dossier were scant on the self-enrichment allegations, further charges against Phosa were also put forward suggesting he had actively encouraged a violent and bitter provincial border dispute that had gained momentum in the town of Bushbuckridge. Falling under the jurisdiction of the Northern Province, residents of the small border town had demonstrated and rioted in an effort to pressure central government to transfer the town into Mpumalanga, Phosa's province.

Those close to Phosa in Mpumalanga felt that a person of Thabo's intellect should have been able to tell that, with elections looming, there was a huge power tussle underway in the province at the time. Their contention was that the matter should have been referred by the ANC president, Thabo, to the Provincial Executive Committee for resolution. Thabo's attitude, however, was that if there was nothing untoward with what the Mpumalanga delegation had to present, there was no reason for him not to meet them. He also stressed at the end of his meeting in Nelspruit that as ANC president he would meet any delegation from any branch, region or province of the ANC. Which was reasonable enough, in theory. But more personal ambitions were at play, argued many Mpumalanga ANC members. They believe the matter not only set in concrete the rift between Thabo and Phosa, but will in all likelihood lead to Phosa's loss of the Mpumalanga premiership. Some already talk of his redeployment, along the lines of Lekota, to some far-off diplomatic or governmental outpost. Ironically, it was Phosa who finally convinced Lekota to swallow the disappointment of his own removal from the premiership of the Free State and take up the chair of the National Council of Provinces.

Far removed from the public eye, it is not always easy to appreciate the motive and method of Thabo's interventions. This is particularly so when the personalities involved are from Thabo's own party and a whole range of unspecified or ill-defined factors are at play, from election manoeuvring to provincial politicking. But whether or not his rivals have been removed by strategy or coincidence, Thabo's ascent to the top of the pile has raised some eyebrows along the way both within and outside the party.

Says Democratic Party MP Colin Eglin: '[Thabo] is an operator. He has cleared the decks of rivals in the period while he has been No 2, not by brutal assaults but by using the levers of power in cooperation with

Mandela, by rearranging the cards the way he wants them. This suggests a certain ability at machination. He disposed of the threat of Bantu Holomisa, Terror Lekota, Tokyo Sexwale, Cyril Ramaphosa (whom he didn't discourage from leaving) and [National Assembly deputy speaker] Baleka Kgositsile not in a brutal way but it does indicate a part of his personality.'

According to Essop Pahad, the accusation that Thabo has a machiavellian streak is not something that bothers the president-in-waiting. 'It was an ANC decision to allow Cyril [Ramaphosa] to lead the constitutional talks,' says Pahad. 'He left on his own accord and was not pushed. I don't think anyone will be able to provide evidence that [Thabo] has gone out to assassinate the characters of Cyril or Tokyo [Sexwale] or any other person. He does not think and worry himself about it because he knows for himself that he has not done any of these things.'

In 1997, Anton Harber, former editor of the *Mail & Guardian*, an independent weekly newspaper which was strongly critical of Thabo, wrote almost admiringly of Thabo's political acumen: 'He played a shrewd behind-the-scenes political game. He anticipated his rival's moves, planning three steps ahead, building up solid defences and putting all his pieces in place for a concerted attack – these are the main game-playing traits of Thabo, making him such a formidable political player.'

Harber continued: 'What Thabo knows he learnt at Tambo's feet. His diplomacy, his style, his speaking manner, his ability to win over enemies – all these traits he picked up from the years of accompanying and watching the highly respected late ANC president. Tambo's greatest achievements were his ability to hold the ANC together under difficult circumstances and his skills at putting a human and friendly face on the organisation. These priorities are deeply ingrained in Thabo from his exile experience. This may explain why Thabo has placed such a high premium on ANC unity, sometimes above sound political judgement.

'When Thabo returned to the country in 1990, he was known to the business community, having been the ANC's front-man dealing with them for some years, and was familiar with the cosmopolitan diplomatic network having headed the ANC's international department. But he did not have a popular base. Nor did he set out to build one. He was seldom seen at ANC branch meetings, he declined many speaking engagements, he kept a low profile and did not make a point of being seen among the homeless and landless, as Chris Hani did. It was as if he knew that his style, his approach, his strength lay elsewhere.'

Harber said Thabo was not the deputy president because of what he stood for but because he was ironically in much the same pragmatic ideological camp as Ramaphosa. 'It is his skills at choosing allies, building up and calling in favours, and playing the end-game in the corridors and on the phone. He is also prone to playing the Africanist ticket when it suits him. It is seldom public, but people around him have said that he knows exactly when and with whom he can successfully play on the sense of an African – rather than a black or a South African – identity.'

We have spoken in earlier chapters of how Thabo, as a young man, made enemies for the simple reason of his intellectual brilliance. Knowledge, in exile, was seen as one of the three sources of power along with position and allies. In the early days, Thabo had knowledge, no position and few allies. Now he has all three. Now, as then, people within the movement are intimidated by Thabo's mental acuity. They envy and fear it. They worry that their deepest convictions will be unravelled by the hypnotic spell of Thabo's arguments; that they will be brainwashed by his logic and coherence. They are concerned they will wake up one morning and find they are, dread of dreads, neo-liberals. They are deeply suspicious of those whom they think have fallen under Thabo's spell, people like Cosatu general secretary Sam Shilowa, who conspicuously refused to oppose Thabo's GEAR policies in spite of widespread union antipathy. Many in the movement avoid one-on-one meetings with Thabo specifically to leave their opinions unchallenged.

But while political enemies come from all sorts of backgrounds and bear all kinds of grievances, friends can be equally dangerous: friends of dubious character or of poor reputation, friends who arouse suspicion or who harbour concealed agendas. These can be as damning to a politician as his or her most overt antagonists. Back in exile, rumours abounded about Thabo's loyalties when he began meeting with Afrikaners and intelligence agents ahead of the ANC's unbanning. His colleagues were suspicious of the ease with which he related to people the movement had been fighting for two decades – even though he related just as easily to the movement's own diverse allies. Some of those with whom he met, in spite of their backgrounds, became close friends over the years. What may have begun as a far-sighted strategy, moved in time onto a personal plane. There is nothing wrong with that in principle, of course. It is human enough and understandable. But question marks remain about the wisdom of Thabo's choice of several people with whom he has had close relationships, especially since his return from exile. These associations have not helped ease the concern that Thabo is prone to some poor judgements of character.

After his arrival back in South Africa in 1990, Thabo met dozens of people who wanted his assistance in one way or another. Not all of them had admirable intentions. The South African Soccer Federation (SAFA) at the time was desperately fighting to gain re-entry into international football, after decades in the wilderness due to the sporting boycott of apartheid teams. A series of fruitless meetings had been held between SAFA's top officials and the world controlling body for soccer, FIFA (*Fédération Internationale de Football Association*). At the head of SAFA was Solomon 'Stix' Morewa, a former Robben Island inmate who spent five years at the famous prison for his political activities. Morewa went to see Thabo with a group of his fellow soccer administrators in an attempt to find the key to unlock the football fields of the world.

The advice offered by Thabo, together with his direct interventions, ensured South African soccer was readmitted to the international fold far quicker than may have been the case otherwise. Thabo suggested that for SAFA to be accepted by FIFA, they had to go via the Confederation of African Football (CAF), a structure SAFA then did not know of or recognise. He also taught them that they could not look at the development of soccer to the exclusion of other sporting codes and urged them to work from within an umbrella body such as the National Sports Council.

When the SAFA delegation was initially rebuffed by Confederation of African Football officials, Thabo and Steve Tshwete – who later became Mandela's minister of sport – came to the rescue by putting Morewa and his colleagues, Abdul Bhamjee, Cyril Kobus and Kaizer Motaung, in touch with influential African political and sporting figures who listened to their case a bit more attentively. Over the months it took for SAFA to gain the recognition it so strongly desired, Thabo befriended Morewa. Thabo, together with Sydney Mufamadi (a close political and personal ally of Thabo's who went on to become the minister of safety and security) and Aziz Pahad (later deputy minister of foreign affairs) soon became regular visitors to the SAFA VIP hospitality suite at Soccer City Stadium outside Johannesburg. The six men watched soccer together, grew closer and began to socialise outside the confines of soccer stadia and functions. They frequented an exclusive upmarket restaurant in Johannesburg, the Carlton Court, and chatted for hours over their food and not inconsiderable volumes of whisky.

During most of these sessions, when Thabo and his colleagues would attempt to inject some humour into the discussions by cracking jokes or talking of lighter subjects, they would always be brought back to more serious political issues by those apparently eager to understand the great minds behind the ANC.

'One thing that I noticed when we socialised was that Thabo would always be quiet, listening to everyone and he would leave his whisky glass untouched for hours on end,' remembers Morewa. 'He could spend hours with one glass. He is unbelievably patient and he thinks before he speaks, no matter how trivial the topic might be. Even his jokes are calculated. One time I said to Kaizer, "The way this man is thinking you can see his brain through his forehead". I was amazed with his attention for detail, no matter how small.'

But Morewa, Bhamjee and Kobus were soon to be tarred with the brush of scandal. A judicial commission of inquiry into the affairs of SAFA was launched by Mandela following numerous allegations of financial impropriety. Though Morewa was never charged, he was forced to resign. Worse fates befell Bhamjee and Kobus. They were tried for fraud and convicted. Bhamjee was handed an eight-year prison sentence, while Kobus received 14 years. The circle of friends had been broken, but not before it had tainted the reputations of all three of the ANC leaders who had chosen to become so close to them.

Another unlikely friendship was one Thabo built with Paul Ekon, a wealthy Johannesburg businessman of Greek extraction. Thabo's relationship with Ekon entered the public domain in 1992 when Holomisa (again) alleged that Thabo's elaborate fiftieth birthday party had been paid for by hotel magnate and bribery fugitive Sol Kerzner. It was Kerzner who built the massive casino resort Sun City in the 'independent' homeland of Boputhatswana during the apartheid era. Casinos and resorts were also established in other homelands such as in the Ciskei. Attempts to force Kerzner to answer charges of bribery have consistently been quashed on the back of the uncertain legal status of the homeland of Ciskei, which, along with Boputhatswana, has now been dissolved and re-incorporated into South Africa. Technically, though, the charges – that he allegedly bribed George Matanzima, the leader of the Transkei homeland, to secure a gambling license – are still outstanding. After he was fired as deputy minister for environmental affairs and tourism, Holomisa claimed Kerzner had financed the birthday party and that other ANC leaders, including Tshwete, had been fêted by Kerzner at Sun City. Tshwete, for instance, had received free accommodation and entertainment while attending a boxing match involving British fighter Chris Eubank, Holomisa alleged.

Reacting to these claims, Cheryl Carolus, acting secretary of the ANC at the time and currently South Africa's High Commissioner in London, said it was nobody's business who paid for Mbeki's birthday party. 'It's unnecessary to say who paid unless it involved taxpayers' money or corruption ... Everyone is entitled to some privacy,' she said.

Amidst allegations that Thabo and other ANC leaders had been discouraged from pursuing the bribery charges levelled against Kerzner, and the furore that resulted, Thabo was forced to come clean about who indeed had paid for his birthday party.

It emerged that the expensive bash had been financed by clothing industrialist Charles Priestbatch, tailor entrepreneur Yusuf Surtee – the supplier of Mandela's famous 'Madiba shirts' – and businessman Paul Ekon. The trio was said to have contributed several thousand rand each in response to a request from the ANC's department of international affairs which Thabo headed at the time of his return from exile.

Ekon first joined the Johannesburg fast set when, as a young man, he inherited a large amount of money from his mother. Friends said he lost most of it gambling or enjoying the high life. In the early 1990s he met Anneline Kriel, Kerzner's former wife through born-again Christian meetings he used to hold at his house. They dated until she met Phillip Tucker who later married, and then divorced, her. Ekon, meanwhile, established a number of businesses, including the Hot Tin Roof, a restaurant in the affluent suburb of Rosebank.

In September 1996, shocking allegations of Ekon's involvement in drugs and hit squad activities were published. It emerged that Ekon, then 38, had brought a R500 000 defamation suit against ANC member and ex-Robben Island inmate Peter-Paul Ngwenya – but withdrew it two days before the matter was heard in court. Papers filed by Ngwenya in response to the charges claimed Ekon was a drug dealer. Worse yet, the papers alleged Ekon had collaborated with former security police chief General Basie Smit in the assassination of anti-apartheid activists.

In spite of these alleged ties with the worst elements of the apartheid security police, Ekon built up extensive contacts with top ANC leaders after the organisation was unbanned in 1990 and this continued until he resettled in London in 1994. He was a prominent guest at the funeral of the late ANC president Oliver Tambo. He attended a cocktail party for singer Paul Simon hosted by Mandela, who also attended Ekon's own wedding. ANC insiders say Ekon acted as a 'fixer' for Thabo's department of international affairs. At a time when the ANC leadership was new to the South African business community, Ekon, sources said, played matchmaker and introduced top ANC officials to key business people. He is also alleged to have given cellular phones and handguns to some ANC officials. He was involved, too, in an attempt to set up a Swedish-based television station in South Africa, in which Dali Tambo, son of Oliver Tambo, would have played a leading role.

Questions have been asked about the circumstances surrounding Ekon's decision to quit South Africa and base himself in London. He has denied that he was the subject of police investigations relating to foreign exchange irregularities or trade in precious materials. In November 1996, South African police sought access to Swiss bank accounts which they believed would link Ekon to a gold syndicate thought to have smuggled more than a billion rands' worth of gold out of the country over the previous ten years. Police believed Ekon played a role in the syndicate which bought unrefined gold stolen from South Africa's mines. They estimate that large shipments of 'veld gold', worth between R3 and R7 million a time, were regularly transported by car to a farm in Mpumalanga where they were loaded onto a light plane bound for Maputo in Mozambique. The allegations were never proven.

Ekon's defamation claim resulted from discussions he had held with Ngwenya in July 1994 during talks on a significant 'black empowerment' initiative for South Africa. An asset manager claims that when considering major investments in black companies, one has to choose between those now associated with Ramaphosa, who until recently was one of the top executives of the largest black company listed on the Johannesburg Stock

Exchange, New Africa Investments Limited, and those falling in the 'Thabo camp'. In any case, the deal – driven by European interests led by Ekon – which had the blessing of the ANC, later collapsed. During the course of the talks, however, Ngwenya had been asked for a reference on Ekon, which he gave after making inquiries in the ANC.

The reference delivered by Ngwenya was considered so defamatory by Ekon that he immediately launched a legal suit. He also appealed to the then Premier of Gauteng, Tokyo Sexwale, to mediate. During the mediation, Ekon offered to withdraw the defamation suit in exchange for an apology. Ngwenya refused, saying he was prepared to meet Ekon in court. Two days before the scheduled court hearing, settlement was reached.

Though the Ekon controversy disappeared with his relocation to London, further evidence of Thabo's alleged ties with some of apartheid's state operatives soon surfaced. Charlie Landman, the suspended commander of the Brixton Murder and Robbery Unit, had been called in by Mufamadi – who was by then the minister of safety and security – to assist in a special investigation into the supply of illegal weapons to Angolan rebels and into the alleged and unauthorised transportation of nuclear materials on domestic flights. Landman claimed he had a special relationship with Thabo and would use this link not only to prove his own innocence but to keep Ferdi Barnard, a convicted murderer who served with the apartheid police's assassination squad, the Civil Cooperation Bureau, out of jail.

Strange alliances? Certainly. Damaging? Only partly. Ever the strategist, Thabo's friends constitute circles within circles within circles. They range from one political extreme to the other and hail from virtually all sectors of society. But who are the characters in the innermost circle, the ones who have the profoundest impact on his day-to-day life and who shape the ideas and goals of the man who will soon lead South Africa into the next millennium?

We have mentioned a few: Sydney Mufamadi, Steve Tshwete and the Pahad brothers, Essop and Aziz, whom he has known for more than 30 years. Add to these Joe Nhlanhla, the deputy minister of intelligence, who served with Thabo in Lusaka, Jackie Selebi, the director-general of foreign affairs, foreign minister Alfred Nzo and South African National Defence Force chief General Siphiwe Nyanda. Tito Mboweni, who was appointed labour minister by Mandela but was later redeployed to the South African

Reserve Bank where he is to replace outgoing governor Chris Stals, and Sam Shilowa, the secretary-general of Cosatu, are also close to the heart of Thabo's inner council.

Though Rev Frank Chikane and Ronnie Mamoepa are responsible, in the main, for Thabo's diary as well as for the day-to-day running of the deputy president's office, perhaps the most central figure of all is Joel Netshitenzhe. Another Lusaka ally, Netshitenzhe was Mandela's press spokesman before accepting the post of chief executive officer of the Government Communication and Information Service. As such he will be responsible, under Thabo, for the dissemination of government policy and information. Netshitenzhe is believed to the most powerful thinker within the ANC, after Thabo, and has made major contributions to the organisation's crucial policy papers over the last decade. He has also studied economics and, by all accounts, is destined for the financial ministership at some stage in the future while en route to the deputy presidency.

Thabo has shown great wisdom in some important appointments during his term as Mandela's deputy, not least that of Trevor Manuel as the minister of finance. ANC insiders insist it was Thabo who had said it was time to appoint an ANC minister of finance if the country was to ever break from the mould in which only a white, non-ANC finance minister was considered a suitable choice to appease the local and international business community.

Mandela agreed to keep on De Klerk's minister of finance, Derek Keys, as a stop-gap measure in 1994 and replaced him after six months with the non-partisan banker Chris Liebenberg. Thabo felt the 'fake stability' provided by Keys and Liebenberg not only tied the ANC's hands but was actually insulting. The underlying assumption was that no black people existed in South Africa who were sufficiently capable of taking over such an important ministry. That is not the kind of assumption that sits easily with Thabo. He felt that foreign investors would just have to deal with a black appointee and that several excellent candidates could be found from within the ANC's ranks. The South African currency became intensely unstable on Manuel's appointment, in spite of the lobbying and introductions conducted both locally and internationally to familiarise the world's bankers, economists and investors with South Africa's new finance minister. It was, by all accounts, a baptism of fire. His steep learning curve has now tapered off. His first budget was hailed by almost all sides of the political spectrum for its prudence and acumen. Thabo was the man smiling on the sidelines. Manuel played a key role in the rethinking of the Reconstruction and Development Programme as well as in changing the loose, mixed-economy plan into the tight, streamlined policy popularly known as GEAR (Growth, Employment and Redistribution strategy).

According to his critics, Thabo is an arch-manipulator who has consolidated his position by disposing of any serious rival. His political style is in part responsible for the mystery and controversy that surround him. He prefers to work quietly behind the scenes rather than leading from the front in a bold, populist way. That has been used by his antagonists to support their assessment of him as a conniving, ruthless politician. But, for his supporters, this is proof that Thabo is a strategic thinker, unwilling to upstage President Mandela. His pragmatic style of leadership unquestionably helped to lower the temperature in violence-torn KwaZulu-Natal in the early 1990s. When Mandela and Inkatha Freedom Party leader Chief Mangosuthu Buthelezi clashed, it was Thabo who was able to step in with a low-profile diplomatic approach. He held a series of face-to-face meetings with the then IFP national chairman Dr Sipo Mzimela and the interaction led to the softening of attitudes between the ANC and the IFP.

Thabo also hosted a series of talks with provincial leaders of both the ANC and the IFP in KwaZulu-Natal, giving further impetus to the new diplomacy with an emphasis on the common experiences and philosophy of the two groups. The *rapprochement* led to the sidelining, within the IFP, of white right wingers and the hardline warlords who relied on strong-arm tactics to rule over shanty town and rural communities in the province.

Certainly, opinions of Thabo are varied and equivocal. The predictions of his presidential achievements span the spectrum from division and outright disaster to a place in the history books even greater in import than the icon he will replace. Analysts weigh up his strengths and weaknesses with few real insights, relying instead on second-hand reports and rumours. In this, Thabo has not been much help. He is closed and private, even to those he knows best and trusts most. He has simply always been that way, the product of a tough childhood, an isolated youth and his submergence in adulthood in a movement that was forced to be clandestine and distant.

And yet, few interested or engaged in politics don't have opinions about Thabo. Analyst Steven Friedman says Thabo is extremely sensitive to criticism. He tends to divide the world into friends and enemies, the former unquestioningly loyal, the latter assumed to be hostile. He also, argues Friedman, surrounds himself with advisers whose chief quality is their inability, or unwillingness, to criticise. A third tendency is a penchant for backing appointments to cabinet of people whose sole asset is their inclination to do as they are told[1].

'He is elusive in spite of the exposure he has had over the last seven years,' says Colin Eglin. 'There's more mystical content to him. In a sense, one knows him and yet doesn't know him and I think it is true for the nation too. But things I don't know about him don't frighten me. I fill in the gaps in a positive way.'

A former cabinet colleague says: 'My sense is that he doesn't have his hands on the administration. Second, he is paranoid about opposition, particularly internal opposition. Bantu Holomisa, Mac Maharaj, Cyril [Ramaphosa], Tokyo Sexwale – all of them left for one reason – either Thabo could not tolerate them or they could not tolerate him. Though Holomisa was expelled, all the others were smoothly manoeuvred out. They left by themselves. They were all individuals who are strong and who could have been competitors in this process. It has been openly speculated that Maharaj left because of tensions with Thabo.

'There are people who think Thabo could be another [Zimbabwean President] Robert Mugabe, but in a far more diplomatic way, in that he will rule out all opposition. He has been busy with Buthelezi in the same way that Mugabe co-opted [ZAPU leader Joshua] Nkomo. Buthelezi will never oppose Thabo. In early 1994, Thabo had a lot to do with bringing Buthelezi back, but then he was the deputy president of the ANC. There were a number of meetings in Durban between Thabo and Buthelezi in which Ramaphosa did not participate. The outcome of the meetings sometimes surprised Ramaphosa because the ANC made concessions that were not part of the negotiation path. We got the message of what had happened in Durban and it was not received well ... My biggest concern is what is he really up to in terms of power? The president is only allowed to serve two terms but he could always do a [Namibian President Sam]

Nujoma. [Nujoma was in the process of amending the Namibian constitution to allow himself to serve another term.] That's why Buthelezi is so important. It assures the two thirds majority.'

Mangosuthu Buthelezi's attitude toward Thabo has changed over the years. In an interview with *The Star* in 1995, on whether he thought Thabo was fit to be president, he said: 'I'm not very sure now. The events of March/April [the issue of whether or not the IFP would participate in the 1994 election and on what preconditions e.g. international mediation and the Zulu king] disillusioned me. Thabo is really a very competent person and I feel that he is the right person in the right place as far as that is concerned. (But) if that is his style then I'm really worried about the future because I'm very worried about that style. That style of doing things is not reassuring.'

Two years later, Buthelezi made the following assessment: 'He is one of the finest brains we have in the leadership of South Africa. He is a listener. He does not rush to react to whatever is presented to him. He listens patiently and then deals with the issue with impressive precision. When he feels that he must intervene, he does so in a way that always reflects his very great mind and commitment.'

The Pan-Africanist Congress of Azania (PAC), the ANC's chief rival during the exile years, though consigned now to a tiny fraction of electoral support, feels Thabo has a tendency to encourage division and that this does not augur well for the future.

Ngila Muendane, the PAC's secretary-general says: 'If anybody is president he must have the ability to unite his party and we don't see [Thabo] as such a person. He tends to set up little cabals within the party. If he can't unite the ANC, what about the country? Thabo has two faces. He appears warm but behind the scenes he is said to be an arch manipulator. He does not inspire me with the confidence that he is honest.'

Mosebudi Mangena, president of the Azanian People's Organisation, is less concerned: 'I'm not sure what is being said about Thabo is fair because as an organisation man myself, I believe it's up to the ANC to ensure that he behaves in a proper manner. Otherwise I have respect for the man, and I'm confident he has the leadership capabilities to continue where Mandela has left off.'

Holomisa, now the leader of a new political party, the United

Democratic Movement, continues to twist the knife of criticism in Thabo's side: 'Recently I was in the Eastern Cape and [Thabo] was there to launch a water project in the Transkei. Only 50 people rolled up to see him. This is not a happy situation. I think the best way is to bring Cyril Ramaphosa back as deputy president. There is nobody else substantial enough to fill that role – all the people mentioned are weak. One effect of Mandela leaving will probably just be that fewer people will vote.'

Political analysts waver over the seemingly contradictory elements of Thabo's nature and the mutability of his core principles. Says respected academic Tom Lodge: 'Thabo has changed his political colours like a chameleon: he was once a communist but moved out of the party when it looked as if it might make him and the ANC vulnerable, he's an Africanist when it suits him, as capable of generating hard-nosed rhetoric as any of the populists – remember his slogan 'make SA ungovernable' – and yet he is also the man who has probably done most to win over to the ANC international and local business, not to mention the white "middle strata".'

Within the ANC, he is equally difficult to predict. After pushing so hard for Zuma to become the party deputy president in 1997 – and ousting Phosa into the bargain – relations between the two men deteriorated immediately. Some ANC insiders say the reason for this is Thabo's desire to consolidate power. According to a National Executive Committee member, between December 1997 and early 1999, Thabo and Zuma – as the two most senior leaders of the ANC – never met person to person. They have occasionally come into contact but always in large groups with the usual retinues of advisers, personal secretaries and hangers-on. But not once in that period did they sit down, one on one, and strategise about the election, the future of the ANC or indeed about anything. Thabo is already on record as saying that just because someone is the ANC deputy president does not mean they were the most obvious candidate for the deputy presidency of the country.

Party insiders deduce that this will indeed be the case come the general election in mid-1999 – with Buthelezi being the man in line for the post – and mutter darkly that Zuma's isolation is more evidence of Thabo's inclination to absorb and consolidate power even in spite of the wishes of the party he represents. Mandela, too, as we have mentioned, has been cut out of the loop quicker than he hoped or the party intended. Their differing attitudes reached stark expression during late 1998 when Thabo took the Truth and Reconciliation Commission to court over the body's final report. 'Thabo sanctioned the court action without talking to [Mandela] and he expressed his views without consulting the president of his organisation,' the NEC member said.

His father, Govan, naturally enough thinks the talk of Thabo's manipulative and scheming nature are unfounded: 'Thabo is still the great reader he was as a youngster. He is able to draw from a whole range of sources in literature. I like poetry, he likes poetry but he reads much more widely than I do. Why should he want to manipulate anybody instead of using their ideas which come from his wide reading? I can't see Thabo playing tricks behind people's backs. He lives within an organisation and for that organisation. It will be bad politics to try and do harm to one or to raise one at the expense of another. If he quotes from the Roman poet Ovid, why should that be an attempt to manipulate?,' asks the 89-year-old veteran, who retired from politics and parliament only months before his son was due to become president. The only weakness that Govan has identified in his son is a possible tendency to be too serious.

Thabo was told in 1998 by the *Financial Mail* that people were worried that they did not know him well enough. Thabo replied, 'Trying to find out who Thabo Mbeki is is irrelevant. It is looking at the wrong thing.' On the allegations he is a schemer and a manipulator, he laughed and responded: 'The first thing I want to say is that people who want to be commentators should make an effort to increase their level of understanding. I don't think the way the ANC operates allows for decisions to be arrived at through manipulation. The ANC does not have ... power of the sort which leads people to say "the leader has decided". Our decisions are arrived at through the process of discussion and debate. So I'm saying any notion that anybody can succeed within the ANC by being manipulative and a schemer is wrong.'

8

Into the future

Thabo's homecoming over the Christmas weekend of 1998 to the rural town of his childhood was like the return of the prodigal son. Everyone, from local peasants to the most colourfully dressed and powerful politicians, descended on his mother Ma Mofokeng's small household next to the Goodwill store in Idutywa to become part of an historic African feast. Two bulls and 20 merino sheep were slaughtered to feed the multitudes that had gathered in the valley of Nceleni, or Ncingwana as the locals prefer to call it.

Ever since he left his home for Johannesburg in the late 1950s and then made his perilous way into exile, Thabo has never had more than an hour or two at a time with his family and with the people with whom he grew up. He chose this Christmas to redress the balance a little, to acknowledge his roots and mark his heritage. For local indigent families, the free meat, samp, vegetables and drinks – courteously made available by a soft drink multinational and a local beer company – were the perfect Christmas present. For those who did not so desperately need the food and drink, it was a time to rub shoulders with the future president, his family, childhood friends and relatives.

Among the guests were Nelson Mandela, whose own home is nearby on the other side of Umtata, and his new wife Graca Machel. Virtually the entire political leadership of the ANC in the Eastern Cape made their way to the modest village, along with half a dozen national cabinet ministers.

But Thabo's homecoming was not about VIPs or civic luminaries. It was not about political alliances or long-term strategic objectives. Thabo, simply, wanted to go home. Home to the lush hills and hidden waterfalls of Nceleni, home to the rustic kraals and welcoming faces of his childhood, home to take his place in his clan, amongst his people.

To those who didn't know of Thabo's return, the first sign was the makeshift police roadblock on the bridge of the Gxaxaka River, at the entrance to Idutywa. Two kilometres down the freshly graded gravel road, two marquees, like roses among thorns, stuck out from the sparse settlement that is Ncingwana.

The weekend feast started in a typically African way. The two bulls bought for the party bolted just before they were slaughtered. The local old folks smiled and the women ululated. It was a good omen, they assured everyone. The grins and singing returned when the beasts had finally been rounded up and bellowed loudly before surrendering to their fate.

Before the slaughter, the clattering of the army helicopter that had brought Thabo, his wife Zanele, and other officials, announced the arrival of this small village's most famous son. Locals sang and danced as Thabo walked from the dusty football grounds which served as a helipad toward the marquees. As the village is without electricity, the state utility Eskom provided some portable power for the huge tents. The local school supplied all its chairs and tables. The national telephone company, Telkom, even arranged for Ma Mofokeng's unreliable party line to be replaced with a state-of-the-art digital connection. It was a party in which everyone wanted their contribution to be noticed. After all, who wouldn't want to please arguably the most powerful person in South Africa?

Hours later, in a vacant lot behind the Goodwill store, a makeshift kraal of grass huts had been erected. Here, Thabo took his rightful place among the Mazizi clan. For his tribesmen and those who gathered to be with him and his family, there is nothing enigmatic about Thabo. He is their kin and their son. For him they danced the traditional dance *(Ukuxhentsa)*, they shared a special piece of meat for clan members only *(ushwama)* and they washed it all down with African beer, brewed meticulously and proudly by the women of Ncingwana.

On Sunday morning, before the high-profile visitors arrived, Thabo and Zanele went down to the banks of the Gxakaxa River where they walked hand in hand. It was a rare moment of peace for the couple. Their life together has always been fraught with tight schedules and travel, business meetings and long weeks and longer months of separation. Even when they were courting, Zanele lived in New York where she worked for the United Nations and Thabo spent most of his time travelling between London and Lusaka. But all agreed it was a wonderful sight to see them together. 'Like teenagers falling in love,' one smiling guest commented.

The weight of the nation's problems, though, are never far away, even on the banks of the Gxakaxa River early on a Sunday morning. The local headman, Sigciniwe Gotyi, barely managed to complete his traditional greetings before getting straight to the point. He was having problems securing his monthly social pension and pleaded with Thabo to intervene. Thabo listened sympathetically to the old man, then replied: 'If you have an identity book we will see what we can do.' He called over a nearby aide who took down Gotyi's details.

A young mother, holding a baby in her arms, approached the couple and appealed for more telephones to help locals during emergencies. Most of the telephones, she explained to Thabo, were installed in shops which closed at 5 pm. If an emergency happened after that, there was no way that people could summon the help of the rescue services, she told them. Thabo nodded and consoled her. More than most, he is deeply aware of the plight of the black masses, and in particular of those living in the rural areas from which he comes. Zanele, too, has made her goal in life the upliftment of black women. It is they that constitute the overwhelming majority of the unemployed and destitute in South Africa. Zanele now heads the Women's Development Bank (WDB) in South Africa, which seeks to do what it can to overturn centuries of neglect and dependence. Through the bank, rural women – often unable to access credit due to their lack of records – can borrow small amounts of money to start businesses. Once the initial loan is settled, larger loans are granted in incremental amounts. The project has assisted thousands of women to become breadwinners and eased their heavy reliance on distant, migrant or unemployed husbands. 'A lot of men who cannot find jobs encourage their women to enlist the help of the WDB so that families can eat,' Zanele said during an overseas trip with Thabo.

Thabo's strong empathy with the plight of the rural peasants, which had its roots in his time spent serving behind the counter of the family trading store as a child, still runs like a golden thread through his speeches and political life. But it is more than just his humanity, and his past, that has persuaded Thabo to take the issue of poverty seriously. He has repeatedly warned that poverty is one of the direst threats to South Africa's future. He is acutely aware that the destitute are a time-bomb waiting to rip apart the fabric of the new society he is trying to build.

'When South Africa stepped through the looking glass [after the elections in 1994], it did not emerge in Wonderland,' wrote American journalist Patti Waldmeir. 'It emerged in the real world, where poverty is the biggest challenge to all democratic governments, and where there are tougher problems to solve than apartheid'[1].

Looking toward his term as South Africa's next president, Thabo is faced with a fundamental paradox. For more than 50 years, the apartheid state sought – and indeed managed – to marginalise and disempower South Africa's black citizens. They were placed far from white cities often without electricity or running water, given inferior education and granted little access to resources or rights. The result, aside from the obvious political implications of non-representation and repression, was that the gap between the rich and the poor in South Africa grew to immense proportions, virtually unequalled anywhere else on the globe. Naturally enough, given apartheid's implicit bias in favour of its white supporters and citizens, the wealth gap is also a racial gap.

The paradox is this: how does Thabo expect to continue the reconciliation of the races so central to the Mandela legacy, while at the same time meeting the expectations and indeed rights of the vast majority of the country's people? Improving the lot of the average citizen goes way beyond the devotion of extra money from an already over-stretched state budget.

A radical transformation of every sector of society will be required. Government, business, civil society, and the economy itself all need to shift from the habits and priorities of apartheid to the demands and needs of a new era. But it is not simply a question of taking away the possessions and assets of the privileged. To many, including Thabo, achieving both reconciliation and transformation is not an easy objective.

'It's a very delicate thing, to handle the relationship between these two elements,' Thabo has observed. 'It's not a mathematical thing, it's an art ... If you handle transformation in a way that doesn't change a good part of the *status quo*, those who are disadvantaged will rebel, and then, goodbye reconciliation'[2]. Instead, he said in 1995, 'durable national

135

reconciliation requires ... the fundamental transformation of the patterns of ownership of wealth, the distribution of income, the management of society and the economy, and the skills profile.'

Five years after democracy was born in South Africa, Thabo remains deeply frustrated by the lack of progress in achieving either reconciliation or transformation.

Toward the end of 1998, Thabo agreed to a National Party request that national reconciliation, or 'nation-building', needed to be debated in the National Assembly. The debate provided the perfect opportunity for him to express his frustrations. The first step toward achieving national reconciliation was a bit like coming to terms with alcoholism or drug addition: the problem had to be acknowledged. Ahead of the speech, now known as his 'Two Nations' address, Thabo consulted with his staff and advisers. Should he couch his words in a palatable, gently chiding manner, or should he go for the jugular and be brutally frank? 'Tell the truth,' his staff urged him. 'People must face reality.'

And it was reality indeed that Thabo brought to a hushed National Assembly chamber at 3 pm on 29 May 1998. He kicked off the address by quoting the preamble of the Constitution, the Bible of politicians in the new South Africa. 'We, the people of South Africa,' he began, 'recognise the injustices of the past ... [and] believe that South Africa belongs to all who live in it, united in our diversity. We therefore adopt this Constitution as the supreme law of the Republic so as to heal the divisions of the past ... [and] to improve the quality of life of all citizens and free the potential of each person.'

As MPs started to wonder where Thabo was taking them, he paused. Everyone had to answer honestly the question of whether South Africa was making the requisite progress toward the creation of a non-racial society, he said. Were South Africans doing enough to build a non-sexist country, to heal the divisions of the past, to achieve the peaceful co-existence of all its people, to create development opportunities for all South Africans, irrespective of colour, race, class, belief or sex and to improve the quality of life of all citizens? 'We also will have to answer the question, again as honestly as we can do, whether our actions have been and are based on the recognition of the injustices of the past and whether our actions have genuinely sought to promote the integrated Constitutional objectives of national unity, the well-being of South Africans, peace, reconciliation between the people of South Africa and the reconstruction of society.'

Thabo then gave the nation his message.

Our answer to the question whether we are making the requisite progress towards achieving the objective of nation building, as we defined it, would be – no! A major component part of the issue of reconciliation and nation-building is defined by and derives from the material conditions in our society which have divided our country into two nations, the one black and the other white. We therefore make bold to say that South Africa is a country of two nations. One of these nations is white, relatively prosperous, regardless of gender or geographic dispersal. It has ready access to a developed economic, physical, educational, communication and other infrastructure. The second and larger nation of South Africa is black and poor, with the worst affected being women in rural areas. Neither are we becoming one nation. Consequently, also, the objective of national reconciliation is not being realised. This follows as well that the longer the situation persists, in spite of the gift of hope delivered by the birth of democracy, the more entrenched will be the conviction that the concept of nation building is a mere mirage and that no basis exists, to enable national reconciliation to take place.

To conclude his speech, Thabo quoted the Afro-American poet, Langston Hughes: 'What happens to a dream deferred?' he asked. 'It explodes.' It's this explosion – the simmering rage among the millions of black South Africans over their continuing deprivation – that Thabo has placed at the top of the national political agenda. For where there is poverty, there is crime, disease, abuse, violence and the breakdown of governance. In order to begin tackling poverty, two areas will require great diligence and attention during Thabo's presidential term: an economic policy that will boost growth and employment and the modernisation and improvement of public administration. One impact of apartheid was the division of governance into multiple levels. Each of the race groups (whites, blacks, coloureds and Indians), the previous four provinces and the more than half a dozen 'independent' homelands had their own administrations. This caused great inefficiencies, duplication and corruption which have proven extremely difficult to change in the years since 1994.

'What Thabo needs to do most of all is to modernise,' argues an ANC member, ' ... and by that I mean results, delivery and the banishment of entitlement and inefficiency. He must bring in powerful people and take a stand against corruption.' Eglin agrees: 'One of Thabo's key problems is the question of management within the public service. The effective management of government must be the second priority after economic growth. If government management is poor, it will not succeed. Thabo will contribute to this. By nature he is more managerial than Mandela.'

But while public service reform will be crucial to Thabo's ability to govern, it is the formulation and implementation of economic policy that many believe will be the make-or-break factor of his presidency. Says Max Sisulu, the ANC's former chief whip who has been redeployed to the state armaments company Denel: 'Under Thabo, the economy – improving the livelihoods of the people – and the leadership of South Africa, will be the key defining needs. He will be judged by completely different yardsticks from Mandela. Mandela was all about reconciliation and democracy. Thabo will be about the economy, how we'll thrive in an economic situation that's not favourable. Thabo has to take the country into the next millennium. We will need to be competitive and education will be vital. We have a very strong economic base. But he did economics, he studied it and he's able to take a more global view of things.'

It is well to remember that Thabo is an economist. He has a Masters degree in economics from the University of Sussex and there are few who have discussed the subject with him who doubt his credentials or his understanding of the issues. One only has to recall the favourable impression he made on the first groups of South African businessmen whom he met while in exile in the mid-1980s to see that this is not a new phenomenon. According to Eglin, Thabo 'understands modern economics. He doesn't necessarily agree with it but he understands it – the interplay between management and labour, between forces within the economy. Through his international exposure he has realised that people who play an important role in the economy are important players. It is crucial to understand the system and to have a relationship with the players, and he has done both.'

Certainly, the fundamentals of the Growth, Employment and Redistribution (GEAR) strategy thought up and implemented by Thabo – with the assistance of Trevor Manuel and finance department deputy-general Maria Ramos – during the last years of the Mandela administration are ample evidence that his economic thinking is in line with free market, global opinion. Says Democratic Party finance spokesman Ken Andrew: 'There is no doubt in my mind that government economic policy, GEAR, would not have been tabled and not in the way it was, without Thabo giving the nod. He was intelligent enough to know, in the long term, that you have got to do what is necessary to create a successful economy. He has studied economics – though there are others who have doctorates but who still want to try socialist policies that have failed – but it is the totality of his experiences which has made him recognise the realities of a successful economy in the twenty-first century'.

While Thabo considers job creation the overwhelming priority and economic growth a necessary prerequisite, he is not prepared to achieve these at the expense of fiscal prudence, nor will he back off easily at the whim of populist opponents. This attitude has already brought him into conflict with the other two components of the governing alliance, the powerful Congress of South African Trade Unions (Cosatu) as well as the South African Communist Party.

GEAR has been consistently criticised by the left wing of the alliance as being 'Thatcherite'. Its opponents have held that its failure to create jobs – the policy promised 400 000 new jobs by the year 2000 – is a clear sign that the policy needs a thorough overhaul. Discounting the severe battering taken by all emerging economies during the global market crash in mid-1998, they argue that an overemphasis on fiscal discipline prevents the state from spending enough to boost the economy. South Africa's debt is considerably lower than many equivalent developing nations and this should be allowed to expand, they argue. Thabo has faced objections over GEAR from provincial premiers too, who have complained bitterly about the tough belt-tightening measures they have been forced to endure. But GEAR's objective is to bring down the national government's budget deficit from 6 to 3 per cent of the Gross Domestic Product and, in so doing, cuts must be made.

The labour unions have made their displeasure increasingly clear during the course of 1997 and 1998. Cosatu, for instance, deliberately omitted Jay Naidoo, a former general secretary of the congress and current communications minister, and Alec Erwin, another former unionist who is currently trade and industry minister, from its nomination list for the ANC's National Executive Committee. But while Thabo has come under pressure from the left regarding his unbending adherence to GEAR, he has also come under attack from opposition parties to his right for not going far enough. The leader of the new National Party, Marthinus van Schalkwyk – who took over the reins of the former ruling party from FW de Klerk in 1997 – told parliament in 1998 that the South African economy had shed 71 000 jobs in the non-agricultural sector in 1996 and between September 1996 and September 1997 had lost a further 116 200 in the formal sector. 'The Government must accept that they're not creating jobs. If we continue with GEAR in this manner then it will go the same way as the RDP.'

Ken Andrew argues that though GEAR is a good policy in principle, it is being sabotaged by ANC ministers and the party's alliance partners. 'When the ANC government and the minister concerned, Trevor Manuel, are put under pressure, they have to be buttressed by someone with Thabo's authority. Otherwise, it will be untenable to pursue GEAR. That is why Thabo is so important in the equation.'

Thabo has argued that GEAR remains on track for the achievement of its objective to structurally transform the South African economy from one characterised by low growth, high inflation, periodic balance of payments difficulties and huge disparities in income and access to services toward a fast-growing economy with stable prices in which opportunity and infrastructure are equitably shared. 'Economics is an imprecise science,' he told his detractors in parliament in 1998. 'So GEAR should not be judged on a set of projections made at a point in time but on the extent to which there is evidence of the structural transformation of the economy.' There was, indeed, considerable evidence of this transformation, he argued. The level of inflation had been consistently brought down since the introduction of GEAR, which augured well for new investment and for the long-term stability of the currency. 'Although we have not achieved the growth targets set out in GEAR, the lower than expected GDP growth must be seen in the context of increased price stability and improved export performance. With these foundations in place, the economy stands well equipped for future growth'.

But the growing frustrations of Cosatu and the Communist Party threaten not only to temper Thabo's enthusiasm for GEAR, but endanger the very alliance that swept the ANC to power in 1994. The inevitable privatisation of state corporations that will gather pace during Thabo's tenure and his pursuance of freemarket policies can only add to the pressures already tugging at the satin ribbons holding the fractious alliance together. There has been talk for some time now of Cosatu breaking away from the alliance during Thabo's term of office to form a more radically left-wing Workers' Party. Should they do this, it would be inconceivable for the communists to remain with a party charged with 'Thatcherite' inclinations. Thabo himself has mused on the subject and feels a break-up of the alliance is, at some point in the future, inevitable. *Millennium* magazine in 1997 recalled his words from an earlier interview: 'As South African society becomes more normal, and the further away it moves from the apartheid past, the closer you will get to the transformation of the ANC. How long this takes depends on the speed with which you transform South Africa. The faster you move to become a normal society, the sooner you will arrive at a situation where people in the ANC will say we have always recognised that this is a broad family that has done what it set out to do, and we can now go our separate ways.'

The first signs of a real rift in the alliance emerged in 1997 when a document was circulated by Peter Mokaba – Thabo's ally from the ANC Youth League who under Mandela was appointed deputy minister of environmental affairs and tourism – in which he called for the purging of all communists from the ANC. The party should be championing the cause of black capitalism, he argued, not pandering to the discredited policies of communism or socialism. Mokaba called on SACP members sitting on the ANC National Executive Committee to resign their posts in one or other of the organisations.

Shortly afterwards, at the SACP's tenth annual congress in Soweto, Thabo himself took up the cudgels. Thabo was incensed at the criticism from the SACP that he was responsible for dumping the Reconstruction and Development Programme in favour of GEAR. He sat stonily quiet as speaker after speaker accused the ANC of treachery, of betraying the revolution and of abandoning the interests of the masses. Then, when his turn came to address the congress, he turned to the attack. 'I would like to suggest that if the SACP is of the view that the ANC is set on a reactionary path of development, it is better that this is stated openly and substantiated with objective arguments, rather than advanced through techniques that are new to our movement, of spreading falsifications about the positions of any of the organisations of the congress movement, so that the accuser can pose as the genuine representative of the progressive movement of our country,' he intoned.

There is no question that, during Thabo's term as president, the ANC/SACP/Cosatu alliance will face its stiffest challenge and may not survive to the next election in 2004. Holding it together, if that is what he wishes, will take all his guile and persuasive talents. Many argue, however, that this is neither possible nor desirable. 'When he is president, he must relax and feel confident,' says one ANC member. 'That's what the country needs. The politics of legitimacy must make way for the normal politicking of factions and interest groups. When he gets to the top he must feel free and start thinking about his place in history. He must abandon sentiment and get on with the job. He must go all-out for modernisation, of the economy, of government and of the whole political culture.'

Within South Africa, economic policy, the state of the alliance, racial reconciliation and the transformation of state and society are but a few of the more important challenges that Thabo will face in the years ahead. Others lurk too that will require no less attention and which may in themselves define the success or otherwise of his efforts. One of these will be his handling of two key dynamics which have repeatedly come to the fore in the history of South Africa over the centuries: African nationalism and Afrikaner nationalism. With both of these, Thabo has already been hard at work. Says the leader of the Afrikaner Freedom Front, General Constand Viljoen: Thabo has been 'very much aware of the crucially important role of finding peace with the Afrikaner ... Many people may not like us, but the Afrikaners were pioneers. They did bad things, such as apartheid, but also good things. We recognise we must share the future and will work with him to achieve it. Thabo carries the can and the responsibility when Mandela goes and the euphoria and the grand miracle has passed and the hard work starts.'

Thabo, as we have said in earlier chapters, made it his personal mission to engage with and involve South Africa's Afrikaners in the transition to democracy. It was Thabo who first started meeting with Afrikaner intellectuals in the 1980s in a bid to understand their fears and needs and it was Thabo who ensured the political parties representing the Afrikaner were included in the 1994 election. It was also Thabo who made room in the Constitution for an Afrikaner council to discuss the creation of a homeland, or Volkstaat. But Viljoen and his cohorts have become frustrated with the progress toward a Volkstaat achieved during Mandela's tenure and are hoping that Thabo's accession will signal a shift in their fortunes.

'I still have a good relationship with Thabo,' says Viljoen, 'and I hope that in the new Mbeki era it will be possible to make some progress ... There are other groups (the Vendas, the Griquas) who have been in solidarity with the idea of anti-apartheid. This has given them cohesion, kept them together. But when that goes, maybe there will be more pressure from others for self-determination and that will make it easier for us.'

Viljoen is determined to pursue the notion of a Volkstaat as well as 'self-determination' for Afrikaners. But while respectful of the role the Afrikaner will play in building a future South Africa, Thabo is not necessarily sympathetic to the idea of a Volkstaat. As he said recently, 'It certainly does not help anybody, least of all the Afrikaners, to be pursuing a notion of a state which will pose a danger to the Afrikaner themselves.' What is important, he argues, is that Afrikaners should be involved in a constructive manner in building the new South Africa instead of remaining on the sidelines waiting to see whether ANC actions constitute a threat.

There is also considerable resistance to the notion of a Volkstaat within the ANC to consider, while the far from homogenous Afrikaner community itself is deeply divided over where such a Volkstaat could or should be. Viljoen remains insistent: 'We will never give up on self-determination. It's the main part of our mission. The Afrikaner people want a home.'

Looming large amongst the black nationalisms for Thabo will be the issue of the huge and powerful Zulu tribe. Already in political control of the province of KwaZulu-Natal, the Zulu-based Inkatha Freedom Party of Mangosuthu Buthelezi will need to become an important ally in Thabo's equation of governance. Here, too, he has already made good headway and many believe Buthelezi's appointment as Thabo's deputy president is as inevitable as it is essential. It was Thabo who brought back Buthelezi and the IFP to participate in the 1994 elections when it looked, until only weeks before the poll, like they would remain out in the cold. Ever since the National Party left the government of national unity in 1996, the IFP and ANC have effectively been working together as a coalition. There has even been talk, including that by some very high-ranking IFP leaders, that a merger of the two parties has been under consideration. Though this seems unlikely, at least for the time being, the partnership looks secure and the violence between supporters of the two parties – which claimed thousands of lives in the 1980s and 1990s – has abated. Buthelezi's cooperation, though, will be crucial to Thabo in the years ahead.

Implicit to Thabo's resolution of both African and Afrikaner nationalism is his own concept of Africanism. Its expression, through his call for an African Renaissance, will become a hallmark of his presidency. Thabo believes that Africa's time has come. For so long portrayed as the dark continent, full of poverty, bloodshed and barbarism, Thabo believes that Africa has much to offer the world. Though suppressed by centuries of colonialism and occupation, the inherent democracy of many of its traditional political systems, its collective knowledge and wisdom, its cooperative humanism and its innovative energy are all elements the world would do well to learn from, he argues. Thabo's Africanism, though, is not of the romantic kind articulated by the former Ghanaian president Nkwame Nkrumah, nor that expressed by the Tanzanian liberator Mwalimu Julius Nyerere. His is hard-edged, realistic and assertive. Thabo has spelt out the path by which Africa can regain its lost pride. Not the resuscitation of quaint traditions or by romantic socialism, but by the infinitely tougher one of economic development, independence, democracy and decency. It is a notion that has caused confusion in some camps, particularly among whites in South Africa who feel they are being excluded.

Says Eglin: 'I don't know whether his concept of Africanness comes across as being inclusive enough; whether whites and others feel included in his notion of Africanness or whether blacks feel that they're the only ones he is talking about. While in general his pronouncements are seen as exclusive, he means to be inclusive. It depends on how you read his lips.'

In a speech delivered in 1998 to a group of high-powered business executives in Hong Kong, Thabo spelt out more clearly what he meant. The Africa of today, he argued, was not the continent that – as portrayed by colonialists – was characterised by political turmoil, social unrest, dictatorship, military coups, genocide, disease, massive displacement of people, cultural backwardness and an unquenchable thirst for misappropriation of public wealth by those who have installed themselves as rulers. Instead, Africa is a continent that has begun its journey out of a period of despair. The will of the peoples of Africa to liberate themselves from corrupt, unaccountable and undemocratic regimes could be demonstrated by the fact that during the present decade more than 25 sub-Saharan countries have established multi-party democracies, he said. The departure from the African political stage of personalities such as General Mobutu Sese Seko, of the former Zaire, symbolised the end of a debilitating era of neo-colonialism in Africa and the resumption of the movement forward which had been interrupted. 'It was for this reason,' emphasised Thabo, 'that we have spoken of the African Renaissance, of the rebirth of the entire continent.'

As his audience listened attentively, Thabo spoke of how countries such as Ghana and Mali in West Africa, which have had their fair share of military dictatorships, were today ruled by democratically elected governments whose policies have resulted in the recovery of their economies. 'Though Somalia in the east disintegrated and ceased to exist as a nation state, strangely, the guns have fallen silent and the contending clans are engaged in searching for a new path to a new Somalia of peace. Hardly four years after the appalling genocide of Rwanda, the peasants of this country of Central Africa are reaching out to one another in an unprecedented drive to achieve national reconciliation, to forgive one another, to rebuild lives of hope out of a shattering experience of inexcusable barbarity.

'After their continuous and deadly chatter for over three decades, the guns have also been silenced in Angola in the south west. Those who had been at war against each other sit together as the government of this sister country which is blessed with extraordinary natural wealth. So too, in the south, has the apartheid blight on the human landscape been overtaken by a new order of democracy and peace and combined efforts of all our people to reconstruct and develop South Africa in a spirit of national reconciliation.' This notion of an African Renaissance, of rebuilding Africa through unity and cooperation, will unquestionably form a key part of South African foreign policy under Thabo in the years ahead. In this he will be aided by the relationships he has already built with the new generation of African and international leaders.

Says Max Sisulu: 'He is part of a new batch of African leaders, many of whom know one another. He has known Festus Mogae, president of Botswana, for years and Benjamin Mkapa, the president of Tanzania. There's a whole new crop of leaders and it will be an advantage to him to have known them.'

As important as domestic and international politics will be to Thabo, other matters of a more civic nature will also require urgent consideration. Crime in South Africa, and particularly violent crime, is high up on the list. South Africa suffers from one of the highest crime rates, including murders per capita, car hijackings, rape and armed robbery, anywhere in the world. The pervasive nature of crime, which under apartheid was kept confined and unreported in the 'black' areas, has diminished national and international confidence in the South African miracle. The causes of this crime wave are complex and varied. Poverty and unemployment play a role. So too does the low value for life spawned over the years by a racist and coercive state. After decades of community mistrust in the police, who carried out – often brutally and cynically – the orders of the apartheid state, the long haul to reversing public attitudes has begun. But containing and decreasing the levels of violent crime will be a fundamental requirement if Thabo is to make any significant impact during his five or ten years as South Africa's president. This applies also to the curtailment of corruption which has been bleeding the state coffers and inhibiting the delivery of basic services for so long. Several institutions have been created, however, which will assist in the tackling of corruption. They include a special investigative unit headed by a judge with the specific brief of looking into corruption within government, the Public Protector and the serious economic crime unit of the police.

While Thabo has not focused especially on either crime or corruption during his deputy presidential term, he has taken the opportunity to deal with other matters of great import. Aids, for instance, will undoubtedly take a heavy toll over the coming years. Southern Africa already has the highest incidence of HIV infection in the world and Thabo is fully aware of the devastating consequences of the disease. In an extraordinary address to the nation at the end of 1998, he had the following to say: 'HIV/AIDS is not someone else's problem. It is my problem. It is your problem. By allowing it to spread, we face the danger that half of our youth will not reach adulthood. Their education will be wasted. The economy will shrink. There will be a large number of sick people whom the healthy will not be able to maintain. Our dreams as a people will be shattered. HIV spreads mainly through sex. You have the right to live your life the way you want to. But I appeal to the young people, who represent our country's future, to abstain from sex for as long as possible. If you decide to engage in sex, use a condom. In the same way, I appeal to both men and women to be faithful to each other, but otherwise to use condoms.' The address, which Thabo took responsibility for at the last moment following Mandela's unavailability, was the first time one of South Africa's top leaders has made such a frank appeal on the issue.

Less critical but important nonetheless has been Thabo's concern with the education and expectations of the youth. Thabo's anger has directed, for example, at young black South Africans who feel they are owed high-paying jobs and all the frills and luxuries of success without having earned them. It is what he calls the culture of entitlement. He has also lashed out, during a national conference of the South African Democratic Teachers Union, at teachers who exhibit general ill-discipline and immoral and unethical behaviour such as arriving at school drunk, when they are expected to lead by example.

When Mandela stepped down as president of the ANC at the organisation's fiftieth national conference in Mafikeng at the end of 1998, an era in South African politics was brought to an end. With Mandela's departure, a whole generation of leaders in South Africa prepared to move aside too, their job done, their time at an end. They are men and women, including Thabo's own father Govan, Walter Sisulu and others, who led the ANC out into exile and back more than three decades later in triumph. Now, though, it is Thabo's turn to build for the future. As head of government, he will need to take a more hands-on approach than the icon of reconciliation and democracy who preceded him. While Mandela's final departure from the national presidency will be a sad emotional loss, Thabo's arrival signals a significant managerial gain. There should be no loss either of the basic philosophy underpinning Mandela's tenure, with which Thabo closely identifies. But Thabo has served his apprenticeship now, both to Mandela and, before him, to Oliver Tambo. He has fought his way to the top and needs no longer to be afraid of bringing into his circle those who are talented or strong enough to make a difference. Perhaps unfairly, though, he will always be judged by the man who led South Africa from apartheid to democracy. After Mandela, says journalist Ingrid Uys, South Africans will demand an impossible excellence of their leaders. Thabo's every action will be automatically scrutinised, and when he fails to be both 'Superman and Mother Theresa' his critics will come bearing down on him[3].

According to minister of justice Dullah Omar, 'Thabo must be less self-effacing, especially in public. He needs to be more assertive. He gives brilliant speeches but he needs to defer less to people and to be more assertive and more confident of his own point of view.'

Mandela was able to get away with a lot of things due to his age, his power and the respect people had for him, says Max Sisulu. This won't be nearly as easy for Thabo. 'I can't see Thabo doing the toyi-toyi like Mandela. He is a different kind of person ... Mandela can get away with a lot of things that Thabo wouldn't. He wouldn't give people a public dressing down. His style is very different. He is quiet, diplomatic.'

When he takes over, Thabo will surround himself with men and women he can trust. This he has always done, from his days in exile to his current high office. He will have an opportunity to make many key appointments following the expected retirement or dismissal of many of those who served under Mandela. Support from the ANC Youth League was key in the battle between Thabo and outgoing secretary-general Cyril Ramaphosa, and one-time fiery Youth League leader Peter Mokaba, now a deputy minister, will probably be rewarded with a full cabinet position for having worked hard to secure for Thabo the deputy presidency, and in the process sidelining Ramaphosa. Mandela's powerful ex-wife, Winnie Madikizela-Mandela, might also be rewarded and recalled to government for reasons not dissimilar to those applying to Mokaba, if her health holds and she stays out of trouble. Look too for those old friends and allies of Thabo's, the Pahad brothers, Joel Nethshitenzhe, Jeff Radebe and Nkosazana Zuma. Buthelezi is certainly in the frame for a senior cabinet post and perhaps will become Thabo's strategic deputy president.

Mandela himself, in spite of some glitches in his relationship with Thabo toward the end of his term, remains optimistic that the ANC, and the country, is in good hands. 'He is a very confident chap,' says Mandela of Thabo. 'He is not afraid of controversy. When he speaks in the National Executive Committee he commands attention ... and everyone listens, even those who might not like him. I don't think it is fair to say that he surrounds himself with weak and sycophantic people.'

Nelson Mandela will always be remembered as the leader whose struggle and dedication inspired South Africa's liberation. Thabo will be remembered in time as the leader who has transformed the apartheid state into a viable and relatively successful liberal democracy. Thabo, as a person, has considerable intellect and talent with an uncanny ability to unite the most disparate strands into a coherent, viable policy direction. Much of the glow around Mandela is a reflection of Thabo's work. In addition, the fact that Mandela's image is yet to be tarnished is due in no inconsiderable measure to the fact that Thabo has had to jump a few yards ahead of the presidential foot, and he has always done so without complaining or excuse.

Thabo has no time for weak people, says Omar, he feels sorry for them. According to him Thabo remains deeply conscious of the fact that 1994 was only a political transformation and is deeply concerned about the lack of transformation at all levels of the economy and in all institutions of society.

Says Thabo: 'What we have tried to do in the last five years is put in place the necessary policies and move away from an apartheid, racist South Africa. There was nothing that was right before. It was necessary to have legislation to give expression to that. We have made much better progress on the policy side than on the transformation and the reformation of the government. I think that we are now in a better position to move forward better and faster with the objectives that we have set for ourselves.'

In his address to Asian businessmen in 1998, Thabo took his audience back nearly 600 years, placing them in the fourteenth century when the Chinese fleet led by Admiral Cheng Ho landed on the east coast of Africa in 1421 to establish relations with the continent. In 1415, Mbeki told the audience, the gift of a giraffe, shipped by an African king, had been sent to the Chinese Emperor of the Ming Dynasty.

'If you asked me why the gentle giraffe rather than an animal obviously representing the prowess and invincibility of the African kingdoms, as would be represented by the elephant, the lion or the leopard, I would answer that the kings of Africa sent a giraffe to the Forbidden City in Beijing to pay tribute to a ruler who could see into the distance, watching to ensure that his kingdom and its people came to no harm. In our own native languages, the giraffe is known descriptively as *indlulamthi* – the animal that towers above trees,' Thabo said.

Top Asian businessman, Ronnie Chand, who was master of ceremonies at the occasion, smiled at his audience and said in his closing remarks: 'Thabo is the giraffe. He is the graceful gentleman who towers above trees looking deep into the distance.'

Speeches

I am an African

Statement of Deputy President TM Mbeki, on behalf of the African National Congress, on the occasion of the adoption by the Constitutional Assembly of the Republic of South Africa Constitution Bill 1996, Cape Town, 8 May 1996

Chairperson, Esteemed President of the democratic Republic, Honourable Members of the Constitutional Assembly, Our distinguished domestic and foreign guests, Friends,

On an occasion such as this, we should, perhaps, start from the beginning.

So, let me begin.

I am an African.

I owe my being to the hills and the valleys, the mountains and the glades, the rivers, the deserts, the trees, the flowers, the seas and the ever-changing seasons that define the face of our native land.

My body has frozen in our frosts and in our latter day snows. It has thawed in the warmth of our sunshine and melted in the heat of the midday sun. The crack and the rumble of the summer thunders, lashed by startling lightening, have been a cause both of trembling and of hope.

The fragrances of nature have been as pleasant to us as the sight of the wild blooms to the citizens of the veld.

The dramatic shapes of the Drakensberg, the soil-coloured waters of the Lekoa, iGqili noThukela, and the sands of the Kgalagadi have all been panels of the set on the natural stage on which we act out the foolish deeds of the theatre of our day.

At times, and in fear, I have wondered whether I should concede equal citizenship of our country to the leopard and the lion, the elephant and the springbok, the hyena, the black mamba and the pestilential mosquito.

A human presence among all these, a feature on the face of our native land thus defined, I know that none dare challenge me when I say – I am an African!

I owe my being to the Khoi and the San whose desolate souls haunt the great expanses of the beautiful Cape – they who fell victim to the most merciless genocide our native land has ever seen, they who were the first to lose their lives in the struggle to defend our freedom and dependence and they who, as a people, perished in the result.

Today, as a country, we keep an audible silence about these ancestors of the generations that live, fearful to admit the horror of a former deed, seeking to obliterate from our memories a cruel occurrence which, in its remembering, should teach us not and never to be inhuman again.

I am formed of the migrants who left Europe to find a new home on our native land. Whatever their own actions, they remain still part of me.

In my veins courses the blood of the Malay slaves who came from the East. Their proud dignity informs my bearing, their culture a part of my essence. The stripes they bore on their bodies from the lash of the slave master are a reminder embossed on my consciousness of what should not be done.

I am the grandchild of the warrior men and women that Hintsa and Sekhukhune led, the patriots that Cetshwayo and Mphephu took to battle, the soldiers Moshoeshoe and Ngungunyane taught never to dishonour the cause of freedom.

My mind and my knowledge of myself is formed by the victories that are the jewels in our African crown, the victories we earned from Isandhlwana to Khartoum, as Ethiopians and as the Ashanti of Ghana, as the Berbers of the desert.

I am the grandchild who lays fresh flowers on the Boer graves at St Helena and the Bahamas, who sees in the mind's eye and suffers the suffering of a simple peasant folk, death, concentration camps, destroyed homesteads, a dream in ruins.

I am the child of Nongqause. I am he who made it possible to trade in the world markets in diamonds, in gold, in the same food for which my stomach yearns.

154

I come of those who were transported from India and China, whose being resided in the fact, solely, that they were able to provide physical labour, who taught me that we could both be at home and be foreign, who taught me that human existence itself demanded that freedom was a necessary condition for that human existence.

Being part of all these people, and in the knowledge that none dare contest that assertion, I shall claim that – I am an African.

I have seen our country torn asunder as these, all of whom are my people, engaged one another in a titanic battle, the one redress a wrong that had been caused by one to another and the other, to defend the indefensible.

I have seen what happens when one person has superiority of force over another, when the stronger appropriate to themselves the prerogative even to annul the injunction that God created all men and women in His image.

I know what it signifies when race and colour are used to determine who is human and who sub-human.

I have seen the destruction of all sense of self-esteem, the consequent striving to be what one is not, simply to acquire some of the benefits which those who had improved themselves as masters had ensured that they enjoy.

I have experience of the situation in which race and colour is used to enrich some and impoverish the rest.

I have seen the corruption of minds and souls as a result of the pursuit of an ignoble effort to perpetrate a veritable crime against humanity.

I have seen concrete expression of the denial of the dignity of a human being emanating from the conscious, systemic and systematic oppressive and repressive activities of other human beings.

There, the victims parade with no mask to hide the brutish reality – the beggars, the prostitutes, the street children, those who seek solace in substance abuse, those who have to steal to assuage hunger, those who have to lose their sanity because to be sane is to invite pain.

Perhaps the worst among these, who are my people, are those who have learnt to kill for a wage. To these the extent of death is directly proportional to their personal welfare.

And so, like pawns in the service of demented souls, they kill in furtherance of the political violence in KwaZulu-Natal. They murder the innocent in the taxi wars.

They kill slowly or quickly in order to make profits from the illegal trade in narcotics. They are available for hire when husband wants to murder wife and wife, husband.

Among us prowl the products of our immoral and amoral past – killers who have no sense of the worth of human life, rapists who have absolute disdain for the women of our country, animals who would seek to benefit from the vulnerability of the children, the disabled and the old, the rapacious who brook no obstacle in their quest for self-enrichment.

All this I know and know to be true because I am an African!

Because of that, I am also able to state this fundamental truth that I am born of a people who are heroes and heroines.

I am born of a people who would not tolerate oppression.

I am of a nation that would not allow that fear of death, torture, imprisonment, exile or persecution should result in the perpetuation of injustice.

The great masses who are our mother and father will not permit that the behaviour of the. few results in the description of our country and people as barbaric.

Patient because history is on their side, these masses do not despair because today the weather is bad. Nor do they turn triumphalist when, tomorrow, the sun shines.

Whatever the circumstances they have lived through and because of that experience, they are determined to define for themselves who they are and who they should be.

We are assembled here today to mark their victory in acquiring and exercising their right to formulate their own definition of what it means to be African.

The constitution whose adoption we celebrate constitutes an unequivocal statement that we refuse to accept that our Africanness shall be defined by our race, colour, gender or historical origins.

It is a firm assertion made by ourselves that South Africa belongs to all who live in it, black and white.

It gives concrete expression to the sentiment we share as Africans, and will defend to the death, that the people shall govern.

It recognises the fact that the dignity of the individual is both an objective which society must pursue, and is a goal which cannot be separated from the material well-being of that individual.

It seeks to create the situation in which all our people shall be free from fear, including the fear of the oppression of one national group by another, the fear of the disempowerment of one social echelon by another, the fear of the use of state power to deny anybody their fundamental human rights and the fear of tyranny.

It aims to open the doors so that those who were disadvantaged can assume their place in society as equals with their fellow human beings without regard to colour, race, gender, age or geographic dispersal.

It provides the opportunity to enable each one and all to state their views, promote them, strive for their implementation in the process of governance without fear that a contrary view will be met with repression.

It creates a law-governed society which shall be inimical to arbitrary rule.

It enables the resolution of conflicts by peaceful means rather than resort to force.

It rejoices in the diversity of our people and creates the space for all of us voluntarily to define ourselves as one people.

As an African, this is an achievement of which I am proud, proud without reservation and proud without any feeling of conceit.

Our sense of elevation at this moment also derives from the fact that this magnificent product is the unique creation of African hands and African minds.

But it is also constitutes a tribute to our loss of vanity that we could, despite the temptation to treat ourselves as an exceptional fragment of humanity, draw on the accumulated experience and wisdom of all humankind, to define for ourselves what we want to be.

Together with the best in the world, we too are prone to pettiness, petulance, selfishness and short-sightedness.

But it seems to have happened that we looked at ourselves and said the time had come that we make a super-human effort to be other than human, to respond to the call to create for ourselves a glorious future, to remind ourselves of the Latin saying: *Gloria est consequenda* – Glory must be sought after!

Today it feels good to be an African.

It feels good that I can stand here as a South African and as a foot soldier of a titanic African army, the African National Congress, to say to all the parties represented here, to the millions who made an input into the processes we are concluding, to our outstanding compatriots who have presided over the birth of our founding document, to the negotiators who pitted their wits one against the other, to the unseen stars who shone unseen as the management and administration of the Constitutional Assembly, the advisers, experts and publicists, to the mass communication media, to our friends across the globe – congratulations and well done!

I am an African.

I am born of the peoples of the continent of Africa.

The pain of the violent conflict that the peoples of Liberia, Somalia, the Sudan, Burundi and Algeria bear, is a pain I also bear.

The dismal shame of poverty, suffering and human degradation of my continent is a blight that we share.

The blight on our happiness that derives from this and from our drift to the periphery of the ordering of human affairs leaves us in a persistent shadow of despair.

This is a savage road to which nobody should be condemned.

This thing that we have done today, in this small corner of a great continent that has contributed so decisively to the evolution of humanity says that Africa reaffirms that she is continuing her rise from the ashes.

Whatever the setbacks of the moment, nothing can stop us now! Whatever the difficulties, Africa shall be at peace! However improbable it may sound to the skeptics, Africa will prosper!

Whoever we may be, whatever our immediate interest, however much we carry baggage from our past, however much we have been caught by the fashion of cynicism and loss of faith in the capacity of the people, let us err today and say – nothing can stop us now!

Thank you.

Issued by: Office of the Deputy President

In search of a national consensus

Speech of Deputy President Thabo Mbeki at the National Assembly, during the debate on budget vote no. 2, 10 June 1997

Madame Speaker, Honourable Members of the National Assembly:

During the year 1987, some of us who are members of this House were privileged to meet a group of Afrikaners in places that seemed, then, to be far away from home.

As the Honourable Members will remember, when that delegation returned home, it was welcomed back with such venomous hostility by the then apartheid regime that we feared for the very lives of these erstwhile visitors to West Africa.

And yet the only crime which these white and mainly Afrikaner compatriots had committed, was that they had engaged other South Africans, who happened to be in exile, in an extensive debate about how to bring about democracy and peace to our then deeply troubled country.

One year before, in 1986, this being one of the events which led to the 'Dakar process' which sought to encourage all of us as South Africans to contribute to the elaboration of a common definition of the 'new South Africa', Prof. Frederick van Zyl Slabbert had resigned his leadership of the Progressive Federal Party as well as his seat in the tri-cameral parliament, arguing that to stay on in that institution would merely serve to lend it legitimacy.

Recognising the historic importance of this decisive break with the apartheid system, by an Afrikaner, the leadership of the ANC made bold to salute Prof. Slabbert as 'a new Voortrekker'.

These events are now 10 years behind us. Sadly, for many of us, they, and other landmarks we passed on our road to the new, are but elements of a dim recollection of a past that is dwarfed by the giant heritage of today's democratic society, towards whose birth the 'new Voortrekkers' made their own, and not insignificant, contribution.

We say sadly because to forget them is to put outside our conscious activity, to omit from our daily agendas the task of confronting the challenge which remains with us – namely, to continue interacting as South Africans, so that we evolve a national consensus about things which will constitute the most fundamental features of the new South Africa and thus define the path which we, as a people, must travel together as the new Voortrekkers.

It is important that we resist the temptation to abandon this path and retreat into a laager, as some recent developments seem to suggest. Certainly, we would not agree with the assertion which has been made, that the steps taken at the beginning of this decade as part of the process of ending white minority rule constituted an act of treachery.

Presumably the question must arise as to whether there can be such a thing as a national consensus on anything, except in the most vacuous sense! Is it possible to have a national agenda – to say in a practical way that these matters make up the national interest to which all can adhere, regardless of partisan interests?

Or are the very concepts of national interest and national consensus nothing more than the dream of fools, an illusion best left to the idle who have nothing to do but build sand castles?

After all, whereas daily we proclaim ourselves a nation, we are a nation, which can share in a national interest, or are we merely a collection of communities that happen to inhabit one geopolitical space?

We are emerging, but only emerging slowly and painfully, out of a deeply fractured society. This is a society which continues to be characterised by deep fissures which separate the black people from the white, the hungry from the prosperous, the urban from the rural, the male from the female, the disabled from the rest.

Running like a structural fault through it all, and weaving it together

160

into a frightening bundle of imbalance and inequality, is the question of race and colour – the fundamental consideration on which was built South African society for 300 years.

It is therefore not an idle thing to imagine that out of this amalgam of inequity, where some have everything and others have nothing, where some instinctively behave as superiors and others know it as a matter of fact that they are seen as inferior, where some must experience change otherwise they perish and others fear they will perish as a result of change – is it not an idle thing to imagine that out of all this there can emerge a national consensus!

But may it not be that the question to pose is whether, for it to survive and develop, a society so deeply fractured within itself does not need to make a conscious, determined and sustained effort to build a national consensus about those matters which will ensure that indeed and in reality, a nation is born!

The birth of that nation demands that we fundamentally transform our society. The new nation cannot come into being on the basis of the perpetuation of the extraordinary imbalances we have inherited from the past. It cannot be founded on the entrenchment of the apartheid legacy.

I am certain that all the Honourable Members of this House will agree with these sentiments, regardless of party affiliation.

After all, we all subscribe to the noble sentiments contained in our Constitution, which commits the country 'to promote and protect human dignity, to achieve equality and advance human rights and freedoms ... to promote non-racialism and non-sexism ...'

I believe that we all supported these constitutional provisions and continue to do so now because we understood that the absence of a settlement containing these objectives would not end the conflict in our country, but would condemn it to a destructive civil war.

By this means, we recognised the fact that there can be such a thing as a national consensus around a national agenda. We accept that the advancement of the very interests of each, regardless of their race, colour, gender or social class, demanded that we bend every effort to ensure that the kind of society described in the Constitution is born.

Together, we adopted a position which recognised that no legitimate sectional interest can be served or aspiration realised unless it was pursued within a society characterised by equality, non-racialism, non-sexism and human dignity.

We are convinced that precisely because we were and are engaged in a complex and all-embracing process of fundamental social transformation, proceeding as we are from our past of division, conflict and mutual antagonism, it was and is important that we develop a national consensus about those matters, such as those reflected in our Constitution, which will define the fundamental and permanent nature of our society.

Our non-racial democracy is three years old. It is but an infant in swaddling clothes. It requires the most careful nurturing to ensure that its ethos, its institutions and its practices mature and take firm root, and that it succeeds to improve the quality of life of all our people.

But I fear that among many of us the mistaken assumption is made that the transition to a stable democracy has been completed. The challenge for us to join hands to build firm foundation for the new edifice is treated as nothing more a matter that can be addressed satisfactorily through mere rhetoric.

Where the question is posed — what is your contribution to the creation of the new society, to the accomplishment of the great goal of reconstruction and development? — the answer is silence.

This is because, to many, the order of the day consists merely in asking the question — what opportunities have emerged for me in this new society to get what I do not have or to preserve, at whatever cost, that which I have already acquired?

To deny the validity of the argument for emergency measures to continue and sustain the offensive for social transformation, bold assertions are made that apartheid is a thing of the past and that to argue otherwise is nothing but to find excuses for the failure of present policies.

After all, that which does not exist does not exist. And since the legacy of apartheid does not exist, there is no call on anybody to uproot it. Fundamental change has occurred. What remains to be done is to achieve measured growth through a process of gradual accretion.

The denial of the stark reality of the defining impact of the past on the present thus constitutes an invitation to abandon the path of fundamental social transformation, to legitimise a socio-economic injustice which our people made enormous sacrifices to abolish.

Needless to say, the adoption of such a position would lead the country back into a destructive situation of conflict from which none would benefit.

During our debates in this House, the issue of affirmative action arises repeatedly. As with other matters on which we all assume there is national consensus, comments on this issue are normally prefaced with professions of support for the objective of creating a non-racial society and understanding for the need to employ affirmative action as one of the means to pursue this objective.

Argument then follows which effectively seeks to rule out such affirmative action in the name of non-racialism, buttressed by further argument about experience and efficiency.

For example, assertions have been made about declining financial management standards in government, which is attributed to inefficient blacks, who, it is said, occupy their positions by virtue of misplaced affirmative action policies.

In reality, we are not far from the day when the diplomatic language will slip and the point will be made openly, that 'the Bantus are not yet ready to govern'.

And this will happen in a situation in which we all continue to assist on our fervent support for the genuine deracialisation and therefore perpetuate the illusion that a national consensus exists on the question of the creation of a non-racial society.

Currently, this House and the country at large are grappling with the thorny question of the revision of the system of welfare benefits for the family and child.

Once more, this debate has firmly brought into the open the question whether a national consensus exists on the objective of creating a non-racial society.

Much of the discussion that has taken place suggests very definitely that such consensus does not, in fact, exist.

At the heart of this matter is the unswerving determination of the government to end the system of racial discrimination in the disbursement of welfare benefits, which in this specific instance resulted in the exclusion of the African mother and child, historically the most disadvantaged sections of our population.

Non-racial equity in these disbursements cannot be achieved on the basis of the level at which these disbursements are today. But the objective of non-racialism has to prevail. It is therefore inevitable that an adjustment will be made, so as to bring into the net the greatest possible number of people and specifically the African destitute, the historic victim of the apartheid system of white minority domination.

If a national consensus on non-racialism did in fact exist, this would not be a matter of debate. And yet it is, because some refuse to accept that the new nation cannot be born on the basis of the perpetuation of the injustices of the past.

Much is also made of the issue of corruption, once again argued on the basis of what one writer in another context described as 'carefully calibrated amnesia' about what our society has inherited from the past.

This is an issue which does indeed require an intensive and extensive national debate because, among other things, it constitutes the bedrock on which rest many ills which afflict our society, including violence and crime.

In themselves, the system and the practice of apartheid constituted the most sustained corruption of our society. Founded on a lie, this system could only be maintained on the basis of the elaboration and sustenance of even further lies.

Where all legitimate states have a societal responsibility to encourage and protect a system of social morality which, in turn, impacts on both public and individual behaviour, a state based by definition on corrupt practice could not but nullify or degrade all social morality.

A direct consequence of this would therefore be to pervert each human being, so that each should believe that the norm or value system which should guide his or her behaviour is the pursuit of self-interest at all costs, without the constraints imposed on each person by a commonly accepted system of social norms.

It is out of this setting of an all-pervasive corruption of society and the individual, characteristic of all other instances where illegitimate states existed, that our society became infected by such problems as white collar crime, corruption within the public service, including the criminal justice system, loss of respect for life and the inviolability of the safety, security and dignity of the individual, depraved personal behaviour and the measurement of personal standing and esteem by the extent of one's personal wealth, however defined.

The task faces all of us to confront this enormous challenge, to restore to our communities the system of social values which create a climate hostile to criminal and other anti-social behaviour.

The first step along this very necessary road is the recognition that we inherited from our past a corrupt society which demands of all of us that we become militant combatants for the moral renewal of our country, as part of the process of its reconstruction and development.

The persistent propagation of the notion that all we require to deal with the problem of crime is merely more police officers and strengthening of the criminal justice system as a whole, critical though these matters are, is not only a fig leaf to hide the reality of a deadly inheritance, but also constitutes an abdication of a responsibility without whose discharge the cesspool which feeds all criminal behaviour will remain and continue to spawn its bitter fruit.

It does nothing to solve the problem, or to build the necessary united national effort, to add insult to injury by suggesting that corruption is endemic to the system of African governance and is, therefore, only three years old in our country.

The great crevices in our society which represent the absence of a national consensus about matters that are fundamental to the creation of the new society are also represented by the controversy which seems to have arisen around the work of the Truth and Reconciliation Commission.

The hatreds and animosities of the past will not go away unless the truth is told about what happened. The telling of that truth is painful to all of us. Where gross violations of human rights have occurred on either side of the conflict, they cannot but diminish anyone of us who were the perpetrators.

We are diminished by the acts which occurred, and not by their recounting to the Commission and the nation. Something of what we are worth will be restored by the courage we show by telling the truth and, admitting that a wrong was done where it was done.

The recognition of the guilt is a necessary part of the commitment to the future not to repeat the past. The refusal to recognise that guilt constitutes a statement that no wrong is seen to have been done and therefore, that it would be permissible that the past should revisit us once again.

The national consensus we thought we had achieved when, together, we adopted the Preamble to our Constitution which says 'We, the people of

South Africa, recognise the injustice of our past, [and] honour those who suffered for justice and freedom in our land ...' seems denied when we act in a manner which says we do not recognise that any injustice was done.

And by that denial we refuse to be co-architects of the national unity and reconciliation without which it is impossible to speak of the new South Africa as a real, an existing or emerging, entity.

Seated on the benches of this House are people who are an important component of the leadership cadre of our country. Collectively and individually, we have a responsibility to contribute to the making of the new democratic, non-racial, non-sexist united and prosperous South Africa, in the common interest of all the constituencies we represent.

I believe that all of us should continually put the question to ourselves – what contribution are we making to the realisation of this objective?

Indeed, I believe this House should also seek to answer the question – does it give itself enough time to discuss such questions as we have raised, which we are convinced are fundamental to the future of our country, and others matters besides?

In this context, we need to make the point that talk of 'restructuring the political landscape' is nothing else but a chimera that is born of a failure to recognise the fact that no new landscape can emerge and hold until our country has made serious forward strides towards its fundamental reconstruction.

The volume of verbiage that issues forth about a new political landscape is little else that a diversion, a pretence at creating a new and better reality for our people where none is intended, the mere bricks and mortar of a fool's paradise.

No conjurer's trick, however well-presented, and no manoeuvring for partisan political advantage, however skilful, will deny the challenge that faces us as political leaders, to effect the fundamental social transformation without which the miracle of our transition to democracy will not survive.

In the end the success of our new democracy to create a people-centred society will be measured by the progress we make as a country to address such questions as job creation, housing, health care, social welfare and education.

Beyond this, and perhaps more fundamentally, it is our collective progress in these areas that must and will underwrite our peace and stability.

As a government, we would be wilfully blind not to have noticed that it is precisely around these issues that those who have no commitment to the success of the new society seek to encourage failure or, at least, the perception of failure.

We would like to take advantage of this opportunity to record our own appreciation to the enormous amount of constructive work the relevant ministers, ministries and departments are making to change our country for the better.

This process of sustained development and transformation from which our government will not depart remains still the provision of a better life for all and the comprehensive deracialisation of our country, among other things, by facilitating the achievement of high and sustained rates of economic growth, further creating the condition for the integration of our economy into the world economy, promoting the creation of new jobs, providing land, clean water and sanitation, making progress towards the elimination of hunger and poverty, improving the quality of and access to educational, welfare and health services, and ensuring the availability of affordable and sustainable energy and the provision of affordable housing.

Simultaneously, we will sustain and improve on the effort to collect the revenues due to the state, manage public resources, reprioritise expenditures and strengthen the public-private sector partnerships, so as to address the pressing developmental needs of our people and country, operating within the context of the necessary fiscal discipline and the appropriate macro-economic balances.

For the information of the electorate, the government will publish a document containing a detailed Programme of Action indicating the targets we have set ourselves for the short-term until the end of 1998, covering the areas we have just indicated and reflecting, among others, the programmes reported on in this House by our various ministers during the course of the debates on their specific budgets.

We will continue to build on such unsung success as those represented by the little township of Boikhutso in Lichtenburg in the North-West, where, among other things, water has been piped into and flush toilets installed in 2 000 houses, replacing the old bucket system, and where 1 000 sites are being prepared to build new houses that will replace the existing shacks and where the streets of the township are currently being tarred.

In this context, it is also necessary to inform the House that the government continues to focus on improving its functionality and effectiveness. Accordingly, the cabinet has taken a decision further to draw on the expertise available in the private sector to increase the government's own management capacity.

An important element of this is the strengthening of the Presidency to ensure that it carries out its constitutional responsibilities as part of the National Executive, bearing in mind the context of the many and important tasks that face us as a country.

The proposed increase to our budget relative to the preceding financial year, which we present to the House, reflect the effort in which we are engaged to discharged to such constitutional obligations as developing and implementing national policy and coordinating the functions of government departments.

I would like to take this opportunity to thank all the leaders and members of the political parties represented in this House, the Speakers and Chairpersons of the Assembly and Portfolio Committees, the Ministers, Deputy Ministers and their Directors-General, the Premiers and the Provincial Administrations, the leaders and members of statutory committees and commissions, and indeed, some of the leaders at local government level, with whom we have cooperated in the collective process of the governance of our country.

My sincere appreciation also goes to my Director-General, the Rev Frank Chikane and the entire excellent team in the Office of the Deputy President which he leads, including my advisers, without whose passionate dedication to their work and to the goal of the fundamental renewal of our country we would fail to discharge our own responsibility to our country and people.

Gradually and perhaps in infinitesimal ways, we are, as a people, making such contribution as we are capable of making towards the creation of a better universe.

The success of our common project to remake South Africa as a stable, non-racial, non-sexist and prosperous democracy depends in good measure on the coterminous existence of an international community, similarly defined.

Among other things, this places on us the obligation to contribute to the common African continental effort, at last to achieve an African

Renaissance, including the establishment of stable democracies, respect for human rights, an end to violent conflicts and a better life for all the peoples of Africa.

This, too, will test our capacity as part of the leadership of this country to discharge this responsibility in our common national interest.

Later this year, the Olympic movement will take a decision about where the 2004 Olympic Games will be held.

We trust that this will be an African Olympics, as a token of the commitment of the world community to see the new century defined as an African century, because it will mark the recovery of our continent from an experience of many centuries, some of whose distinguishing features have been the slave trade, colonial domination and exploitation, apartheid, bad African governance and the identification of what is bad with the colour black.

Our first step towards our own entry into that century must consist in our capacity together to transform our own country into a place which all our people would be proud to call home.

The African Renaissance, South Africa and the world

Speech by Deputy President Thabo Mbeki at the United Nations University, Tokyo, Japan, 9 April 1998

We must assume that the Roman, Pliny the Elder, was familiar with the Latin saying, *Ex Africa semper aliquid novi!* (Something new always comes out of Africa). Writing during the first century of the present millennium, Pliny gave his fellow Romans some startlingly interesting and supposedly new information about Africans. He wrote:

> Of the Ethiopians there are diverse forms and kinds of men. Some there are toward the east that have neither nose nor nostrils, but the face all full. Others that have no upper lip, they are without tongues, and they speak by signs, and they have but a little hole to take their breath at, by the which they drink with an oaten straw ... In a part of Afrikke be people called Pteomphane, for their King they have a dog, at whose fancy they are governed ... And the people called Anthropomphagi which we call cannibals, live with human flesh. The Cinamolgi, their heads are almost like to heads of dogs ... Blemmyis a people so called, they have no heads, but hide their

mouth and their eyes in their breasts.
(Cited in: *Africa: A Biography of the Continent* by John Reader. Hamish Hamilton, London, 1997.)

These images must have frightened many a Roman child to scurry to bed whenever their parents said, 'The Africans are coming! The strange creatures out of Africa are coming!'

Happily, fifteen centuries later, Europe had a somewhat different view of the Africans. At the beginning of the 16th century, Leo Africanus, a Spaniard resident in Morocco, visited West Africa and wrote the following about the royal court in Timbuktu, Mali:

The rich king of Timbuktu ... keeps a magnificent and well-furnished court ... Here are great stores of doctors, judges, priests, and other learned men, that are bountifully maintained at the king's cost and charges. And hither are brought diverse manuscripts or written books out of Barbarie, which are sold for more money than any other merchandise. (Reader, *op cit.*)

Clearly, this was not the Dog King of which Pliny had written at the beginning of the millennium, but a being as human as any other and more cultured and educated than most in the world of his day. And yet five centuries later, at the close of our millennium, we read in a book published last year:

I am an American, but a black man, a descendant of slaves brought from Africa ... If things had been different, I might have been one of them (the Africans) – or might have met some ... anonymous fate in one of the countless ongoing civil wars or tribal clashes on this brutal continent. And so I thank God my ancestor survived that voyage (to slavery) ... Talk to me about Africa and my black roots and my kinship with my African brothers and I'll throw it back into your face, and then I'll rub your nose in the images of the rotting flesh (of the victims of the genocide of the Tutsis or Rwanda) ... Sorry, but I've been there. I've had an AK-47 (automatic rifle) rammed up my nose, I've talked to machete-wielding Hutu militiamen with the blood of their latest victims splattered across their T-shirts. I've seen a cholera epidemic in Zaire, a famine in Somalia, a civil war in Liberia. I've seen cities bombed to near rubble, and other cities reduced to rubble, because their leaders let them rot and decay while they spirited away billions of dollars – yes, billions – into overseas bank accounts... Thank God my ancestor got out, because, now, I am not one of them.

(*Out of America: A Black Man Confronts Africa* by Keith B. Richburg. Basic Books, New York, 1997.)

And this time, in the place of the Roman child, it is the American child who will not hesitate to go to bed when he or she is told, 'The Africans are coming! The barbarians are coming!'

In a few paragraphs, quoted from books that others have written, we have traversed a millennium. But the truth is that we have not travelled very far with regard to the projection of frightening images of savagery that attend the continent of Africa.

And so it may come about that some who harbour the view that as Africans we are a peculiar species of humanity pose the challenge: How dare they speak of an African Renaissance? After all, in the context of the evolution of the European peoples, when we speak of the Renaissance, we speak of advances in science and technology, voyages of discovery across the oceans, a revolution in printing and an attendant spread, development and flowering of knowledge and a blossoming of the arts. And so the question must arise about how we – who, in a millennium, only managed to advance from cannibalism to a 'blood-dimmed tide' of savages who still slaughter countless innocents with machetes, and on whom another, as black as I, has turned his back, grateful that his ancestors were slaves – how do we hope to emulate the great human achievements of the earlier Renaissance of the Europe of the 15th and 16th centuries?

One of our answers to this question is that, as Africans, we recall the fact that as the European Renaissance burst into history in the 15th and 16th centuries, there was a royal court in the African city of Timbuktu which, in the same centuries, was as learned as its European counterparts.

What this tells me is that my people are not a peculiar species of humanity! I say this here today both because it is true, but also because I know that you, the citizens of this ancient land, will understand its true significance. And as we speak of an African Renaissance, we project into both the past and the future. I speak here of a glorious past of the emergence of *homo sapiens* on the African continent.

I speak of African works of art in South Africa that are a thousand years old. I speak of the continuum in the fine arts that encompasses the varied artistic creations of the Nubians and the Egyptians, the Benin bronzes of Nigeria and the intricate sculptures of the Makonde of Tanzania and Mozambique. I speak of the centuries-old contributions to the evolution of religious thought made by the Christians of Ethiopia and the Muslims of Nigeria.

I refer also to the architectural monuments represented by the giant sculptured stones of Aksum in Ethiopia, the Egyptian sphinxes and pyramids, the Tunisian city of Carthage, and the Zimbabwe ruins, as well as the legacy of the ancient universities of Alexandria of Egypt, Fez of Morocco and, once more, Timbuktu of Mali. When I survey all this and much more besides, I find nothing to sustain the long-held dogma of African exceptionalism, according to which the colour black becomes a symbol of fear, evil and death.

I speak of this long-held dogma because it continues still to weigh down the African mind and spirit, like the ton of lead that the African slave carries on her own shoulders, producing in her and the rest a condition which, in itself, contests any assertion that she is capable of initiative, creativity, individuality, and entrepreneurship. Its weight dictates that she will never straighten her back and thus discover that she is as tall as the slave master who carries the whip. Neither will she have the opportunity to question why the master has legal title both to the commodity she transports on her back and the labour she must make available to ensure that the burden on her shoulders translates into dollars and yen.

An essential and necessary element of the African Renaissance is that we all must take it as our task to encourage she who carries this leaden weight, to rebel, to assert the principality of her humanity – the fact that she, in the first instance, is not a beast of burden but a human and African being.

But in our own voyage of discovery, we have come to Japan and discovered that a mere 130 years ago, the Meiji Restoration occurred, which enabled your own forebears to project both into their past and their future. And as we seek to draw lessons and inspiration from what you have done for yourselves, and integrate the Meiji Restoration into these universal things that make us dare speak of an African Renaissance, we too see an African continent which is not 'wandering between two worlds, one dead, the other unable to be born.'

But whence and whither this confidence? I would dare say that that confidence, in part, derives from a rediscovery of ourselves, from the fact that, perforce, as one would who is critical of oneself, we have had to undertake a voyage of discovery into our own antecedents, our own past, as Africans. And when archeology presents daily evidence of an African primacy in the historical evolution to the emergence of the human person described in science as *homo sapiens*, how can we be but confident that we are capable of affecting Africa's rebirth?

When the world of fine arts speak to us of the creativity of the Nubians of Sudan and its decisive impact on the revered and everlasting imaginative creations of the African land of the Pharaohs — how can we be but confident that we will succeed to be the midwives of our continent's rebirth? And when we recall that African armies at Omduraman in the Sudan and Isandhlwana in South Africa out-generalled, out-soldiered and defeated the mighty armies of the mighty and arrogant British Empire in the seventies of the last century, how can we be but confident that through our efforts, Africa will regain her place among the continents of our universe?

And in the end, an entire epoch in human history, the epoch of colonialism and white foreign rule, progressed to its ultimate historical burial grounds because, from Morocco and Algeria to Guinea Bissau and Senegal, from Ghana and Nigeria to Tanzania and Kenya, from the Congo and Angola to Zimbabwe and South Africa, the Africans dared to stand up to say the new must be born, whatever the sacrifice we have to make — Africa must be free!

We are convinced that such a people has a legitimate right to expect of itself that it has the capacity to set itself free from the oppressive historical legacy of poverty, hunger, backwardness and marginalisation in the struggle to order world affairs, so that all human civilisation puts as the principal objective of its existence the humane existence of all that is human!

And again we come back to the point that we, who are our own liberators from imperial domination, cannot but be confident that our project to ensure the restoration not of empires, but the other conditions in the 16th century described by Leo Africanus: of peace, stability, prosperity, and intellectual creativity, will and must succeed! The simple phrase 'We are our own liberators!' is the epitaph on the gravestone of every African who dared to carry the vision in his or her heart of Africa reborn.

The conviction therefore that our past tells us that the time for Africa's Renaissance has come, is fundamental to the very conceptualisation of this Renaissance and the answer to the question: Whence this confidence? Unless we are able to answer the question 'Who were we?' we will not be able to answer the question 'What shall we be?' This complex exercise, which can be stated in simple terms, links the past to the future and speaks to the interconnection between an empowering process of restoration and the consequences or the response to the acquisition of that newly restored power to create something new.

If, at this point, you asked me whether I was making a reference to the Meiji Restoration and its impact on the history and evolution of this country, my answer would be: Yes! However, I would also plead that you should not question me too closely on this matter, to avoid me exposing my ignorance.

But this I would like you to know: that in the depth of my ignorance I am moved by the conviction that this particular period in the evolution of Japan, to the point, today, when her economic problems are those of a surfeit rather than the poverty of resources, has a multiplicity of lessons for us as Africans, which we cannot afford to ignore or, worse still, not to know. And if we as students are badly informed, you have a responsibility to be our teachers. We are ready to learn and to become our own teachers as a result.

We would also like you to know that our determination to learn is exemplified by the willingness we have demonstrated to learn on our own from our experiences. I refer here, in particular, to the period since the independence of many of our countries. Among many Africans, this has been referred to as the neo-colonial period.

This constitutes an honest admission of the fact that an important feature of African independence at that stage was that the development of these independent states was determined by the reality that the fundamental, structural relationship between the independent states and the former colonial powers did not change. As a consequence of the acquisition of independence, new state symbols had been adopted and were displayed daily. New state institutions were created. Political and other decision-making processes commenced, which represented and signified the formation of new nation-states. At last, Africans were governing themselves.

However, reality, including the purposes of the Cold War, dictated that the former colonial powers continued to hold in their hands the power to determine what would happen to the African people over whom, in terms of international and municipal law, they no longer had any jurisdiction. The mere recognition that this signified a neo-colonial relationship, rather than genuine independence, affirmed the point that the peoples of our continent had not abandoned the determination to be their own liberators!

Much of what you see reported in your own media today represented, for instance, by the exit from the African stage of a personality such as General Mobutu Sese Seko of the former Zaire, represents the death of neo-colonialism on our continent. And so we must return to the question, 'Whence the confidence that we, as Africans, can speak of an African Renaissance?'

What we have said so far is that both our ancient and modern history as well as our own practical and conscious deeds convey the same message: that genuine liberation, in the context of the modern world, is what drives the Africans of today as they seek to confront the problems which for them constitute a daily challenge.

The question must therefore arise: What is it which makes up that genuine liberation? The first of these [elements] is that we must bring to an end the practices as a result of which many throughout the world have the view that, as Africans, we are incapable of establishing and maintaining systems of good governance. Our own practical experiences tell us that military governments do not represent the system of good governance which we seek.

Accordingly, the continent has made the point clear that it is opposed to military coups and has taken practical steps, as exemplified by the restoration to power of the elected government of Sierra Leone, to demonstrate its intent to meet this challenge when it arises. Similarly, many governments throughout the continent, including our continental organisation, the OAU, have sought to encourage the Nigerian government and people to return as speedily as possible to a democratic system of government.

Furthermore, our experience has taught us that one-party states also do not represent the correct route to take towards the objective of a stable system of governance, which serves the interests of the people. One of the principal demands in our liberation struggle, as we sought to end the system of apartheid was: 'The people shall govern!' It is this same vision which has inspired the African peoples so that, during the present decade, we have seen at least 25 countries establish multi-party democracies and hold elections so that the people can decide on governments of their choice.

The new South Africa is itself an expression and part of this African movement towards the transfer of power to the people. At the same time, we are conscious of the fact that each country has its particular characteristics to which it must respond as it establishes its democratic system of government.

Accordingly, none of us seeks to impose any supposedly standard models of democracy on any country, but we want to see systems of government in which the people are empowered to determine their destiny and to resolve any disputes among themselves by peaceful political means.

In our own country, conscious of the need to properly handle the contradictions and conflicts that might arise among different ethnic and national groups, aware also of the fact that such conflicts have been an important element of instability on the continent, we have made it a constitutional requirement to establish a Commission for the Promotion of Cultural, Language and Religious Rights.

In this context, we must also mention two initiatives which the continent as a whole has taken through the agency of the Organisation of African Unity. We refer here to the establishment of the inter-state Central Organ for the Prevention and Resolution of Conflicts which is empowered to intervene to resolve conflicts on the continent and which is currently working on the design of an instrument for peace-keeping to increase our collective capacity to intervene quickly, to ensure that we have no more Rwandas, Liberias or Somalias.

The second initiative to which we refer is the adoption of the African Charter of Human and People's Rights, which sets norms according to which we can judge both ourselves and our sister countries as to whether we are conducting ourselves in a manner consistent with the defence and promotion of human and people's rights. Like others throughout the world, we too are engaged in the struggle to give real meaning to such concepts as transparency and accountability in governance, as part of the offensive directed against corruption and the abuse of power.

What we are arguing therefore is that, in the political sphere, the African Renaissance has begun. Our history demands that we do everything in our power to defend the gains that have already been achieved, to encourage all other countries on our continent to move in the same direction, according to which the people shall govern, and to enhance the capacity of the OAU to act as an effective instrument for peace and the promotion of human and people's rights to which it is committed.

Such are the political imperatives of the African Renaissance which are inspired both by our painful history of recent decades and the recognition of the fact that none of our countries is an island which can isolate itself from the rest, and that none of us can truly succeed if the rest fail.

The second of the elements of what we have described as the genuine liberation of the peoples of Africa is, of course, an end to the tragic sight of the emaciated child who dies of hunger or is ravaged by curable diseases because their malnourished bodies do not have the strength to resist any illness.

What we have spoken of before, of the restoration of the dignity of the peoples of Africa itself, demands that we deal as decisively and as quickly as possible with the perception that as a continent we are condemned forever to depend on the merciful charity which those who are kind are ready to put into our begging bowls.

Accordingly, and again driven by our own painful experience, many on our continent have introduced new economic policies which seek to create conditions that are attractive for domestic and foreign investors, encourage the growth of the private sector, reduce the participation of the state in the ownership of the economy and, in other ways, seek to build modern economies.

Simultaneously, we are also working to overcome the disadvantages created by small markets represented by the relatively small numbers of people in many of our nation states. Regional economic associations have therefore been formed aimed at achieving regional economic integration, which in many instances would provide the necessary condition for any significant and sustained economic growth and development to take place.

In our own region, we have the Southern African Development Community, which brings together a population of well over 100 million people. The community has already taken the decision to work towards transforming itself into a free-trade area and is currently involved in detailed discussions about such issues as the timetable for the reduction of tariffs to encourage trade among the member states and thus to take the necessary steps leading to the creation of the free-trade area to which we have referred.

We are also engaged in other initiatives aimed at the development of infrastructure throughout the region, both as an expression of development and to create the basis for further development and therefore a sustained improvement in the standard of living of the people.

As part of the determined offensive to achieve integrated and mutually beneficial regional development, we have taken other initiatives to deal with common regional problems, going beyond the directly economic. I refer here to the establishment of a regional instrument to address questions of regional security, peace and stability, including the building of regional peace-making and peacekeeping capacity. I refer also to the development of a regional system of cooperation to combat crime, including trade in narcotics and illegal firearms, as well as the evolution of common programmes and legislative frameworks to deal with such challenges as violence against women and children.

We are therefore determined to ensure that we end the situation according to which, for many years, Africa recorded the slowest rates of economic growth and, in many instances, actually experienced economic decline. Already, a significant number of countries have shown relatively high rates of growth as a direct consequence of changes in economic policy and, of course, the achievement of stability within our countries as a result of the establishment of democratic systems of government.

These economic objectives, which must result in the elimination of poverty, the establishment of modern multi-sector economies, and the growth of Africa's share of world economic activity, are an essential part of the African Renaissance. We are certain that the movement towards their achievement will also be sustained precisely because this movement represents an indigenous impulse which derives from our knowledge of the mistakes we have made in the past and our determination to put those mistakes behind us.

I say this to emphasise the point that necessarily the African Renaissance, in all its parts, can only succeed if its aims and objectives are defined by the Africans themselves, if its programmes are designed by ourselves and if we take responsibility for the success or failure of our policies.

As South Africans, we owe our emancipation from apartheid in no small measure to the support and solidarity extended to us by all the peoples of Africa. In that sense our victory over the system of white minority domination is an African victory. This, I believe, imposes an obligation on us to use this gift of freedom, which is itself an important contribution to Africa's Renaissance, to advance the cause of the peoples of our continent.

The first thing we must do, clearly, is to succeed. We must succeed to strengthen and further entrench democracy in our country and inculcate a culture of human rights among all our people, which is indeed happening.

We must succeed to rebuild and reconstruct our economies, achieve high and sustained rates of growth, reduce unemployment, and provide a better life for the people, a path on which we have embarked.

We must succeed to meet the needs of the people so as to end poverty and improve the quality of life by ensuring access to good education, adequate health care, decent homes, clean water and modern sanitation, and so on, again a process on which we have embarked.

We must take decisive steps to challenge the spread of HIV/AIDS, of which Africa accounts for two-thirds of the world total of those infected. Our government has taken the necessary decisions directed at launching and sustaining a big campaign to confront this scourge.

We must discharge our responsibilities to ourselves, future generations and the world with regard to the protection of the environment, cooperating with all nations to meet what is, after all, a common challenge.

We must rise to the critical challenge of creating a non-racial and non-sexist society, both of which objectives are also contained within our constitution. I believe that we, who were exposed to the most pernicious racism represented by the system of apartheid, have the historic possibility and responsibility indeed to create a non-racial society, both in our own interest and as our contribution to the continuing struggle throughout the world to fight racism, which remains an unfortunate feature of many societies.

Similarly, we have a real possibility to make real advances in the struggle for the genuine and all-round emancipation of women and have, with this objective in mind, established a constitutional commission for gender equality which will help our society as a whole to measure the progress we are making to secure gender equality.

Many African peoples throughout southern Africa sacrificed their lives to help us secure our freedom. Others further afield ignored the fact of their own poverty to contribute resources to guarantee our emancipation. I am convinced that this immense contribution was made not only so that we end the apartheid crime against humanity, but also so that we build a society of which all Africa would be proud because it would address also the wrong and negative view of an Africa that is historically destined to fail.

Similarly, the peoples of Africa entertain the legitimate expectation that the new South Africa, which they helped to bring into being, will not only be an expression of the African Renaissance by the manner in which it conducts its affairs, but will also be an active participant with other Africans in the struggle for the victory of that Renaissance throughout our continent.

Necessarily therefore, we are engaged and will continue to be engaged in Africa's efforts to guarantee peace for her children, to feed and clothe them, to educate them and to bring them up as human beings as human as any other in the world, their dignity restored and their equal worth recognised and valued throughout our universe.

We would like you to join us in the noble struggle to achieve these objectives. The process of globalisation emphasises the fact that no person is an island, sufficient to himself or herself. Rather, all humanity is an interdependent whole in which none can be truly free unless all are free, in which none can be truly prosperous unless none elsewhere in the world goes hungry, and in which none of us can be guaranteed a good quality of life unless we act together to protect the environment.

By so saying, we are trying to convey the message that African underdevelopment must be a matter of concern to everybody else in the world, that the victory of the African Renaissance addresses not only the improvement of the conditions of life of the peoples of Africa but also the extension of the frontiers of human dignity to all humanity. Accordingly, we believe that it is important that the international community should agree that Africa constitutes the principal development challenge in the world. Having made this determination, we believe that we should then all join forces to ensure that we elaborate and implement practical programmes of action to respond to this principal development challenge.

Urgent steps are required to bring about debt relief to the many countries on our continent which suffer from an unsustainable debt burden. Measures must be taken to encourage larger inflows of capital into the continent, taking advantage of the fact of changed economic policies and improved political circumstances which have brought many of our countries into the mainstream of world developments with regard to the creation of circumstances which make for high and sustained economic growth.

The developed world has to follow more generous trade policies, which should ensure easier access of African products into their markets. Further, we still require substantial flows of well-directed development assistance. Accordingly, we believe that steps should be taken to reverse the decline in such assistance which has occurred in many countries of the developed world.

Similarly, as the process of globalisation develops apace, enhancing the need for a multilateral process of decision making affecting both governments and the non-governmental sector, it is necessary that, acting together, we ensure that Africa, like other regions of the developing world,occupies her due place within the councils of the world, including the various organs of the United Nations.

It is our hope and conviction that this important member of the world community of nations, Japan, will see itself as our partner in the practical promotion of the vision of an African Renaissance. By acting on the variety of matters we have mentioned and others besides, we trust that

Japan will continue to place herself among the front ranks of those who are driven to act not only within the context of a narrowly defined national interest, but with the generosity of spirit which recognises the fact that our own humanity is enriched by identifying ourselves especially with those who suffer.

When once more the saying is recalled, *Ex Africa semper aliquid novi!* – Something new always comes out of Africa! – this must be so, because out of Africa reborn must come modern products of human economic activity, significant contributions to the world of knowledge in the arts, science and technology, new images of an Africa of peace and prosperity.

Thus shall we, together and at last, by bringing about the African Renaissance depart from a centuries-old past which sought to perpetuate the notion of an Africa condemned to remain a curiosity slowly grinding to a halt on the periphery of the world. Surely those who are the offspring of the good that sprang from the Meiji Restoration would not want to stay away from the accomplishment of so historic a human victory!

Thank you.

South Africa: Two nations

Statement of Deputy President Thabo Mbeki at the opening of the debate in the National Assembly, on reconciliation and nation building, Cape Town, 29 May 1998

Madame Speaker, Honourable Members of the National Assembly;

I would like to thank our presiding officers, the whips and all the parties represented in the Assembly for giving all of us the opportunity to discuss the important matter of reconciliation and nation building for which we have convened this morning.

The 1993 Constitution of the Republic of South Africa ends with an epilogue entitled 'National Unity and Reconciliation'.

Among other things, it says:

This Constitution provides a historic bridge between the past of a deeply divided society characterised by strife, conflict, untold suffering and injustice, and a future founded on the recognition of human rights, democracy and peaceful coexistence and development opportunities for all South Africans, irrespective of colour, race, class, belief or sex.

'The pursuit of national unity,' it continues 'the well-being of all South African citizens and peace require reconciliation between the people of South Africa and the reconstruction of society.'

For its part, the 1996 Constitution of the Republic of South Africa has a preamble which among other things, says:

We, the people of South Africa, recognise the injustices of our past... (and) believe that South Africa belongs to all who live in it, united in our diversity.

We therefore... adopt this Constitution as the supreme law of the Republic so as to heal the divisions of the past... (and) to improve the quality of life of all citizens and free the potential of each person.

In its 'Founding Provisions', this Constitution also says that our Republic has as one of its values 'commitment to promote non-racialism and non-sexism.'

I believe that as we discuss the issue of national unity and reconciliation today, we will have to do a number of things.

The first of these, to which I am certain we will all respond in the same manner, is that we should commit ourselves to the pursuit of the objectives contained in these constitutions for a democratic South Africa.

The second is that we will have to answer the question honestly as to whether we are making the requisite progress:

to create a non-racial society;
to build a non-sexist country;
to heal the divisions of the past;
to achieve the peaceful coexistence of all our people; to create development opportunities for all South Africans, irrespective of colour, race, class, belief or sex; and to improve the quality of life of all citizens.

Thirdly, we will have to answer the question, again as honestly as we can, as to whether our actions have been and are based on the recognition of the injustices of the past, and whether our actions have genuinely sought to promote the integrated Constitutional objectives of:

national unity;
the well-being of all South Africans;

peace;

reconciliation between the people of South Africa; and

the reconstruction of society.

In the light of these prescriptions contained in the two Constitutions to which I have referred, let me declare some of the matters to which the government I represent is committed.

We are interested that, as a people, we move as rapidly and as consistently as possible to transform South Africa into a non-racial country.

We are interested that our country lives up to its constitutional commitment to transform itself into a non-sexist society.

We are interested that together, as South Africans, we adopt the necessary steps that will eradicate poverty in our country as quickly as possible and in all its manifestations, to end the dehumanisation of millions of our people, which inevitably results from the terrible deprivation to which so many, both black and white, are victim.

We are interested that we must deal with our political past honestly, frankly and without equivocation, so that the purposes for which most of us agreed to establish the Truth and Reconciliation Commission are achieved.

We are interested that our country responds to the call to rally to a new patriotism, as a result of which we can all agree to a common national agenda, which would include:

a common fight to eradicate the legacy of apartheid;

a united offensive against corruption and crime;

concerted action to advance the interests of those least capable to defend themselves, including children, women, the disabled and the elderly;

an agreement about how we should protect and advance the interests of all the different cultural, language and religious groups that make up the South African population;

a commitment to confront the economic challenges facing our country, in a manner that simultaneously addresses issues of high and sustained growth and raising the living standards of especially the black poor;

an all-embracing effort to build a sense of common nationhood and a shared destiny, as a result of which we can entrench into the minds of all our people the understanding that however varied their skin complexions, cultures and life conditions, the success of each nevertheless depends on the effort the other will make to turn into reality the precept that each is his or her brother's or sister's keeper; and

a united view of our country's relations with the rest of the world.

We believe that these are the issues we must address when we speak of reconciliation and nation building. They stand at the centre of the very future of South Africa as the home of a stable democracy, human rights, equality, peace, stability and a shared prosperity.

Accordingly we must attend to the question whether with regard to all these issues and at all times, all of us behave in a manner which promotes the achievement of the goals we have mentioned, and therefore take us forward towards the realisation of the objective of reconciliation and nation building, without which the kind of South Africa visualised in our Constitution will most certainly not come into being.

So must we also pose the questions – what is nation building and is it happening?

With regard to the first of these, our own response would be that nation building is the construction of the reality and the sense of common nationhood which would result from the abolition of disparities in the quality of life among South Africans based on the racial, gender and geographic inequalities we all inherited from the past.

The second question we posed is – are we making the requisite progress towards achieving the objective of nation building, as we have just defined it?

If we elected to answer this question in a polite and reassuring manner, we would answer – yes, we are making the requisite progress.

However, I believe that perhaps we should answer this question honestly and deal with the consequences of an honest response, however discomforting it may be.

Accordingly, our answer to the question whether we are making that requisite progress, towards achieving the objective of nation building, as we defined it, would be – no!

A major component of the issue of reconciliation and nation building is defined by and derives from the material conditions in our society which have divided our country into two nations, the one black and the other white.

We therefore make bold to say that South Africa is a country of two nations.

One of these nations is white, relatively prosperous, regardless of gender or geographic dispersal. It has ready access to a developed economic, physical, educational, communication and other infrastructure.

This enables it to argue that, except for the persistence of gender discrimination against women, all members of this nation have the possibility to exercise their right to equal opportunity, the development opportunities to which the Constitution of 1993 committed our country.

The second and larger nation of South Africa is black and poor, with the worst affected being women in the rural areas, the black rural population in general and the disabled.

This nation lives under conditions of a grossly underdeveloped economic, physical, educational, communication and other infrastructure.

It has virtually no possibility to exercise what in reality amounts to a theoretical right to equal opportunity, with that right being equal within this black nation only to the extent that it is equally incapable of realisation.

This reality of two nations, underwritten by the perpetuation of the racial, gender and spatial disparities born of a very long period of colonial and apartheid white minority domination, constitutes the material base which reinforces the notion that, indeed, we are not one nation but two nations.

And neither are we becoming one nation. Consequently, also, the objective of national reconciliation is not being realised.

This follows as well that the longer this situation persists, in spite of the gift of hope delivered to the people by the birth of democracy, the more entrenched will be the conviction that the concept of nation building is a mere mirage and that no basis exists, or will ever exist, to enable national reconciliation to take place.

Over the four years, and this includes the period before the elections of 1994, we have put forward and sustained the position that the creation of the material conditions that would both underpin and represent nation building and reconciliation could only be achieved over a protracted period of time.

I would like to reaffirm this position. The abolition of the apartheid legacy will require considerable effort over a considerable period of time.

We are neither impressed nor moved by self-serving arguments which seek to suggest that four or five years are long enough to remove from our national life the inheritance of a country of two nations which is as old as the arrival of European colonists in our country, almost 350 years ago.

Let me digress briefly and say something about the ongoing process of German unification.

As the Honourable members are aware, the two post-war German states united into one country in 1990.

After 45 years of division into two states with competing social systems, the German leaders and people understood that, truly to become one country and one people, they, like ourselves, would have to address the central questions of national unity and reconciliation.

This was despite the fact that here we speak of a people who share the same language, colour and culture.

The seriousness with which the German people treated that process of the promotion of German national unity and reconciliation is reflected, among other things, by the extraordinary volume of resources which the richer, developed West Germany transferred to the poorer and relatively underdeveloped East.

During the first five years of unification after 1990, $586,5 billion of public funds were transferred from West Germany to East Germany to underwrite Germany's project of national unity and reconciliation. This exceeded East Germany tax revenues for the same period by a factor of 4.5.1.

Further to illustrate the enormity of this effort, these transfers amount to 70 times the size of the national budget which this House is currently debating.

To help finance this extraordinary expenditure, a 7,5 per cent surcharge on individual income tax was imposed in 1991 and extended in 1995 for an unspecified period of time. Correctly and interestingly, this was designated a 'solidarity tax'.

It might also be of interest to note that despite the huge flow of German public and private funds into the East, at the end of this first five year period, per capita income in the East still amounted to 74 per cent of income in the Western part of the country.

In our case, the reality is that in the last five years, the national budget has increased by a mere 10 per cent. In other words, to all intents and purposes, taking into account the increase in population, we are spending the same volume of money to address the needs of the entirety of our population as were disbursed to address the needs of essentially the white minority before the democratic transition.

Our own 'solidarity tax' was imposed for one year only, accompanied by much grumbling from some sectors of our society.

Before we digressed to Germany, we were making the point that four or five years are not enough to weld the two nations which coexist in South Africa as a consequence of a long period of the existence of a society based on racism.

To respond to all of this, in conceptual terms we have to deal with two interrelated elements.

The first of these is that we must accept that it will take time to create the material base for nation building and reconciliation.

The second and related element is that we must therefore agree that it is the subjective factor, accompanied by tangible process in the creation of the new material base, which must take the lead in sustaining the hope and conviction among the people that the project of reconciliation and nation building will succeed.

Given the critical importance of the subjective factor, therefore, we must return to the question we posed earlier during this intervention.

That question is — are we all, as the various parties in this parliament and our society at large, behaving in a manner which promotes the objectives of reconciliation and nation building, within which the kind of South Africa visualised in our Constitution will most certainly not come into being?

Again, my own answer to this question would be a very definite — no!

Clearly, it would be irresponsible for me to make such a statement without substantiating it.

Let me therefore cite openly some of the interventions or non-interventions which, over the last four years, have not helped to move us more speedily towards the attainment of the objective of reconciliation and nation building.

Unlike the German people, we have not made the extra effort to generate the material resources we have to invest to change the condition of the black poor more rapidly than is possible if we depend solely on severely limited public funds, whose volume is governed by the need to maintain certain macro-economic balances, and the impact of a growing economy.

What this throws up, inevitably, is the question – are the relatively rich who, as a result of an apartheid definition, are white, prepared to help underwrite the upliftment of the poor, who as a result of an apartheid definition, are black?

If we are serious about national unity and reconciliation and treat the obligations contained in our Constitution as more than words on paper, we have to answer this question practically.

The South African Revenue Service is engaged in a difficult struggle to ensure that every individual and corporate entity meet their tax obligations.

I am informed that so far SARS has established that something in the order of 30 per cent of our corporations are not registered for tax purposes. These are people who, by honouring their legal obligations, could make an important contribution to addressing the material challenges of national unity and reconciliation.

They deliberately choose not to but will not hesitate to proclaim that the Government has failed to 'deliver'.

Many of us in this House find it very easy each time we speak to demand that the Government must spend more on this and that and the other.

At the same time, we make passionate demands that taxes must be cut and the budget deficit reduced.

The constant and, in some instances, dishonest refrain for more funds, in many instances incanted for party political gain, re-emerges in our streets as when, only a few days ago, public sector workers marched behind posters which bore the words – 'give us more, give us more'.

In the majority of cases, the call for the transformation of both public

191

and private sector institutions and organisations, in particular to address the issue of racial representativity, has been resisted with great determination.

Indeed, one of the issues of great agitation in our politics is the question of affirmative action.

To ensure that it does not happen, some of what is said that 'black advancement equals a white brain drain' and 'black management in the public service equals inefficiency, corruption and a lowering of standards'.

In many instances, correctly to refer to the reality that our past determines the present is to invite protests and ridicule even as it is perfectly clear that no solution to many current problems can be found unless we understand their historical origins.

By this means, it comes about that those who were responsible for or were beneficiaries of the past absolve themselves from any obligation to help do away with an unacceptable legacy.

The current situation suggests that the TRC will be unable to complete its work especially with regard to the full disclosure and attribution of many acts of gross human rights violations.

This will leave the law enforcement agencies with no choice but to investigate all outstanding cases of such violations, making it inevitable that our society continues to be subject to tensions which derive from the conflicts of the past.

Some of our country, including some who serve within the security forces, are prepared to go to any length to oppose the democratic order, including the assassination of leaders and destabilistation by all means.

These include the now well-known story of the alleged involvement of former freedom fighters in plans to carry out a *coup d'état* as well as other disinformation campaigns which the intelligence services are investigating involving allegations that Minister Mufamadi is involved in the cash-in-transition robberies, while Deputy Minister Kasrils and myself are responsible for the murder of white farmers.

Last week, I mentioned in the House the negative impact of such events as the recent appearance of the President of the Republic in court, the SARFU [South African Rugby Football Union] saga and the matter of the appointment of the Deputy Judge President of the Natal bench.

I am certain that many of us can cite many examples of interventions which have not contributed to the goal of national unity and reconciliation, including the many instances of resistance to pieces of legislation which seek to transform our country away from its apartheid past.

And yet we must make the point that the overwhelming majority of our people have neither abandoned this goal nor lost hope that it will be realised.

An important contributory factor to this is that there are, indeed, significant numbers of people in our society, including people among the white and Afrikaner community who, by word and deed, have demonstrated a real commitment to the translation of the vision of national unity and reconciliation into reality.

Again last week, in this House, I said that much of what is happening in our country which pushes us away from achieving this goal is producing rage among millions of people. I am convinced that we are faced with the danger of a mounting rage to which we must respond seriously.

In a speech again in this House, we quoted the African-American poet, Langston Hughes, when he wrote — 'what happens to a dream deferred?'

His conclusion was that it explodes.

Thank you Madame Speaker.

On national unity and reconciliation

Statement of Deputy President Thabo Mbeki on the occasion of the debate on the budget vote of the office of the Deputy President, National Assembly, 3 June 1998

Madame Speaker, Honourable Members of the National Assembly:

Our Constitution enjoins the President of the Republic to 'promote the unity of the nation and that which will advance the Republic'.

In that context, we would like to devote this intervention on the budget of the Office of the Deputy President further to reflect on the matter of national unity and reconciliation which we started discussing last week.

As the Honourable Members are aware, our mass media has, quite correctly, also joined this discussion.

Accordingly, and with apologies to the Members who have read these opinions, I would like to quote some of the editorial comment which has appeared in the newspapers since Friday.

In its issue of June 1st, *The Citizen* wrote:

Thabo Mbeki has grossly oversimplified the divisions in South Africa by talking about two nations: rich whites and poor blacks. In doing so, he has not helped foster the reconciliation he purports to be striving for. If anything, he has set down a marker, showing a

194

clear distinction between the mainly conciliatory approach of
President Mandela and his own brand of Africanism which
highlights racial differences ... The overall impact of his message
has been to cast a damper on the prospects of reconciliation ... But
Mr Mbeki especially asked for time to be set aside in parliament
where he could disseminate his negative message. Considering that
parliament has a large volume of work to get through, his was an
unnecessary and fruitless intervention. It will take more than that for
the poor to believe he is their champion.

The *Cape Argus* wrote on June 1st:

As Mbeki pointed out, in seeking to change this historic imbalance,
all in South Africa have a duty to make a contribution, especially
relatively affluent whites. But Mr Mbeki and his government also
have a duty: to recognise the limitations of what can reasonably be
contributed by whites, and to recognise the obligation which falls on
the government to utilise and nurture that contribution with wisdom
and good leadership ... One way is to accept that opposition parties
in South Africa which, more because of our contorted history than
their own inclinations, happen to speak for the relatively wealthy,
and have a democratic right and obligation to represent the interests
of those who support them ...

The *Beeld* said on May 30th:

From a cynical point of view, one would say this debate
demonstrated the importance of reconciliation to the person in the
street and that it is too important to be left to the politicians whose
job is to differ rather than to seek common ground ... In this
process, politicians are trapped in their own corners, with their
starting point being mutual accusation and self-exculpation. If this
tendency persists, with no one moving closer to the other end, the
end result in all likelihood will be the explosion of which Mr Mbeki
warned ... Only if there is genuine understanding in both "nations"
for each other's progress and suffering, ideals and fears, can there be
hope in the country, with all its nations and interest groups, of being
able to address its problems in a common effort.

On May 31st, the *Sunday Times* said:

> Deputy President Thabo Mbeki's speech in parliament on Friday on reconciliation has launched an important and long overdue debate on South Africa's racial divide ... To heal the deep divides in our society, we will need a sustained focus on breaking the stereotypes that underlie racial tension. Opposition parties need to ask themselves what they are doing to break these stereotypes ... Business must ask what it is doing to break racial stereotypes about the economy. Affirmative action, window dressing and carping about declining standards must give way to a real effort to remove the real, if somewhat crude, suspicion that the South African economy is still all about rich whites who have made their profits at the expense of poor blacks ... Mbeki ... needs to ask himself what he is doing to defuse racial hostility in his speeches and to produce those all-important public gestures that speak of a single united nation ... The government needs to recognise [the challenge of job creation] by jettisoning every piece of legislation – including some of its cherished labour laws – that impede job creation. More than that, Mbeki and the ruling ANC need to make sure that government works.

Rapport of May 31st commented:

> [Mr Mbeki] again confirmed that his main priority as an African is addressing poverty among the black masses, and no one should hold it against him since the millions of black voters, still living in terrible conditions, voted the ANC into power and Mr Mbeki and the ANC are dependent on their vote ... However, nation building and reconciliation will remain a dream for so long as crime persists and white farmers are killed day in and day out and week after week by blacks ... Naturally, the government does not have the necessary funds to do everything that has to be done, but surely government should ask the question on how much of the available funds are spent well and how much is lost due to mismanagement and corruption ... The only definite way of ensuring the upliftment of the blacks is by creating more jobs through economic growth ... The ANC is at loggerheads with its alliance partners regarding the

macro-economic policy and serious violent crime remains a deterrent to potential investors ...

The *Sunday Independent* commented on May 31st:

The parliamentary debate on reconciliation on Friday was a refreshing indication that our elected representatives are able to rise above political point-scoring when it comes to matters affecting the very survival of our delicate emerging democracy ... This newspaper has consistently argued that a national forum – similar to the Codesa that produced South Africa's political compromise – is needed to reach a national consensus on how to fund the developmental challenge. The already heavily taxed private sector would clearly need to take a central role in such an initiative.

Business Day wrote in its own editorial on June 2nd:

But what is also striking about Mbeki's speech is its exclusive focus on the duties of whites – there is no mention of the growing black business, professional and political élite, of which he is a member. A schizophrenic attitude may be observed in governing circles on this issue: sacrifices are demanded from whites while black businessmen are encouraged to enrich themselves without a word being uttered about their social responsibilities ... A socially responsible black élite, and a government that cracks down, regardless of race, on all freeloading, incompetence and graft, are also a vital part of the equation.

Again, we must express our appreciation for the serious responses of the editors as reflected in these editorial extracts.

But it is also necessary that we return to the reality of the South Africa of two nations to which we referred.

Accordingly, let us restate some of the stark truths which define our common South Africa.

According to the report on 'Poverty and Inequality in South Africa' issued only a few weeks ago, 61 per cent of the Africans are poor with the figure among Whites being 1 per cent. The figures for Coloureds and Indians are 38 and 5 per cent respectively.

In 1993, 59 per cent of the national income accrued to the 13 per cent who are white, with the figure for Africans who were 76 per cent of the population being 29 per cent, representing a white-black disparity of 11,8 to 1.

In 1995, while 50 per cent of white households had after tax income of R60 000 per annum, only 6 per cent of African households enjoyed the same standard of living.

Ninety-three per cent of the unemployed poor are African.

Of those who are employed but earn less than R1 000 a month, 42 per cent are African while 4 per cent of whites fall into this category.

If we speak about the quality of life more broadly, the same basic feature of two nations emerges. For example, 85 per cent of white households have a telephone line compared to 14 per cent for African households.

The infant mortality rate for whites was 7.3 per 1 000, and 54.3 for Africans, this being the same as Zimbabwe and Kenya.

As those who seek a proper understanding of the serious problem of crime and understand the relationship between poverty and crime would know, Africans are 20 times more at risk from death through murder, while, in 1995, 95 per cent of reported rapes were of African women.

We must also consider these crime statistics bearing in mind that in 1996, 75 per cent of all police stations were in historically white areas.

A point has also been made about the place and role of the black élite.

Again, it is necessary to get the facts right.

The introductory remarks to the Employment Equity Bills say, among other things:

In the three-year period to 1997, the number of black senior managers increased by 2,3 per cent, with a paltry 1,6 per cent among middle managers.

It goes further to say, drawing on a 1997 survey of the Public Service:

Whites (who are 21 per cent of the public service) are 62 per cent of management ... The survey found that the percentage of Africans in senior management, at 47 per cent, was just above that of whites who stood at 43 per cent.

In figures published in September 1997, the 'Breakwater Monitor' of the University of Cape Town Graduate School of Business, covering virtually the entire South African economy, stated that 87,43 per cent of management was white, while Africans occupied 6,18 per cent of management positions and blacks, as a whole, 12,57 per cent.

With regard to the issue of black business, McGregor Information Services puts the percentage of market capitalisation on the Johannesburg Stock Exchange under 'black control' at 10,3 per cent as at February 1998.

The organisations falling under this category are described as those 'where the predominant number of individuals is black with sufficient directors to veto or approve a motion at a board meeting.'

Whatever our views about the figures given, let us nevertheless accept the figure that when we talk of black business at this level of the economy, we speak of 10 per cent of national wealth, as well as black participation in management to the tune of 13 per cent of the cadre of managers in the country.

Undoubtedly, these figures represent an improvement on the past, but also illustrate the reality of the two nations of which we spoke.

We have given these statistics to say that the fact of the gross racial disparities in our country is not the creation of the fertile imagination of an individual who is driven by a desire to be nasty in order to gain political advantage.

It helps nobody, except those who do not want change, to argue that the difference in income between a senior black manager and an unskilled black worker is as high as the difference in income between an equivalent senior white manager and an unskilled black worker, and therefore that, like many other countries, we are now faced with the challenge of class differentiation rather than the racial differentiation which is the heritage of white minority rule.

During the debate last Friday, the Honourable Tony Leon posed a question as to whether some of the remarks I made constituted a threat and, I suppose, an attempt at intimidation therefore.

One of the fond slogans of China during the Mao years was – 'let a hundred flowers bloom! Let a hundred schools of thought contend!'

Given the complexity of the issues we have to address, I would like to believe that we too face the challenge of allowing a hundred flowers to bloom and a hundred schools of thought to contend!

Responding to the Honourable Melanie Verwoerd's appeal to all of us to listen and to hear, we must also learn to allow ourselves to speak to one another.

The question we posed – 'what happens to a dream deferred?' – was an inquiry which had to be made. The menacing vision it might evoke is not a fault of the questioner, but is inherent to the social conditions which gives birth to the question.

Let none of us pretend that the debate about change will be capable of being handled in the manner of a cosy chat around a bountiful dinner table.

Because of the nature of what we have to do, it will be rough and painful and drive many of us to shout at one another, to curse and use misunderstood and hurtful words that were only meant to soothe, if only they were understood!

Some intellectuals have sought to teach all of us to understand how a person who is white and South African might respond to the national challenges of our day.

What has been said I cannot vouch for but that you and I have to reflect upon it, I do not doubt.

In an article in the *Sunday Independent* 'Higher Education Supplement' of 15 September 1996, David Williams of the University of the Witwatersrand wrote:

> What interests me is the way in which education people are prepared to swallow so readily these legends about (falling) standards.

> I suspect it has nothing to do with medical degrees at all, but is a symptom of a psychosis in white society ... It is as if white people feel so deeply threatened they dare not allow themselves hope for the future, because the pain of having it dashed will be too great. So they look everywhere for evidence of decline, in order that they cannot be disappointed.

Elements of white society to the current vogue, according to which everybody demands that the Government or somebody else other than myself, must do this or the other, David Williams, who is white, concludes his article with the words:

It is up to the great universities to prove (this army which has lost its morale) wrong. As with many difficult jobs, nobody else is going to do it.

Two intellectuals, both with Ph. Ds, James M Statman and Amy Ansell, have also made their own effort to help us understand the inchoate images that pass through our minds.

In a paper presented at the Second Annual Congress of the Psychological Society of South Africa in September 1996, they write:

Like the first rumblings of an earthquake, the case of "MW Makgoba versus 13 academics at the University of the Witwatersrand" was profoundly unsettling not simply because it revealed and perhaps heightened the terrible "racial", political and class faults suddenly found lying so close beneath the dominant discursive patina of reconciliatory rainbowism, but more so because in its discovery of a failure of fundamental social consensus even on the question of what was at issue, it exposed a clash of seemingly incompatible and perhaps irreconcilable paradigms, discursive systems, or realities.

Particularly for those who had for so long set the terms of the dominant South African political and social discourse, those used to determining the "public transcript", that such power came to be experienced as the natural order of things, this stark assertion of other realities and other's power threatened to erode a coherent sense of social, psychological and, perhaps most fundamentally, of ontological security.

The Makgoba affair presents a brief instance when conflicts otherwise repressed, hidden, disguised, barely recognised or acknowledged suddenly appear, momentarily revealing the terrifying shape of an alien landscape, a discordant parallel epistemological universe that challenges the basic assumptions of the construction of our world. And like the pathological family system, all collude to quickly deny the forbidden knowledge, to restore the social/ psychological mythic reality to its familiar state of covert conflict.

Doctors Statman and Ansell then go on to argue that by July 1996, nine months after 'the Makgoba Affair' had burst into the open, it was being 'dismissed with a kind of bored weariness as "old news", replaced by excitement about crime and Pagad, the fall of the Rand or Trevor Manuel and the Springboks (itself a nice little example of symbolic conflict).'

Then they speak about how the South African Sociological Association virtually ignored the Makgoba affair at its July 1996 annual meeting and write:

> That a sociological congress should choose to systematically ignore what was arguably the most emotive, volatile and contentious conflict of the past year, to itself evidence a kind of social amnesia, is remarkable testimony to the powerful stake of all in maintaining a shared macro discursive consensus ...

> Strewn beneath Desmond Tutu's hoped-for rainbow canopy, the fragmented discursive ruins of the Makgoba affair litter our social landscape. And if in the end the ubiquitous way forward is blocked by such debris, there can be no avoiding these obstacles.

What these authors say is that the repressed, hidden, disguised and barely recognised conflicts of our society will erupt, as did the Makgoba affair, into a world which seeks the consensus of incompatible paradigms in which some came to see their exercise of power as the natural order of things.

The only escape for those who seek the absence of turbulence, and strive to maintain their positions of privilege by stealth, will be the artificial imposition of a social amnesia, until the next conflict emerges above the gentle waves.

I do not believe that any one of us wants to live in this fake and unreal world peopled by ostriches with heads hidden in the sand of the Kgalagadi.

And so, what must we do?

I believe that there are practical steps we can take in the immediate future.

First, all of us, the government, the private sector, the unions and the rest of the non-governmental sector, must combine to ensure that the projected Presidential Job Summit leads to a serious programme of action which will result in increasing the number of newly created jobs.

Among others, I am pleased to inform the House that we are currently involved in detailed and constructive discussions with especially the major players in the private sector, concretely to realise this objective.

Secondly, we must take advantage of the opportunity thrown up by the need for reparations arising from the process of the Truth and Reconciliation Commission to join in a major effort that will simultaneously address the issues of reparation, reconciliation and sustainable development.

Again, I am happy to inform the House that those we have spoken to in the private sector have responded very well to the proposal that the necessary effort will have to be made to provide the resources to make this possible.

Thirdly, later this year, our religious leadership will convene what they have christened the 'Moral Summit', to address the serious problem of the collapse of moral values in our society, which gives birth to the crime, corruption and immorality which make it so difficult to inspire the millions of our people, both black and white, to respond to the vision encapsulated in the call – 'Masakhane'!

The preparation for and the holding of the Summit will provide all of us with the possibility to act together for the moral renewal of our society, without which the noble goals of nation building and reconciliation cannot be achieved.

The fourth point – all of us who lead any constituency among the black people, however big or small, have an obligation to communicate the message that, as much as we were our own liberators, so are we all the architects of our destiny.

Accordingly, we must each ask ourselves the question – what have I done to be the architect of that better life for the country and myself? Only a few days ago African students burnt down offices at the University of Venda. What they were demanding, which, correctly the university administration would not concede, was that the university should give them about R500 000 for a student party, described as 'the Freshers' Ball', allow that each student should, on average, have 30 cans of beer at this ball and readmit to the university the president of the SRC and a leader of AZASCO who, in four years, had only completed four courses.

The time has come to call and impose a halt to the abuse of freedom in

THE LIFE AND TIMES OF THABO MBEKI

the name of an entitlement, said to arise naturally from our having been the victims of apartheid, especially by those elements among the black élite which have a voice, precisely because they are better off.

Clearly, now, these seek to hijack the sacrifices which millions of ordinary people made to liberate our country for noble purposes, in order to satisfy a seemingly insatiable and morally unbound greed and personal thirst for wealth and individual comfort, regardless of the cost to our society.

In this context, I would like to take advantage of this opportunity to express the Government's and my own gratitude for the steps taken by both NAFCOC and FABCOS, after discussion with ourselves, to ensure that their members and the constituency they represent meet their tax obligations.

Similarly, this I must say, that we felt proud when black medical students stood up to say that they were fully in agreement with the Minister of Health, the Honourable Dr Nkosazana Zuma, and the government, that they would do community service on completion of their studies.

Fifth, we have to take all necessary steps to transform the machinery of state to ensure that while being lean, it nevertheless serves the people efficiently, effectively and with dedication.

Again, in this regard, as we look forward to an amicable solution of current problems, I would like publicly to recognise the fact of the acceptance by three public sector unions, NEHAWU, SADTU and POPCRU, after discussions with ourselves, of the obligation to act together with the government to promote the concept of public servants as workers who must be driven by the imperative to serve the people.

Clearly this commitment must be translated into more visible movement forward with regard to the performance of government.

There is a Xhosa expression – *ukuthundez'ubityo* – to coax along the most emaciated and therefore the weakest ox in a span. As government, we are ready to live up to this expression – *sithundeze ubityo* – so that all of us, as South Africans, can pull our weight in pursuit of a common national agenda.

A leader of the NG Kerk writes 'the church owes the nation hope!'

Former Generals of the SADF, including Generals Jannie Geldenhuys and George Meiring, write:

We are patriots. We love our country and its people. We would like to see our country acquire international acknowledgement and status. We respect the Constitution and would like to fulfil our part in keeping it intact ... We would like to make our contribution towards conciliation and harmony.

I am inspired by these sentiments and have profound respect for the white and Afrikaner South Africans who have the courage to make them.

In our schools our children are beginning to work and play together. The exceptions are reported in the mass media for one reason only – because they are news, because they are the exceptions and not the rule.

The craftsperson who handles an uncut and unpolished diamond has a vision of what that stone may become, imagination that must bend to the reality of the contours of the given stone. He or she knows that it takes dedicated search for excellence to achieve the final result.

The diamond has true value when it gives life to light and all its faces gleam, when the diversity of its surfaces glitter and sparkle in unison and rejoice in their symmetry and beauty in a multi-faceted unity, such as the South Africa for which we must all strive.

At the end, we must repeat what the *Beeld* said:

Eers as daar in albei nasies werklike begrip is vir die ander se voorspoed en ellende, ideale en vrese, kan daar hoop wees om die land – met al sy nasies en belangegroepe – se probleme in 'n gesamentlike poging aan te pak.

Muito obrigado!

Notes

Introduction

1. Sapa-AFP news service profile, 18 December 1997.
2. Patti Waldmeir. *Anatomy of a Miracle.* (London: Penguin, 1997), p. 281.
3. Nelson Mandela. *Long Walk to Freedom.* (Randburg: MacDonald Purnell, 1994), p. 592.
4. Howard Barrell. 'Conscripts to their Age: African National Congress Operational Strategy, 1976-86'. Unpublished Ph.D. thesis, University of Oxford, 1993, p. 12.

1: Family life and beginnings

Information for this chapter (and for Chapter 2) was obtained through a range of interviews, including with Thabo Mbeki, Govan Mbeki, Epainette Mbeki, Linda Mbeki, Micky Nama and Sonwabo Mphahlwa. Reconstructions were based on these interviews as well as on extensive transcripts of interviews with Govan Mbeki done for a 90 minute video documentary on his life entitled *Heart and Stone* by Bridget Thompson, as well as video and film archive material which is held in the Mayibuye Centre at the University of the Western Cape. Some of Govan's remarks come from the transcripts. Colin Bundy's introduction to *The Prison Writings of Govan Mbeki* gave a useful historical perspective of Thabo's forbears and some of the information used here was sourced directly from

Bundy's work. The speeches of Albert Luthuli and various historical documents accessible on the ANC's internet site, such as the resolutions and speeches of the 1943 ANC Annual Conference in Bloemfontein, were also helpful. As was Hassen Ebrahim's *The Soul of a Nation* which also contains important historical documents.

1. Govan Mbeki. *The Prison Writings of Govan Mbeki.* (Cape Town: David Philip, 1991), p. (x). From the introduction by Colin Bundy. This section leans heavily on Bundy's work.
2. Ibid. p. (xiv).
3. Ibid. p. (xiv).
4. Ibid. p. (ix).
5. From transcripts of interviews with Govan Mbeki, recorded in December 1991 by Bridget Thompson for the documentary *Heart and Stone*, held by the Mayibuye Centre, University of the Western Cape, p. 6.
6. Mbeki, G., p. (xi).
7. Ibid. p. (xiii).
8. Thompson, p. 15.
9. Ibid. p. 27.
10. Ibid. p. 29.
11. Mbeki, G., p. (x).
12. Thompson, p. 69.
13. Mbeki, G., p. (xiii).
14. Ibid. p. (xiv).
15. Ibid. p. (xiv).
16. Thompson, p. 71.
17. Ibid. p. 71.
18. Ibid. p. 69.

2: Political awakenings

1. Mbeki, G., p. (xv).
2. Mbeki, T. *Africa: The Time has Come.* (Cape Town: Tafelberg and Mafube, 1998), pp. (iv)-(v). From the foreword by Willie Esterhuyse.
3. Ibid. p. (v).
4. Albert Luthuli. From a speech given after he was dismissed from his

position as chief of the Abase-Makolweni tribe for refusing to resign from the ANC, November 1952.

5. Mbeki, G., p. (xvii).
6. Interview in *The Star*, Johannesburg, 18 July 1998.
7. Hassen Ebrahim. *The Soul of a Nation*. (Cape Town: Oxford University Press, 1998), p. 3.
8. B. Bunting. *Moses Kotane: South African Revolutionary, A political biography*. (London: Inkululeko Publications, 1975), p. 260.

3: Exile

A range of interviews were carried out for this chapter. Howard Barrell's doctoral thesis for the University of Oxford, 'Conscripts to their Age: African National Congress Operational Strategy, 1976–86', was a particularly helpful text.

1. Interview in *The Star*, Johannesburg, April 1996.
2. Mbeki, T., pp. (x)-(xi).
3. Barrell, H., p. 163.
4. Mbeki, T., p. (xii).
5. Barrell, H., p. 110.
6. *The Battle for South Africa*, video series by CBS. Mayibuye Centre, University of the Western Cape.
7. Allister Sparks. *The Mind of South Africa – The story of the rise and fall of apartheid*. (London: Mandarin, 1990), pp. 245–6.
8. Barrell, H., p. 191.
9. Ibid. p. 292.
10. Ibid. p. 352.
11. Ibid. p. 369.
12. Waldmeir, P., p. 66.
13. Ibid. p. 67.
14. Ibid. p. 65.
15. Ibid. p. 65.
16. Barrell, H., p. 383.
17. ANC resolution, Kabwe Consultative Conference, Kabwe, Zambia, June 1985.
18. Barrell, H., p. 384.

19. Waldmeir, P., p. 73.
20. Ibid. p. 74.
21. Barrell, H., p. 399.
22. Ibid. p. 443.
23. Waldmeir, P., p. 63.
24. Ibid. p. 63.
25. Ibid. p. 69.
26. Allister Sparks. *Tomorrow is Another Country.* (Johannesburg: Struik Book Distributors, 1994), p. 72.
27. Ibid. p. 74.
28. Ibid. p. 72.

4: The return

Information for this chapter was compiled with the assistance of two key interviews conducted by the authors with Maritz Spaarwater and Mike Louw. We have also leaned heavily on the accounts in Waldmeir's *Anatomy of a Miracle* and Sparks' *Tomorrow is Another Country.* Johann van Rooyen's analysis of the threat from the white right wing, *Hard Right,* was a useful reference work. An interview with General Constand Viljoen, the leader of the Freedom Front, was also conducted by the authors.

1. Waldmeir, P., p. 86.
2. Mbeki, T., p. (xviii).
3. Sparks, A., p. 78.
4. Waldmeir, P., p. 75.
5. Sparks, A., p. 78.
6. Ibid. p. 78.
7. Ibid. p. 79.
8. Ibid. p. 81.
9. Ibid. p. 82.
10. Ibid. p. 79.
11. Ibid. p. 61.
12. Waldmeir, P., p. 82.
13. Ibid. p. 74.
14. Ibid. p. 78.
15. Sparks, A., p. 85.

16. Ibid. p. 87.
17. Mbeki, T., p. (xviii).
18. Sparks, A., p. 111.
19. Lester Venter. *When Mandela Goes, The coming of South Africa's second revolution.* (Johannesburg: Doubleday, 1997) p. 71.
20. Sparks, A., p. 110.
21. Ibid. p. 112.
22. Interview in *The Star,* Johannesburg, 1993.
23. Ibid.

5: The right wing

1. Johann van Rooyen. *Hard Right, The New White Power in South Africa.* (London: IB Taurus & Co.: 1994), p. 171.
2. Ibid. p. 192.
3. Ibid. p. 164.
4. Ibid. p. 167.
5. Ibid. p. 194.
6. Ibid. p. 194.
7. Ibid. p. 196.
8. Ibid. p. 198.
9. Mbeki, T., p. (xiv).
10. Van Rooyen, J., p. 164.
11. Ibid. p. 196.

6: The Deputy President (1994–1999)

A range of interviews were conducted by the authors for this chapter, including with the deputy minister in the office of the deputy president, Essop Pahad, minister of justice Dullah Omar, Democratic Party MP Colin Eglin, minister for posts, telecommunications and broadcasting, Jay Naidoo, and with a variety of sources within the ANC and opposition parties who preferred to remain anonymous.

1. Waldmeir, P., p. 82.
2. Interview in *The Star,* Johannesburg, November 1997.
3. Mbeki, T., p. (xxi).

4. From a speech delivered by Thabo Mbeki, 8 January, 1996. Accessed from the ANC's Internet site at www.anc.org.za.
5. R. Schrire. 'Thabo's Republic', *Leadership magazine*, vol. 17 (4), 1998, pp. 14–18.
6. Interview in *Finance Week*, June 1996.
7. Venter, L., p. 78.
8. Interview in the *Sowetan*, Johannesburg, August 1996.

7: The enigma

Along with a broad range of interviews, some of which were conducted under conditions of anonymity, we have relied heavily in this chapter on published press cuttings from a variety of newspapers, most particularly *The Star*, the *Sowetan* and the *Mail & Guardian*.

1. S. Friedman. *In the Wings, Portfolio of South Africa* (Gauteng: Portfolio Business Publications: 1996–7), pp. 13–14.

8: Into the future

The authors accompanied Mbeki on his trip home in late 1998. Again, a broad range of interviews were conducted for this final chapter, some named and some not.

1. Waldmeir, P., p. 281.
2. Interview by Ingrid Uys in *Millennium* magazine, May 1996, pp. 32–8.
3. Ibid.

Index